NOT FADE AWAY

by Walter Rimler

*A Comparison of
Jazz Age with Rock Era
Pop Song Composers*

pierian press
1984

ISBN 0-87650-159-5
LC 84-60268

780.92
R576N

Copyright © 1984 by
Walter Rimler

All Rights Reserved

THE PIERIAN PRESS
Post Office Box 1808
Ann Arbor, MI 48106

For
Peg Rimler

Contents

Illustrations ix
Acknowledgements xi
Introduction xiii

Chapter One: SONGWRITING COMMUNITIES 1
Chapter Two: PARTNERSHIPS 31
Chapter Three: POP ORCHESTRATION 51
Chapter Four: THE SONGWRITER AS PERFORMER 67
Chapter Five: LYRICS 79
Chapter Six: PRODUCTIVE LONGEVITY
    George Gershwin: 25 Last Songs 91
    Jerome Kern: Beautiful Pranks 101
    Richard Rodgers: The Sweetest Sounds 107
    Irving Berlin: Reaching For It 113
    Cole Porter: True Grit 121
    Harold Arlen: Always the Bridesmaid 127
    John Lennon: The Great Swan of Liverpool 135
    Paul McCartney: Keeper of the Flame 143
    George Harrison: Fall From Grace 153
    Mick Jagger and Keith Richards: Poseurs 163
    Bob Dylan: Tunesmith 171
    Carole King: The Perils of Philosophy 179
    Holland-Dozier-Holland: The Thousand Days 189
    Paul Simon: Contemporary Lieder 195

Afterword 207
Index 211

Illustrations

The Broadway songwriting fraternity (pre-World War I) xii
The Gershwin brothers in Hollywood in 1937 20
The Beatles in 1964 36
Richard Rodgers and Lorenz Hart circa 1925 38
Richard Rodgers and Oscar Hammerstein II working
    on "The King and I" in 1951 40
George Gershwin orchestrating "Porgy and Bess" in
    Palm Beach, Florida, February 1935 58
Harold Arlen and Ira Gershwin in 1936 92
Oscar Hammerstein II and Jerome Kern 100
Richard Rodgers in 1975 106
Irving Berlin in the 1960s 112
Irving Berlin and Ginger Rogers on the set of "Top Hat"
    in 1935 118
Cole Porter 120
Harold Arlen in the 1960s 128
John Lennon in 1968 134
Paul McCartney in the 1970s 144
George Harrison at the "Concert for Bangladesh" in 1971 154
Mick Jagger and Keith Richards 162
Bob Dylan in 1978 170
Bob Dylan with Joan Baez in 1963 175
Carole King in the early 1960s 181
Carole King in the early 1970s 184
Holland-Dozier-Holland shortly after they left Motown 190
Paul Simon in 1982 196
Simon and Garfunkel in the late 1960s 200

Acknowledgements

For their kinds words and encouragement, thanks to Samuel and Ruth Rimler, Jack and Cindy Switalla, Rona Arato and family, Ed and Marilyn Gendason, Tom Schultheiss, Judi Reigel O'Mara, Vivian Wills, Paula Lozar, Joan Alexander Applebaum, Judy Sanders, Diane Athearn and Randy Black. I am also grateful to Edward Jablonski, Michael Kerker, Jerry Gardner, the offices of Rodgers and Hammerstein and those of Paul Simon for providing photographs, and to Robert Kerwin, Donna Kerwin, Jerry Salzman and Jon Thomas, who were generous with recordings, sheet music, books and other reference materials. Thanks also to Jethro Leiberman for his advice and counsel.

A pre-World War I portrait of the Broadway songwriting fraternity. Jerome Kern is at the extreme left, Irving Berlin is at the far right. Others include Rudolf Friml (fourth from the left), Oscar Hammerstein I (seated), and John Phillip Sousa (sixth from the right).

INTRODUCTION

When musical comedy began supplanting operetta after World War I, the new writers, led by Jerome Kern and Irving Berlin, managed to co-exist with members of the old school, led by Sigmund Romberg and Rudolf Friml. Not only was there no animosity between them, some writers, such as Oscar Hammerstein II, commuted successfully between one form and the other.

But things were not so amicable forty years later when the show composers of Broadway and Hollywood were faced with upstart songwriters whose work was rooted in rock and roll. Something drastic had happened to popular music — something which, to survivors of the older generation, was clearly a turn for the worse. It seemed to them as if their lyrical, harmonic and structural discoveries had been tossed aside in favor of nonsense lines which, set to three-chord ditties, were being played in ear-splitting fashion by inept guitarists. Like Roman senators at the approach of the Vandals, they mourned for civilization.

At the same time, the younger songwriters, led by the Beatles, Bob Dylan and the Rolling Stones, were equally certain that theirs was the truly bold and innovative form of popular song. It seemed to them that their compositions were more vital than the mannered works of the earlier composers and that, in serving no masters but their own muses (the theater composers had often been at the mercy of Broadway producers and Hollywood moguls), they had freed popular song from a straitjacket imposed by earlier, more timid times.

Now that more time has passed, the line of demarcation between these two generations is less clearcut. Frank Sinatra sings George Harrison's "Something," Harrison records Cole Porter's "True Love," and one is not surprised to hear "Begin the Beguine" and "Norwegian Wood" played back to back in office buildings and restaurants and supermarkets — Muzak having become a common boneyard for the songs of both generations.

Now there is a patina of nostalgia upon the songs of both eras. Many radio stations are currently devoted exclusively to the music of one or the other of these two pasts, reflecting a situation in pop that is analogous to the one that has long stymied the world of highbrow concert music. Not only do our symphony orchestras play museum pieces, so do more and more of our pop music stations. It seems as if the best has come and gone all across the musical spectrum.

Members of the baby boom generation, those one-time Vandals, are themselves now afraid for civilization. Gamely, they try to keep up with the new writers but deep down they believe that the song composers of today just don't have the right stuff. As proof, they can point to all those radio stations that play only '60s music, and to the still powerful presence in the Top 40 of writers like Mick Jagger and Paul McCartney. Of course, they do not pretend that those venerables are as good now as they used to be. On the contrary, there is a feeling — largely unexpressed, but it is there — that their generation has been gypped, that the sudden decline and fall of almost every one of the great songwriters of their youth has robbed them of pleasures that they had a right to expect. Dylan, the Stones, the surviving ex-Beatles, Carole King, John Sebastian, Brian Wilson, Jimmy Webb, Donovan Leitch, David Crosby, Stephen Stills, Graham Nash, Neil Young, Eddie Holland, Lamont Dozier, Brian Holland and nearly all of their peers have not yet recovered from the unfortunate sea change that overtook them in the 1970s. On the other hand, men like Irving Berlin and Jerome Kern were able to stay in top form for a very long time. Berlin, for instance, wrote his first big hit, "Alexander's Ragtime Band," in 1911 — thirty-five years before composing his greatest stage work, *Annie Get Your Gun*.

The odd and exasperating decline of the great '60s songwriters has so far been meekly accepted as an inescapable fate, a meekness that goes hand in hand with the generation's passive acceptance of mediocrity in many other, non-musical, areas. But was the decline of these writers inevitable? And are their glory days necessarily over? Those questions are the heart of this book and I have tried to answer them in two ways: first, by identifying the musical differences between these two generations of pop songwriters and, second, by showing how those differences accounted for the disparities in productive longevity.

I have not made a comprehensive analysis of all of the music of the two eras, but have instead looked at the careers of a handful of the most gifted writers: Kern (1885--1945), Berlin (1888--), Cole Porter (1891–1964), George Gershwin (1898--1937), Richard Rodgers (1902--1979) and Harold Arlen (1905--), who dominated the earlier generation, are my choice to represent the group that I have called, collectively, the theater or show writers (since almost everything they wrote was for a theater or a show of one kind or another — on the Broadway stage or in movie houses). I have also, on occasion, dubbed them "The Six," since they were tied to one another in a way that recalled other knots of composers, such as the French Six and the Russian Five. As for the '60s generation, I have called them the studio writers, since it was in recording studios that their music came to life. Representing them in this book are John Lennon (1940--1980), Paul McCartney (1942--), George Harrison (1943--), Bob Dylan (1941--), Mick Jagger (1943--), Keith Richards (1943--), Paul Simon (1941--), Carole King (1941--), Eddie Holland (1939--), Lamont Dozier (1941--), and Brian Holland (1941--). Because the Beatles, Dylan and the Rolling Stones presided over their era in much the same way as The Six dominated theirs, their presence in this book was inevitable. Simon, King and Holland-Dozier-Holland were chosen because they too were great and prolific songwriters at work during the decade, though their influence was less profound. Some talented writers, such as Joni Mitchell, Randy Newman and Stevie Wonder, were not included on the grounds that they really came into their own in the '70s, not the '60s.

These choices make it obvious that I have concentrated on the musical side of the songwriting equation and not on lyrics. This is due to my belief that popular songwriting is a musical more than a literary form, and because the decline in the quality of the work of the '60s writers was primarily a musical decline.

Nor have I paid much attention to the sociology of the two eras. While it can be argued that the fall of the '60s writers was due to non-musical factors, such an argument would inevitably push music into the background and concentrate on vague generalities.

I have not dwelt on the role that drugs played in the music of the studio writers, except in the one case, that of Keith Richards, where they directly affected a writer's output. It is my guess that, with Richards as a possible exception, drugs did not significantly enhance or diminish the talent of any of them. Occasionally, the subject of a song was affected — but even there, the influence of narcotics and psychedelics was probably less important than one might think, despite so much publicity to the contrary.

I have also ignored the business end of popular music. Certainly, corporations are fit subjects for discussion but their machinations rarely have much of an effect on truly talented writers.

Other terms besides "theater writers" and "studio writers" have been used consistently throughout this book and they ought to be defined here, at the beginning. One, "highbrow," has been chosen to denote those composers who are usually mislabeled "classical" or "serious" or "longhaired." Strictly speaking, "classical" ought to apply only to Mozart, Haydn, C.P.E. Bach and others of the late 18th century. "Serious" wrongly implies that the work of highbrows is always dour and forbidding and that, conversely, the music of pop writers is always silly. "Longhaired" is inaccurate for obvious reasons. Since it means nothing at all, "highbrow" seemed to be the best choice.

"Dummy lyric" is not a pejorative but refers to those lines which are temporarily attached to a melody only because their syllables fit the notes.

"Release" is a term used to denote the "B" section of a song. In a 32-bar tune this is the third eight-bar section, after the refrain and its repetition. As used here, "release" is synonymous with "middle eight" or "bridge."

The title of this book is taken from a song by a man, Buddy Holly, who ought to have been part of the '60s generation, but who never had a chance to fade away, having died in an air crash in 1959 at the age of twenty-two.

Though I have concentrated on musical comparisons between the two generations, it has been impossible not to notice and discuss certain traits — perhaps superficial, perhaps not — that seem to be common to many great songwriters. For instance, the theater and studio writers were mostly of the same physical type: of average or less than average height, slightly built and thin. They were also very similar in personality: intelligent, free of immobilizing neuroses, personable and undogmatic (there wasn't a Richard Wagner or an Ezra Pound in the lot). None of The Six wanted much of anything to do with organized religion or even personal religion. And the same was true for the studio writers until 1967, when George Harrison introduced Indian mysticism into pop — an act which invited the more familiar tenets of Christianity into the mainstream (it had heretofore confined itself to country and gospel music). Dylan's counsel in the '60s had been "don't follow leaders." But by the end of the 1970s he was singing "Gotta Serve Somebody." Carole King was also entering the "I found it" sweepstakes by then, though on a line closer to Harrison's. It may or may not be a coincidence, but pop music seems to grow weaker when it is written by the devout.

Another similarity between these two groups of composers was that, with the exception of Cole Porter, every one of them was a solid success by his or her twenty-fifth birthday. Porter had to wait until his mid-thirties for general acceptance, although his songs were being sung on the Broadway stage as early as 1915, when he was twenty-four. But no great pop songwriter has ever been discovered late in life or posthumously.

And there is one other phenomenon that has something to do with chronology. The theater writers, whose birthdates ranged over twenty-one years, all reached their peak at just about the same time — circa 1935. The studio writers also hit their peaks simultaneously, thirty years later, but they were much closer in age, all having been born within four years of one another.

Before my astrologically-minded readers get too excited, I ought to move on to more substantial matters. The word "genius," though it is not used much during the course of this book, is always at least a spectral presence. Considering the amount of brilliance and pleasure that they brought into the world, it is tempting to say that every one of these theater and studio composers was at all times nothing less than a full-blooded genius. But that would be misusing a word that has suffered more than its share of abuse and inflation. To state it simply, a genius is someone who produces something that no one else could, can or will ever be able to produce. In a sense, then, we are all geniuses, since every one of us is a unique creature. But, as applied to the arts, "genius" is a word that must be used with great circumspection. Irving Berlin could conceivably have written many of Cole Porter's songs and vice versa. The same can be said of all the theater composers: any one of The Six could have written at least half the output of any of the others. These writers displayed their genius only on occasion, in songs which were not only masterpieces, but quintessential expressions of themselves as conscious thinking authors. No one but Kern could have written "All the Things You Are," no one but Gershwin could have written "Summertime," and it is through such songs that these composers became something more than hit-makers. They became authors whose progress could be followed and appreciated from one work to the next.

Because the studio writers composed for their own performing specifications and because they were allowed much more latitude in expressing their own individual personalities, this definition of genius, when applied to them, is apt to be confused with style and idiosyncracy. Still, they too had moments of undiluted genius, such as Dylan's "Subterranean Homesick Blues" and the Beatles' "Penny Lane." And it is because of such songs that so large an audience became drawn and attracted to them.

Genius is a tropism. Everyone turns to it, whether it is manifested in sports, politics, science or the arts. All people, no matter how humble, identify with it and are able to cast aside envy in its presence. The genius that produced so many great songs in the 1960s — that turned so many songwriters into authors — is all but gone now. Yet those composers are not yet chronologically old. They should be entering their primes, not their dotage. That is why I have written this book: to show that a songwriter's future can unfold, that it does not have to unravel, and to prove that great pop composers do not have to fade away. If the music made by the studio writers in the 1960s was art — something that is now commonly acknowledged — then they ought to be living the lives of artists — lives of continuing exploration and growth.

Chapter One

SONGWRITING COMMUNITIES

Take the city of Vienna from the history of highbrow music and one is left without Beethoven, Schubert, Brahms, Mahler, the Strauss family and Schoenberg. Take New York City from the history of popular song and you lose Jerome Kern, Irving Berlin, George Gershwin, Richard Rodgers, Harold Arlen, Bob Dylan, Paul Simon and Carole King. In both categories the loss would be devastating. New York City has been the Vienna of twentieth century popular song — a fact that is not surprising when one remembers that it has been home to Tin Pan Alley, the Broadway theater, Greenwich Village, the Yiddish theater and to innumerable publishing houses and record companies. It would have been odd had this city *not* been the locus. But if one considers these songwriters more carefully, an unexpected pattern does emerge: every one of them was Jewish. For some reason, New York Jews became songwriters the way their Irish neighbors became cops.

It is impossible to know for certain why this was so. Jewish composers had never been dominant in the concert hall. The cumulative weight of those who made it into the highbrow pantheon — Mendelssohn, Offenbach, Mahler and Schoenberg — does not offset any one of the Three Bs. Why then their dominance as songwriters? One can point to the squalor of the Lower East Side and talk about upward mobility. But the fact is that this steady eruption of talent is as inexplicable as was the sudden flowering of drama in 17th century London or of literature in late 19th century Russia. And, just as there are those who long for a time-traveller's ticket to the Globe Theatre of Shakespeare's day or to Tolstoy's estate when Chekhov was a dinner guest, so there are people who would give much to be transported to a Saturday night poker game attended by Kern, Gershwin and Arlen.

To understand the origins of this group one has to go back to March of 1881. In that month the Tsar of Russia, Alexander II, was assassinated — an event which proved to be one of the luckiest breaks

1

in the history of American popular music. Alexander had been a relatively moderate ruler — he was the one who freed the serfs in 1861 — but his son and successor, Alexander III, was a reactionary and an anti-Semite. Under his regime a new round of pogroms began and tens of thousands of Jews came to America to escape it.

Among them was Moses Baline, whose house in Temen, Siberia had been burned to the ground by Cossacks. Baline was able to get his wife and eight children beyond the Jewish Pale of Settlement, to a steamship waiting on the Baltic Coast and thence to a window-less apartment on Monroe Street on New York's Lower East Side. It was from there that one of his sons, Isadore, managed, in the by now familiar route, to make his own escape, first by selling news-papers in the streets and later by earning nickels as a singing waiter in the grubby cafes of the Bowery. Eventually he began singing his own lyrics, usually parodies to the popular melodies of the day. In 1905, when he was seventeen, the pianist in a rival Chinatown saloon wrote a hit Italian dialect song called "My Murriuccia Take a Steamboat" and Baline tried to cash in on a new fad by writing an Italian number of his own, "Marie from Sunny Italy." It was published the day after it was written (with music by Nick Nicholson) — in so much of a hurry, in fact, that the publisher mistakenly credited the words to I. Berlin. Baline, liking that better, fleshed the "I" into Irving and thus began one of the great names and careers in songwriting.

Berlin set many precedents for the Jewish songwriters who would follow him. Like him, almost all of them would change their names. Like him too, most of them would be uneasy about their religious background, though unwilling to abandon it. In this regard, Berlin's story was larger than life. Upon achieving his first huge success, "Alexander's Ragtime Band" (named not in gratitude to the late Tsar but for a bandleader named Jack Alexander), he had appeared one day at his mother's doorstep to sweep her off to the Bronx, where a new home was waiting, complete with a maid who had just laid a hot kosher meal on the table. It was a scene which would become *de rigueur* for rags-to-riches songwriters throughout the century. The next year, however, Berlin gave his mother a profound shock by marrying Dorothy Goetz, a non-Jew. He was forgiven but the bride died five months after the wedding, having caught typhoid while on their honeymoon in Cuba.

In 1926 Berlin married again, this time to Ellin Mackey. Her father was Clarence Mackey, head of the American Postal Telegraph Company and an unabashed anti-Semite. The romance of an East Side Jew to a Long Island socialite caught the fancy of the pub-lic and it helped sell many a newspaper and tabloid. It even inspired a song (not by Berlin) entitled "When a Kid Who Came from the East Side Found a Sweet Society Rose." But the prospect of Berlin

2

as his son-in-law was anything but inspirational to Mackey. In 1924 he took his daughter to Europe hoping that a separation would help her forget her songwriter-beau. He even got her an audience with the Pope. In the meantime, Berlin, by now a world-famous composer and lyricist, remained stateside writing sentimental waltzes such as "All Alone," "What'll I Do?" and "Remember." When, upon Ellin's return, the romance resumed and the couple eloped, Mackey disowned his daughter and her name quickly disappeared from the *Social Register*. Two years later, on Christmas Day 1928, when the Berlins' month-old son died of a heart ailment, some of Ellin's society friends even went so far as to express the thought that this was divine retribution for her having married a Jew. Clarence Mackey was not so intractable and he wrote the couple a letter of sympathy. But he would soon be needing some of the same. After exchanging his controlling interest in Postal Telegraph for shares in ITT the stock market crash of 1929 caused him to suffer what one Wall Street analyst called "the greatest reversal of fortune of any rich American." Berlin, who lost most of his money too, had recouped enough by 1934 to bail his father-in-law out.

Throughout his creative life Berlin was adamant about remaining musically uneducated. He was famous for his limited knowledge of harmony and piano. A special upright piano had been built for him which, by means of a lever, allowed him to change keys without taking his fingers off the black notes. He called it his "Buick" and certainly no other Buick has ever given anyone so much mileage. Nevertheless, to capture the increasingly complex harmonies underpinning his songs, Berlin needed a musical secretary at whom he would whistle, hum, or, by some more mysterious means, convey the tune or chord that was in his head. One day in 1917 the applicant for this job seemed to be a worthy young man but Berlin turned him down — he realized that the fellow was just too talented to serve as someone else's musical amanuensis.

This job-seeker's American citizenship was also due to Alexander II's demise. His father, Morris Gershowitz, had fled St. Petersburg at about the time that Berlin's father was leaving Siberia. Shortly after arriving in New York in 1895, Morris married Rose Bruskin, whom he had known in St. Petersburg, and the couple had three sons and a daughter. The first son, Israel (later Ira), became one of the musical theater's finest lyricists. The second, Jacob, became a tunesmith, inspired in part by the craze stirred up by Irving Berlin's "Alexander's Ragtime Band." Jacob left high school to take a job selling the songs of a Tin Pan Alley publisher to vaudeville acts who were in constant need of new material. At the age of fifteen, calling himself George Gershwin, he became the youngest piano pounder in Tin Pan Alley history.

3

Gershwin's connection with popular music was, unlike Berlin's, never entirely free of the Old World. He was particularly influenced by the Yiddish Theater, located on New York's Second Avenue. As a very young man he had been attracted to the music of Joseph Rumshinsky and Abraham Goldfadden, both of whom wrote for Boris Thomashefsky's National Theater. In fact, Thomashefsky had asked Gershwin to collaborate with another composer, Sholom Secunda, on a Yiddish opera (Secunda had refused due to his reluctance to work with so youthful a partner) and much later, after he had established himself on Broadway, Gershwin returned to the idea of a musical work based on Jewish themes. In 1929 he signed a contract with New York's Metropolitan Opera Company to compose an opera based on S.A. Ansky's play *The Dybbuk* but the project had to be shelved when Gershwin learned that the rights to the play had been assigned to another composer. Had the way been clear it had been his intention to travel to Europe and study Jewish music there — a step which might have been gratuitous since Gershwin's music, with its insistent use of the minor third interval, already had Jewish qualities.

Charles Schwartz, in his biography of the composer, has gone so far as to suggest that such Gershwin tunes as " 'S Wonderful" and "Funny Face" are really Yiddish melodies dressed up in Broadway harmony, that Gershwin's dance tunes resemble Jewish wedding *frailachs*, and that other Gershwin songs, notably "My One and Only," clearly boast melodic traits derived from the cantor's art. But Schwartz may have been pushing his thesis too hard. The minor third, after all, is also crucial to the blues scale, while the most famous pop song use of the cantorial style occurs not in any of Gershwin's songs but in Cole Porter's "My Heart Belongs to Daddy," where the melody parodies cantillation on the syllables "da-da-da." Gershwin never got around to writing his Jewish opera but that Second Avenue strain continued in his melodies, reaching its culmination in his last stage work, *Porgy and Bess*.

Still another emigrant from East European repression was Moses Arluck, who moved his family from Vilna, Poland to Louisville, Kentucky in 1885. Moses' son Samuel became a cantor at the Clinton Street Synagogue in Buffalo, New York, and Samuel's son Hyman sang in the choir. Early on the boy showed musical ability. He had inherited from his father a natural and pleasant singing voice and he quickly showed talent at the piano. Another strong trait was his urgent need to leave the environment of Orthodox Judaism and make his way in the world at hand, through music. He quit high school to play in a band and later, after an abortive attempt at running away to sea, he became a movie house pianist. Then he joined a group called the Snappy Trio and, at the age of fifteen, he was playing piano in the local red-light district. Eventually, he landed in New York City where, Americanizing his name to Harold Arlen, he became a singer, pianist and arranger for a group called the Buffalodians. They played in a walkdown nightclub called The Monte Carlo whose floor show featured Ray Bolger. Arlen and Bolger became friends and, for a time, roommates. Fourteen years later Arlen would write the music for Bolger's most memorable film, *The Wizard of Oz*.

After a stint in vaudeville as a singer accompanying himself, Arlen was signed to sing and act in a Vincent Youmans show, *Great Day*. He substituted for the rehearsal pianist one day and it was while he was fooling around with the introduction to one of Youmans' songs that he came up with his first great tune, "Get Happy." The number was the beginning of a very profitable partnership with Ted Koehler, who wrote the lyrics. Arlen and Koehler wrote a succession of memorable songs in the early 1930s for revues staged in Harlem's Cotton Club. "Get Happy," however, had proved to be a turning point for him in another way. It was interpolated into a show called *Nine-Fifteen Revue*, to which Gershwin was also a contributor and Gershwin, upon hearing the song, became one of Arlen's greatest admirers. Arlen, for his part, returned the compliment to the point of hero worship. Many years later, when his house caught fire, he rushed back inside despite the flames to rescue a portrait of Jerome Kern that had been painted by George Gershwin. It was an odd moment: one songwriter risking his life to save the painting that his hero, another songwriter, had made of *his* hero, still another songwriter.

As for Kern, he was the elder statesman of this group, having made his first contribution to a Broadway show in 1904, in the days of Victor Herbert. His background was slightly different from that of Berlin, Gershwin and Arlen. Kern's father had left Baden-Baden for New York in the 1850s and he established a solid upper-middle class household on East 56th Street. Kern's mother's family had come from Bohemia and his maternal grandfather had been a beadle at New York's Temple Emanu-El. But Kern took his religious cue from his father, who was a secular man. When he referred to his Jewishness he usually did so with a laugh, in the style of the Jewish comedians of the day. His most quoted remark in this manner occurred in the early 1930s when he and Oscar Hammerstein II were thinking about doing a musical about Marco Polo, to be adapted from Don Byren's play *Messer Marco Polo*. "Jerry," said Hammerstein, "here's a story laid in China about an Italian and told by an Irishman — what kind of music are you going to write?" "It'll be good Jewish music," Kern replied.

It was Kern's "They Didn't Believe Me," a hit from the 1914

5

play *The Girl from Utah*, that inspired Gershwin to set his sights on Broadway, as opposed to the vaudeville market served by Tin Pan Alley. And it was Kern's music for *Very Good, Eddie*, produced in 1915, that made another young man, Richard Rodgers, decide to devote himself and his music to the theater, as had Kern. Rodgers had grown up on West 120th Street in New York. His mother's family had been in the United States since the mid-1860s and had become rich in the silk business. His father's parents had come from Russia somewhat later but had also achieved wealth, and Rodgers' father was a successful doctor. They were assimilated Jews — orthodoxy had left the household upon the death of Rodgers' great-grandmother — and it was with little sense of Jewishness and none of poverty that he went out into the world to pursue his ambitions in the theater. His route was different from the one taken by the other four. He was the only one of them to earn a college degree and it was in college, writing for Columbia varsity shows, that his career received its grounding. This may or may not have been a factor in his having had little to do with the others socially. However, it is true that they — Kern, Berlin, Gershwin and Arlen — were constantly in and out of one another's homes and lives, especially in the Hollywood years of the 1930s, while Rodgers more or less went his own way. His path does not seem to have crossed that of Irving Berlin much at all until as late as 1946 when he hired Berlin to write the songs for *Annie Get Your Gun*, a show that he and Hammerstein were producing. This is not to imply any animosity between Rodgers and the others. Far from it. Each man knew that he was related to the rest. Assimilated to the point where their Jewishness was almost subliminal, they were nevertheless a community, one based on talent, certainly, but also, in an unmeasurable way, upon heritage.

Another name must be added to this group, although he was not Jewish but Presbyterian and though he was born not in New York but in Peru, Indiana. This was Cole Porter, whose family was wealthier by far than either Kern's or Rodgers'. J.O. Cole, the composer's grandfather, had earned a fortune in the California goldfields by selling water to thirsty miners. Back in Indiana he used this money to buy land and run a brewery. Cole Porter inherited $250,000 from him and then went on to marry into even greater wealth.

It is really an irony that he was the only one of The Six to consciously make use of Hebrew melodic style. That he did so is attested to by Rodgers, to whom Porter explained his strategy when they first met in 1927. Rodgers and his partner Larry Hart had been travelling in Europe and, upon arriving in Venice, they were introduced to Porter by Noel Coward. Up to that time Porter had achieved little success or recognition. His attempts to crack Broadway had brought him little but failure and his songs were known only to aficionados. He had made one attempt at highbrow composition, a ballet called *Within the Quota* (it had been premiered in Paris along with the Milhaud's *Creation of the World*), but here too he had found failure.

Porter had consoled himself by spending the 1920s in Europe, consolidating his position as the consummate American playboy. In Paris he and his wife made their home at 13 rue Monsieur which became a nexus for the nabobs of two continents. They liked to ride through the Parisian streets attended by a brood of little dachshunds. For a time they also lived in a series of extravagant Venetian palazzi and Porter had the distinction of being one of the first to operate a speedboat on that city's canals.

In Venice Rodgers and Hart were escorted by the Porters' personal gondalier to the Porter residence where, after an elegant meal, the two composers took turns at the piano. Upon hearing Porter's works for the first time, Rodgers immediately saw that here was no dilettante but a melodist and a wordsmith of high originality, not to mention commercial potential. It was at this point that Porter told Rodgers that he had discovered the secret that would enable him to write hits. "I'll write Jewish tunes," he said. Rodgers laughed, thinking it a joke, but he soon realized that Porter was very serious indeed. Shortly after that evening Porter did, in fact, achieve his first success, a Broadway musical called *Paris*, whose big song, "Let's Do It," is not without Jewish overtones, especially in the chromatic descent repeated over and over again on the words "do it." It was the first of many great Cole Porter songs whose strains have an unmistakably Jewish flavor. "Love for Sale," "In the Still of the Night," "So In Love," and "I Love Paris" are just a few which take advantage of that paradoxical but familiar Oriental/occidental quality that is characteristic of Jewish melody.

That is the irony of this group of six: a cornfed Presbyterian was the one American popular songwriter who consciously tried to uphold the musical tradition that had been uprooted from Tsarist Russia. He did not do this, of course, for ethnological reasons but because he, like the other five, was out to write hit songs. It also may have been due, at least in part, to the fact that he had broken away from and rejected his midwestern origins in a much more dramatic and fundamental way than the others had rejected their Judaism. Irving Berlin had gotten out of the Lower East Side but he went only as far as a luxury apartment on Beekman Place by the East River. Porter, in forsaking Indiana, not only got all the way to Europe, he even served a brief hitch in the French Foreign Legion (or so the legend goes). Moreover, his determination was not simply to put geographical distance between himself and middle-America. He eschewed its spiritual anchor as well. Whenever a reference to the

Divine was called for he referred not to God but to "the gods" and then only in jest, for he was an atheist. A horseback riding accident in 1937 left him crippled and in severe pain for much of the rest of his life but he never abandoned his non-believer status. In 1964, upon entering the hospital for the last time, the long-suffering Porter still refused to fill in the blank for "religion" on his admittance form.

Between the end of the First World War and the mid-1950s, popular music was dominated by these six men. Even after the advent of country, folk and rock, the city of New York and a new generation of Jewish songwriters who lived and worked there continued to play a full, even a commanding role in pop song. They were at the heart of the Greenwich Village folk movement which, at the beginning of the 1960s, tried to take songwriting out of the hands of "the professionals" (those who wrote for the slick productions of Broadway and Hollywood) and give it back to "the people," from whence, they believed, it had come. This movement was led by songwriter/performers who played and sang the heartfelt but unpretentious tunes they had discovered on expeditions into the countryside.

Few of them were New York-born. They had been drawn to the city and to the Village by its Bohemian image and because of folk-singing elders such as Woody Guthrie, Burl Ives and Josh White, who had made the place a Mecca for folksingers in the 1940s. A community of transplants, they still had more in common than the love of folk music. Phil Ochs came from a Jewish family in El Paso, Texas. Ramblin' Jack Elliott, born Elliott Adnopoz, had roots in the Jewish community in Brooklyn. Bob Dylan, born Robert Zimmerman, was the son of Jews who had settled in Hibbing, Minnesota. Others in the group, of course, were not Jewish at all — Buffy Sainte-Marie was a full-blooded Cree Indian from Saskatchewan, Canada. Nevertheless, the folk movement, because it was centered in New York City and because of Bob Dylan, its most talented son, had much in common, both geographically and ethnically, with the Broadway composers of a generation past.

Taking the stage in Gerdes, the Gaslight, the Village Gate and other bars and cafes, these singer/songwriters adopted a common style of dress, speech and thought and each of them found the glitter of traditional show business an anathema. In the press their names usually appeared one after the other, as if they were not individuals but different sections of a single creature. There was more unity in this clique than there ever had been among the New York show composers.

To join their ranks one needed only possess a guitar, an unbounded desire to discover and make up songs and to have spent some time on America's backroads. In these stipulations they had

8

again taken their cue from Woody Guthrie and his peers, who had all earned their credentials by riding the rails and meeting the people. Typical of this older generation was Billy Hill, who punched cattle in Montana, mined ore in Death Valley and worked as a Fifth Avenue doorman before writing the hit songs, "The Last Roundup" and "Wagon Wheels." The young writers of the 1960s were much more liable to look up to him than to Jerome Kern or Cole Porter — men who showed absolutely no inclination to spend any time in a boxcar.

To this new generation, songwriting had little to do with art and it was not even much of a craft. Far more important were one's living style and social orientation. The conscious shaping of melodic lines was rejected outright, as was harmonic innovation. Melodies were often lifted or remade from what they had found in their musicological diggings. "Just write — don't worry where the tune comes from," was Woody Guthrie's advice to Bob Dylan — advice which he himself had followed on many occasions. He most famous tune, "This Land Is Your Land," is really an amalgam of the melodies of two folk songs: "When the World's on Fire" and "Little Darling of Mine."

But lax as these writers were about melody, harmony and rhyme, they were strict in other ways, aiming for an ascetic, almost Spartan purity. For instrumentation, the guitar, sometimes the banjo and occasionally a related stringed instrument like the dulcimer or the ukelele were deemed appropriate. Pianos, brass and electrically amplified instruments were not. Some experimentation was permitted in lyrics or verse, as words to them were more important than melodies. But they wanted nothing to do with clever rhyme schemes, urbane wit and the unbounded euphoria so prevalent in the songs of the show writers. In a way, the work produced by this community had severe, Amish overtones.

It was in January of 1961 that Bob Dylan arrived in the Village. His father, a hardware store owner, had moved the family from Duluth to Hibbing when Bob was six. A few years later the boy was playing piano, guitar and harmonica — though he had already made up his mind to refuse all offers of formal training. His first hero was country singer and songwriter Hank Williams but he went on to admire rhythm and blues artists such as Muddy Waters and Jimmy Reed and then rock and roll writers like Little Richard, whom he would imitate at the piano, backed by a band called The Golden Chords. But the most profound influence was that of Woody Guthrie. In 1960, after reading Guthrie's autobiography *Bound for Glory*, Dylan found his first musical anchor. Shortly thereafter he went to seek out not only his hero, who lay hospitalized in New Jersey, but his hero's disciples who had congregated in New York City. By that time, however, there had been one other influence, albeit a nonmusical one.

9

This was James Dean. As had happened to many millions of teen-agers in the 1950s, a thrill had shuddered through Dylan upon Dean's sudden death. As it was for many others, this was Dylan's first en-counter with the exotic brand of death which was to become all too familiar in the next few years: that of a symbolic public figure. Dean inspired Dylan to cultivate a new sense of himself — misunderstood, poetic, star-crossed. The fact that his parents were kindly middle-class folk and that he was able to get from them almost everything that he wanted was a sore irritation to him and he seems to have worked very hard at appearing, both to himself and to others, the very opposite of them. He became obsessed with the idea of in-venting himself, of recreating himself from head to toe. "I hurt a lot," he would say. "I don't even know if I'm normal." Seething with intrigue, strangeness and the indecipherable, he made his way to the Village where it quickly became obvious that, in addition to be-ing an unusual fellow, he was one of those very rare singers who is able to speak to the heart. When it later became clear that he was a fine songwriter as well, the combination of mystery, voice and crea-tivity set the tone that popular music was to take in the 1960s.

In his need to break away from his background, Dylan was more desperate than any of the Broadway songwriters had ever been and he did something that had never occurred to any of them: he made up a past. Only twenty years old, he could not match the other folk-singers in boxcar/field-hand experience. In fact, outside of a few weeks performing in a honky tonk in Central City, Colorado, he had hardly done anything colorful at all. So when people asked where he was from he claimed to be an orphan, sometimes from New Mexico and other times, out of deference to Woody, from Oklahoma. The name Dylan had been produced out of thin air when he had found it impossible to say Zimmerman to a coffee house manager in Min-neapolis. Sometimes he bragged about having hopped a freight car to Mexico with Big Joe Williams. On other occasions he claimed to have toured with Bobby Vee. Sometimes he claimed to *be* Bobby Vee. To Dylan, anything was preferable to being a middle-class Jew. So it was that in Greenwich Village he found the perfect home. There it was okay, even fashionable, to make up one's own identity. And there a babyfaced youth of twenty could play wastrel, sleep in crash pads and charm his way into a free dinner.

But Dylan was more than charming. His talent was as obvious as it was huge. On the evening of the very day that he arrived in New York he was already up on the stage of Macdougal Street's Cafe Wha? A few weeks later he was playing regularly at Gerde's Folk City, joining in on Monday night hootenannies which featured such established names as Dave van Ronk, Phil Ochs, Tom Paxton, Jack Elliott and Paul Clayton. On April 11, 1961, only three months after arriving in the city, Dylan was signed to a Columbia records recording contract by John Hammond. In September of that year *New York Times* critic Robert Shelton, after watching Dylan at Gerdes, wrote, "There is no doubt that he is bursting at the seams with talent." Soon interviewers began knocking at his door, reporting statements like, "The less hair on the head, the more inside. Wear a crewcut and you have all that hair cluttering around your brain." By the end of the year he had recorded his first album for Columbia and had signed a seven-year contract with Albert Grossman, who also managed Peter, Paul and Mary. In April of 1962, fifteen months after he had suddenly appeared out of the north country, Dylan wrote "Blowin' in the Wind." "The song was there before I came along," he told Pete Seeger. "I just sort of came and just sort of took it down with a pencil." He was now on his way — as a singer, as a writer and as a personality.

Dylan's songs, aided by his extraordinary talent as a performer (on recordings, the line between the song and its performance was soon to get very blurry), had more style, more of an author's presence than the ersatz folksongs which were being turned out by his Village brethren. In a way, he was a writer of the old school — not lyrically or musically so much as in the personality that is present in even his earliest efforts. There was an intensity and an élan about everything he sang and wrote. His work had the aura of authorship and one was thus able to follow it and grow with it. But there was another side to this coin — for Dylan, being so different from his peers, was probably the most solitary of all this century's great songwriters. Even the best of the Broadway writers had his equals. The same was true of the talented men and women who crowded Hollywood in the 1930s. Later in the century other communities — Liverpool and London in England, San Francisco, Los Angeles and Detroit in the United States — produced crops of talent but none produced a lone genius. (The Beatles may have had no real rivals in Liverpool but they were matched by one another.) The Village, on the other hand, produced many fine songs but only one great songwriter. Dylan was alone and his background — the concatenation of forces that shaped him — has come to have a unique look, as if he, of all the geniuses who are the concern of this book, evolved separately, like a creature on the Galapagos Islands.

With success, his relationship to the Village became schizophrenic. On the one hand, he seemed to genuinely love the place. On the other, he did his best to stand apart from it. When Jack Elliott, a Guthrie protege, told him in 1962, "You're really like the Woody of today," Dylan spoke heresy, saying, "I've gone way beyond Woody." Later that year he thumbed his nose at all of them when, on his first single, "Mixed Up Confusion," he chose to be backed by a rock band. Though the record was quickly withdrawn from the market to forestall protests from the purists, it pointed to the big break which was to come two years later.

The barrier between himself and the others continued to grow. It was like the Berlin Wall — wire at first, later solid brick and of an increasingly ugly cast. He had disrupted not only the musical purity of the movement but its egalitarian purity as well. As the first of the group to achieve stardom, he became the first to inspire envy, to attract sycophants. He drew them into his orbit as planets in the heavens draw satellites, on the basis of his cosmic bulk. Eric Anderson, Dave van Ronk, Tom Paxton, Phil Ochs and others always seemed to be surrounding him, following him at night from club to club. Dylan would preside over them, sometimes sullenly, sometimes like a raucous king. They were at his mercy. He might sneer at them or ignore them altogether.

But pecking orders based on talent were nothing new among songwriters. There is the often told story from the 1920s about a game of catch between George Gershwin and Harry Ruby (composer of "Three Little Words," "Hooray for Captain Spaulding" and others). Gershwin, impressed by Ruby's ability to throw a baseball, exclaimed, "I could do very well too if I tried but I must be careful of my hands. With you it doesn't matter." The fact that Ruby also made his living at the piano had not occurred to Gershwin, whose egocentricity was as well known as it was guileless. Even so, such an interchange was quite rare among show composers, and the kind of derision that Dylan heaped on his inferiors was unheard of. In this way too Dylan was an innovator.

Increasingly, he would set out to tweak not just an individual but the folk movement as a whole. When he appeared at the 1964 folk festival in Newport he chose to sing only personal songs about love gone sour, even though the war in Vietnam had become a paramount issue. Then, in March 1965, he released an album, *Bringing It All Back Home*, on which he was accompanied by electrically amplified instruments. A few months later he brought this apostasy back home to Newport itself where, in addition to electric guitars and a back beat, he further inflamed the audience by eschewing workmen's jeans for mod English clothing.

Still, his relationship with the Village continued to have its loving side too. As late as 1963, when he was selling more than ten thousand albums a month, he was still living in his West Fourth Street apartment, sleeping on a floor mattress and eating at a card table. Eventually he had to get out, for his fame had flared up beyond all reckoning. But in 1969 he returned, moving into a townhouse on Macdougal Street, around the corner from Gerdes and the other old clubs. By then he had made a journey as exotic as any made by the epic heroes of old. But, unlike Ulysses', this homecoming was not to bring much peace. A fallow period in his songwriting ensued; after the *New Morning* album of autumn 1970 he did not release a collection of new songs until 1974. By then he was rootless once again, having moved with his wife and children to Malibu, California — only to have his marriage break up.

At the time of Dylan's first arrival in the Village, Tin Pan Alley — or a new incarnation of it — suddenly came to life again in New York city. This was primarily through the success of Aldon Music, a publishing house formed by guitarist Al Nevins and songwriter Don Kirshner. Its address was 1619 Broadway, the Brill Building — and "Brill Building Pop" soon became a phrase denoting a brand of music which sought to bridge the gap between the stylish, hand-crafted Tin Pan Alley fare and the good time impulsiveness of rock and roll. Aldon Music's stable of songwriters consisted of several composer/lyricist teams, most of them Jewish. Carole King, who had married her lyricist, Gerry Goffin, was born Carole Klein in Sheepshead Bay, Brooklyn. She met Goffin while at Queens College and together they wrote songs for an eclectic list of performers, including the Drifters ("Up on the Roof"), Steve Lawrence and Edie Gorme ("Go Away Little Girl") and Bobby Vee ("How Many Tears"). This was yet another way in which they were a throwback to Tin Pan Alley days — for the writers of that bygone era had hawked songs wherever they could: to vaudeville acts, to Broadway revues, to circuses, anywhere. Because Goffin and King's songs were recorded and re-recorded by so many different groups ("Chains," initially sung by the Cookies, was later covered by the Beatles), they were among the first of the rock and roll era which could be called standards.

King and Goffin worked in a windowless cubicle. In another booth just a few feet away a second husband and wife team was doing the same thing. They were Barry Mann and Cynthia Weill, composers of "Uptown," "Who Put the Bomp," "Blame It on the Bossa Nova," "Walking in the Rain," "You've Lost That Lovin' Feeling" and many more. They, in turn, shared a wall with Neil Sedaka and Howie Greenfield, recent graduates of Brooklyn's Lincoln High School and the creators of a number of hits, including "Oh! Carol" (Sedaka wrote this song about Carole King, who had been a childhood friend and neighbor), "Stupid Cupid" (for Connie Francis), "Charms" (for Bobby Vee) and "Foolish Little Girl" (for The Shirelles). Some of their best songs were sung on record by Sedaka himself, including "Stairway to Heaven," "Calendar Girl" and "Breaking Up Is Hard to Do." A piano prodigy and a graduate of the Juilliard School of Music, Sedaka brought a musically sophisticated touch to the songs that Kirshner was directing to the teenage market.

Several other successful songwriting teams were at work in New York during this period. Though not employed by Aldon Music, their style was similar in spirit to the music made at the Brill Building — and they too were Jewish. Burt Bacharach, another pop composer with classical training, combined with lyricist Hal David to write a string of hits for singer Dionne Warwick. Doc Pomus and Mort Shuman wrote hits for Fabian ("Turn Me Loose"), The Drifters ("This Magic Moment") and Elvis Presley ("Surrender"). Jerry Leiber and Mike Stoller gave Aldon Music a real run for its money with a barrage of classic rhythm and blues numbers, including "Hound Dog," "Young Blood," "Yakety Yak," "Poison Ivy," "Fools Fall in Love," "Jailhouse Rock," "Love Potion Number 9," "Kansas City," "Stand By Me," "Is That All There Is" and many others. Jeff Barry and Ellie Greenwich were yet another successful husband and wife songwriting team in New York City during this period, writing, producing and sometimes singing such songs as "Da Doo Ron Ron" (written with Phil Spector), "Chapel of Love" (with Spector), "Do Wah Diddy Diddy," "Leader of the Pack" and "River Deep, Mountain High" (with Spector).

With the coming of the Beatles in 1964 and with the simultaneous blossoming of the golden age of Motown, the influence of these New York writers began to wane. Neil Sedaka and Carole King would achieve highly successful comebacks as singer/songwriters in the 1970s but, for the remainder of the 1960s, the pendulum of pop swung away from New York. Mid-1960s New York City did, however, manage to produce one more songwriting great. This was Paul Simon. Born in Newark, New Jersey to a Jewish/Hungarian family, he grew up in the Kew Garden Hill section of New York City. While still in high school Simon wrote his first hit song, "Hey! Schoolgirl," recorded by himself and school friend Art Garfunkel under the stage name of Tom and Jerry (on Thanksgiving Day of 1957 they sang the song on the same edition of American Bandstand on which Jerry Lee Lewis sang "Great Balls of Fire"). But they could produce no follow-up. At Queens College Simon met Carole King and recorded some demonstration records with her (she played piano and drums, he played guitar and bass) but nothing much came of that either. In 1964 Columbia Records put out Simon and Garfunkel's debut album *Wednesday Morning 3 A.M.* but the record went nowhere and Simon returned to Europe where he had been singing in folk clubs and coffee houses. It was in his absence that Tom Wilson, the producer of the album, added electric guitar, electric bass and drums to one of the songs, "The Sound of Silence," thereby propelling it to number one on the U.S. charts. Simon had arrived. Subsequently, he was to become the best American composer/lyricist since the days of Cole Porter and Irving Berlin and, unlike King, Sedaka and the

14

others, his popularity remained consistently high. Like them, however, he was never quite comfortable with the Woodstock generation. He was not visceral enough to challenge the triumvirate of the Beatles, Dylan and the Rolling Stones in the late 1960s. Only when distinctions between the underground and the aboveground became imprecise and a little ludicrous in the 1970s did his talent stand unencumbered by extra-musical considerations. "When I started writing I didn't think there was any space for me between Dylan and the Beatles — they had it all covered," he told *Newsweek* in 1975. "I was writing little psychological tunes based on wandering melodies. Now I'm trying to get closer to Tin Pan Alley. It's no fluke that me, Berlin, Gershwin and Kern are all Jewish guys from New York who look alike."

Another chapter in the history of twentieth century pop songwriting communities was written by rich and successful New Yorkers who emigrated to the sometimes more lucrative, always more sunshiny state of California. Dylan, as has been seen, relocated to Malibu in the early 1970s and he was only one of a number of famous songwriters who established residences along a Malibu-Laurel Canyon axis. Carole King also arrived, as did Joni Mitchell (from Alberta by way of Toronto, Detroit and New York) and Graham Nash (from Blackpool, England). Even more than Gershwin, Kern and Arlen nearly forty years before, they sought in one another social and musical companionship, appearing as session players on each other's albums, joining in on one another's tours and participating in one another's political causes. But this was a community that was in decline from the beginning: some of the residents, such as Joni Mitchell, did do their best work after coming to Laurel Canyon. But, for most, the song catalogues of bygone days were richer than the additions made here. And even Joni Mitchell who, by her willingness to experiment, was able to keep her fans guessing and off-balance, was not always able to keep them whistling — that first and most magical of a songwriter's responsibilities. They were like the Village crowd in that they were, for the most part, singer/songwriters who preferred acoustic instrumentation and civilized, civilizing lyrics. But, by being rich, they were unlike either the Village or that more recent songwriter's commune, San Francisco's Haight/Ashbury. They were about as interested in sharing the communal life with unwashed peers as Cole Porter and Richard Rodgers had been. They lived near and around one another but in a way that recalled the manner in which the upper classes of Europe would vacation together in St. Tropez. Great songwriting can certainly arise amidst great wealth — Cole Porter's career proved that — and yet this pocket of songwriters, wealthy as oil sheikhs, has yet to produce songs worthy of its talent.

Forty years earlier the six great Broadway composers had made a similar trek — one that was not always so pleasant, but one which was ultimately more successful. When Depression-era hard times turned the lullaby of Broadway into a lull, the New York songwriting community had moved bodily to Hollywood. Awaiting them there were the moguls, whose ranks included Irving Thalberg, Louis B. Mayer and Jack L. Warner, to whom they surrendered some of their pride and much of their autonomy. In return, they received lucrative, Depression-defying contracts and one another's company. Present in mid-1930s Hollywood was a vast array of talent, including composers Kern, Berlin, Gershwin, Arlen, Rodgers, Porter, Arthur Schwartz, Harry Warren, Hoagy Carmichael, Vincent Youmans, Sigmund Romberg and Harry Ruby as well as such lyricists as Y.A. Harburg, Buddy De Sylva, Dorothy Fields, Howard Dietz, Larry Hart, Oscar Hammerstein and Ira Gershwin.

Hollywood was very different from New York. Back east they had been big wheels; here they were just cogs in the wheel. On Broadway the names Berlin, Porter, Kern and Gershwin had long meant at least as much and usually more than the names of the stars who sang their songs — even when the performers were as renowned as Gertrude Lawrence, Fred Astaire and Ethel Merman. In Hollywood, however, the composers played second fiddle to the stars — who were themselves moved about like chess pawns by studio executives. It was an odd, disquieting atmosphere, with little of the quiescent, self-satisfied ambience of Laurel Canyon in the '70s. Still, the Broadway writers were making more money in California than they ever had in New York and on far easier assignments; not only that, here there were palm trees, orange groves and Hollywood parties — in short, the good life. And, best of all, they were together — a hotbed of songwriting talent such as had never been seen, even in New York. Yet, nearly everyone was vaguely miserable.

Berlin fared best. His songs were in the movies as early as 1927 when Al Jolson sang "Blues Skies" in *The Jazz Singer*. Berlin contributed music to several other films before writing his first full score in 1935 for the memorable Astaire/Rogers film *Top Hat*. He followed that up the next year with another successful Astaire/Rogers film, *Follow the Fleet*, and his tunes were in *On the Avenue* in 1937. In 1938 there was a third Astaire/Rogers film, *Carefree*, which contained the hit "Change Partners," and that same year Twentieth Century Fox came up with *Alexander's Ragtime Band*, featuring 28 Berlin oldies plus three new compositions. In 1939 there was *Second Fiddle*, starring Sonja Henie and Tyrone Power, and in 1942 came *Holiday Inn* with its mega-hit "White Christmas." Because of these successes, the moguls treated Berlin with more deference than any other songwriter. A canny businessman himself, Berlin always more than held his own with them and, for the rest of his career, while successfully dividing his time between Hollywood and the Broadway stage, he was careful to maintain his residence in New York.

Things did not go quite so well for Jerome Kern. He had received his first indication of what work on the West Coast would be like in 1931, when he came to California with lyricist Otto Harbach to work on the film *Men in the Sky*. The studios discarded every song that they wrote (though a couple were used as background music). Kern, who was already the doyen of American popular songwriters, was not used to such treatment. When he returned to California in 1934, settling in a sixth floor suite at the Beverly Wilshire Hotel, he was unwilling to take any additional guff from the studio executives. In 1936 David O. Selznick, who was producing a new film called *Ebb Tide*, called Kern into his office, mentioned the need for a musical score, and asked to hear some of the composer's melodies. "I don't play samples," Kern replied and then he walked out. Nevertheless, he bore the studios no grudge. It was in Hollywood that he wrote "I Won't Dance" and "Lovely to Look At" for the screen version of his Broadway show *Roberta*, as well as the classic score for the 1936 Astaire/Rogers film *Swingtime*, which included the Academy Award-winning "The Way You Look Tonight."

In 1937 Kern left the Beverly Wilshire and moved into a white brick house at 917 Whittier Drive in Beverly Hills. Shortly thereafter, he suffered a heart attack which put him out of commission for more than a year. That same year Cole Porter had his riding accident and George Gershwin, living just a few blocks away from Kern in Beverly Hills, died from a brain tumor. None of these events was caused by Hollywood (though Gershwin's headaches had for a time been mistakenly attributed to his dissatisfaction with the studios) but they somehow added to the unpleasant aura of the place.

Harold Arlen came to Hollywood in the mid-'30s, made his home there and, except for a few forays back to Broadway (some of them notable, including *St. Louis Woman, Bloomer Girl* and *House of Flowers*), spent the remaining thirty-five years of his career there. In all that time, he received just a couple of good assignments: *The Wizard of Oz* in 1939 and *A Star Is Born* in 1954. The genesis of his most memorable movie song, "Over the Rainbow," is typical of what a composer — even one of Arlen's stature — was up against in the Hollywood of that era. The tune had an auspicious beginning — it came to Arlen as he was driving past Schwab's Drugstore on Sunset Boulevard on his way to Grauman's Chinese Theater. But it quickly ran into trouble. Arlen's lyricist, H.A. "Yip" Harburg, thought it more suited to a Jeanette MacDonald operetta than to the plangent voice of Judy Garland. The two men took the tune to Ira Gershwin for arbitration and, when the latter pronounced it good, Harburg proceeded to write a lyric. But the real impasse proved to be the MGM front office. The studio heads objected to the octave leap between "some" and "where" as well as to the middle of the song ("Someday I'll wish upon a star"), which one bigwig likened to a child's piano exercise. Three times the song was deleted from the movie and three times it had to work its way back in before it could stay, unchallenged.

Bigger names than Arlen were treated in the same cavalier fashion. Cole Porter's first foray into the world of moviemaking was strange, even by the standards of the day. The twists and turns of work on MGM's *Born to Dance* were bizarre enough to prompt him to keep a diary. That is how we know that on December 20, 1935, Executive Producer Sam Katz promised him that all would proceed smoothly, that the script, to be written by Jack McGowan and Sidney Silvers, would be based on the real-life romance between John Barrymore and Elaine Barrie and that it would star Clark Gable and Jean Harlow. Three weeks later Porter learned that the Barrymore story was out, that Gable and Harlow had been scotched, that writers McGowan and Silvers had been fired and that the new producer would be Jack Cummings, a relative of Louis B. Mayer. The film would now be about two reporters, one male and the other female, competing for the Pulitzer Prize while covering a story in Tibet. Then the Tibetan angle was ruled out and months passed while writers and executives wrangled over story ideas. Finally it was decided that *Born to Dance* would be about a lonely hearts club in Honolulu. For some reason, the studio was pleased that this would allow for dance numbers aboard Navy battleships.

But Porter's troubles did not end there. Like Kern and Arlen, he found that the studio could veto his songs. One number, "Goodbye Little Dream Goodbye," suffered such a fate, though it had won everybody's heart at first. MGM executives were so moved by it that they immediately offered to extend Porter's contract, and when Paramount got wind of the tune it offered Porter the next Bing Crosby picture. Nevertheless, "Goodbye Little Dream Goodbye," true to its title, was eventually thought wanting and it never made it into the film. Another song, "Swingin' the Jinx Away," irritated Director Roy Del Ruth and Dance Director Seymour Felix. The fate of this tune had to be decided at a meeting of directors, actors and technicians that resembled a jury trial. Only the positive testimony of orchestrator Eddie Powell and of the dancing star Eleanor Powell tipped the scales in its favor. Somehow, despite this chaos, *Born to Dance* was a success. Jimmy Stewart sang the big hit, "Easy to Love," and Porter, chuckling at the absurdity of it all, was happy to sojourn in Hollywood again and again.

18

Richard Rodgers and his partner Larry Hart were not so easily amused. Like the others they too washed up on California's shores in the 1930s. Between 1930 and 1931 they worked on four films. Only one of them, *Love Me Tonight*, was successful. Then, in late 1932, they signed with Irving Thalberg of MGM for a single picture, *I Married an Angel* — a movie which was suddenly and whimsically cancelled by Thalberg's boss, Louis B. Mayer, shortly after the music and the script had been written. (*I Married an Angel* eventually was made into a movie by MGM, but only after Rodgers and Hart had turned it into a successful Broadway show.)

Now the team was in a quandary. Months of work in California had come to nothing. The situation on Broadway was still bleak. Rodgers had a wife and a baby to support. Hart, with no family, wanted money for needs that were less upright. They were sorely tempted when Thalberg offered them another year's contract but the document did not specify a project and they were afraid that they would be given nothing to do. Should that prove to be the case and should they complain about it, they knew that they would be told, "You got your check, didn't you?" Still, they signed.

As it turned out, they *were* given an assignment. It was a film called *Hollywood Party* which featured every available MGM comedian from Jimmy Durante to The Three Stooges. Perhaps the nature of the cast had something to do with the fact that every day brought a new director to the set (no director was ever named in the film credits). As for Rodgers and Hart, only three of their twelve songs were used in the film, although one of the discards later turned up with new lyrics as "Blue Moon."

After this fiasco the team was all but inactive. Hart spent his time in barrooms while Rodgers, unable to think of anything else to do, risked sunstroke on the tennis courts. Because they could not abrogate their contract, they were forced to wait out the rest of the year. On his last day in Hollywood Rodgers went to Thalberg's office to offer a diplomatic handshake and a gentlemanly goodbye. Thalberg, however, had no idea who he was.

But the saddest Hollywood tale befell the Gershwin brothers. George and Ira had first visited the film capital in 1931 when, for $100,000 they had written the score for just one film, *Delicious*. It had been a half-hearted effort — the songs they used had been discards from various Broadway shows. Even the title tune had been written six months before they set foot in California.

Not that they had been unwilling to work. They had hoped, even expected to be included in script conferences, in the recording and editing of the music and in the filming process itself. After all, they were used to being involved in every phase of a Broadway production and they had expected that Hollywood would want their advice too.

The Gershwin brothers in Hollywood in 1937.

But the script did not call for their attention — half a dozen writers were already at war over it — and the performance and recording of the music were also outside their purview. Even the songs did not seem all that necessary. The film only required two — as opposed to the dozen or more contained in a typical Broadway score.

So it was that on their first visit to Hollywood the Gershwins mostly sat in their rented Beverly Hills house and tried to think of how to pass the time. When they worked, it was on non-Hollywood matters: George composed a second rhapsody and the two of them wrote some songs for the upcoming Broadway play *Of Thee I Sing*.

Five years later, after a succession of flops on Broadway (*Let 'Em Eat Cake, Pardon My English* and, with Dubose Heyward, the opera *Porgy and Bess*), the Gershwins found it necessary to come to Hollywood again. But now they could no longer bargain with the studios from a position of strength. Having advised their New York agent that their fee for a Hollywood picture would be $100,000 plus a percentage of the profits, they were told not to expect that much. There was, the agent explained, "an ill-founded belief that George Gershwin would only be interested in writing so-called 'highbrow' material."

A few months later the Gershwins received a wire from a Hollywood agent reiterating that the studios were "afraid you will only do highbrow songs." George wired back: "Rumors about highbrow music ridiculous stop am out to write hits." They finally settled for $55,000 (Irving Berlin, who had just written the score for *Follow the Fleet*, was being paid $75,000 plus a percentage of the profits).

When the brothers arrived in Hollywood on August 1 they checked into the Beverly Wilshire Hotel (Kern was living there at the time and Cole Porter would establish himself there at the end of the year) and quickly went to see the latest Astaire/Rogers picture, *Swingtime*. Not having written hit songs together in so long (some of the melodies from *Porgy and Bess* were just starting to catch on) they were nervous about their ability to compete with such high-quality material.

Then came the familiar problems with the studio, this time RKO. Weeks passed, then months and still there was no script. The Gershwins, unconsulted by the producers, felt like lackeys, despite the high pay and the perquisites that went with life in Beverly Hills. It was in such an atmosphere that George Gershwin lived his last days and wrote his last songs. Surrounded by friends but unhappy with Hollywood's style, constantly planning his return to New York (with a new opera, a new show, a new concert work), filling his spare time with dates as a piano soloist (as well as dates with Paulette Goddard and Simone Simon), he earned his keep by writing a series of very great songs: "They Can't Take That Away from Me," "A

Foggy Day," "They All Laughed," "Nice Work If You Can Get It," "Let's Call the Whole Thing Off," "Love Walked In," and "Love Is Here to Stay."

This material, along with the other songs written for Depression-era Hollywood films, forms the backbone of American popular song literature. Just why it was that these writers rose to such heights at that time is a question that is worth pondering. This century's only other gathering of rich and established songwriters was the one in Laurel Canyon in the 1970s. But they, unlike the Broadway transplants of Hollywood in the 1930s, were beholden to no one. No film executives breathed down their necks; no record company chieftains rejected their songs. They were able to work as they chose — in solitude or with a few close friends — and they were in complete control of what they produced, from the choice of a bass player to the art work on an album sleeve. It had been different for the songwriters in 1930s Hollywood. They were under considerable pressure — not only from the omnipotent and whimsical studio heads, but from the fellow who was pounding his piano in the mansion next door.

Twentieth century pop tunesmithing did not entirely escape the clutches of New York City until the late 1950s, when a significant musical community arose in the British west coast seaport of Liverpool. No one from outside this town ever used to give it a thought but now its byways are part of everyone's heritage because of a few songwriters known collectively as the Beatles. Their story is as well known to this generation as the stories of the Greek gods were to ancient Athenians. Everyone has heard about their beginnings in grimy Liverpool; about the day that Paul McCartney pedaled his bicycle across town to be introduced to John Lennon and to hear the latter's skiffle group, the Quarrymen; about ships from the New World which docked in mid-'50s Liverpool bearing the latest rhythm and blues records; about George Harrison's first £3 guitar and the way he practiced it until his fingers bled; about Ringo Starr's childhood hospitalizations and loneliness; about John Lennon's exhortations of "Sieg Heil!" to German nightclubbers in Hamburg's Reeperbahn and "rattle your jewelry" to royalty at the Prince of Wales Theatre in London; about the extraordinary love between these men.

Because of them, much is also known about the sudden and extravagant outpouring of musical yearning on the part of Liverpool's young citizenry in the mid-'50s. This craze is usually credited to Lonnie Donegan's recording of "Rock Island Line" which, because it made use of such extemporaneous instruments as a washboard and a tea chest, inspired a taste for southern U.S.-style skiffle music among Liverpool boys who were too poor to buy proper instruments. With the advent of Elvis Presley and the latter's recording of "Heartbreak Hotel" in 1956, the musical ambitions of Liverpool youth were further inflamed. But Donegan and Elvis notwithstanding, one cannot really know for sure why this generation chose music as its craze; the mania might as easily have been for gang warfare or for punting along the Mersey River. That the Beatles, roughs themselves of a sort, did choose music and that they found themselves not only successful at it but touched with a magical genius, is something which can never adequately be explained.

Given their talent, it was inevitable that they would rise above such Liverpool competition as Rory Storm and the Hurricanes (Ringo had been their drummer) and Gerry and the Pacemakers. But they continued to rise — above all competition in England and then all competition in America. Certainly they had peers in the craft of songwriting: Carole King and Gerry Goffin, Holland-Dozier-Holland, Jagger and Richards, Bob Dylan, Paul Simon — but they rose above these peers in much the same way that Gershwin went beyond Berlin, Kern and Rodgers. Like Gershwin, they seemed to have an inexhaustible supply of not just good but surprising musical ideas. There was also a distinct parallel between Gershwin and the backbone of the Beatles, John Lennon. Both had the reputation of having been born poor, though neither ever knew want. Each was in his teenage years before turning to music (though Gershwin, at the age of six, was momentarily waylaid by Anton Rubenstein's *Melody in F* while roller-skating past a mechanical piano in Harlem) but both, when they did take up music, proceeded to learn their instruments, write songs and strive blindly toward the top, like spawning salmon. Each, though quite capable of cranking out innumerable hit tunes, wanted to do something more, something new. Gershwin's *Rhapsody in Blue* and the Beatles' *Sgt. Pepper* represent two of the rare occasions in which popular music suddenly and successfully stretched itself. The Gershwin piece, written in 1924 when the composer was 25, startled a hall full of concert-goers and went on to send ripples around the musical world. For all of its tunefulness, for all of its inoffensive palatability, it was still a shocker. Forty-three years later the Beatles released *Sgt. Pepper* (Lennon was 26, McCartney, 25) and the same thing happened again, though this time the ripples travelled from east to west. *Sgt. Pepper* enthralled in much the same way as had the *Rhapsody* and, with it, the Beatles left their peers behind, as Gershwin had done with Berlin and Kern.

Liverpool was the Lower East Side of its day, producing counterparts not only to New York's Jewish songwriters but to its Jewish comedians as well. Names like Tommy Handley, Ted Ray and Arthur Askey may never have had any currency in the United States, but they and other Liverpudlian music hall comedians were to England

23

what George Jessel, the Marx Brothers and other New Yorkers were to the United States. And the Beatles were probably the best comedians that Liverpool ever produced. After the success of their films *A Hard Day's Night* and *Help!* it seemed that they might even turn into a modern-day version of the Marxes (who, in turn, had been musicians of a sort). While that did not happen, their ad libs at press conferences and in interviews stand up well beside some of Groucho's best quips. After the decline of its cotton industry and prior to the music boom, such humor was Liverpool's best crop.

By 1965 the hub of English popular music had moved away from Liverpool and south to London. The Beatles too relocated to the capital where they joined the other songwriting bands that had come into prominence: the Kinks, the Who and, most important, the Rolling Stones. The story of that group is another part of this generation's folklore. In a sense, it is an even more tantalizing tale than that of the Beatles, for it has more dark edges. The jealous tension that the Beatles had faced when Stu Sutcliffe and Paul McCartney were vying for John Lennon's favor were put to rest long before the group came to prominence. Sutcliffe left the fledgling band in 1961 and he died of a brain tumor in 1962. The Stones, on the other hand, lived with such a rivalry even into their years of superstardom. Mick Jagger and Keith Richards, born within six months of one another in 1943, first met when they were both in primary school, though their paths did not cross again until 1960, when they discovered a mutual interest in rhythm and blues music. They eventually ended up playing at the same London club as Brian Jones, who was a year older and from a more middle class background (Jagger and Richards were born in Dartford; Jones, in the posh suburb of Cheltenham). By 1963 the lineup of the band was complete with drummer Charlie Watts and bass player Bill Wyman, but the primary tensions within the group, both creative and personal, were between Jones and Jagger, with Richards' alliance as the prize. Jagger, much the stronger of the two, was the inevitable winner. By 1969, when Jones left the group (he was to die a few weeks later), Jagger and Richards had become the heart and soul of the Stones, as well as songwriters *par excellence*.

In the meantime, this band had carved out a niche for itself as the underside of the Beatles. Dark, menacing, unrepentant, they understood that odd but inevitable duality which often asserts itself in the popular arts (i.e., Hemingway and Fitzgerald) and they played an angry yang to the Beatles' gentle yin. Privately, however, the Beatles and the Stones intermingled. Occasionally, a member from one would cross the line and assist in the other's recording sessions (the Beatles sang on the Stones' "We Love You," while Brian Jones played saxophone on The Beatles' "You Know My Name") and, for

24

a time, there was even talk that the two bands would merge under the same business management. But rivalry did continue to exist. At a party in late 1968 Jagger was playing an advance pressing of the Stones' as yet unreleased album *Beggar's Banquet* when Paul McCartney entered and upstaged him with an acetate of the new Beatles' single, "Hey Jude."

This social intermingling of songwriters in mid-'60s London was similar to what had taken place in mid-'30s Hollywood. In fact, there was probably even more creative electricity in the London scene, since the Hollywood composers had had to work in the shadows of movie stars — while the Beatles and the Stones were second to none in glamour. They, the Who, the Animals, the Hollies and the Kinks brought the spotlight of pop culture away from America and to London; at the same time they turned the pop music of London away from the pseudo-Broadway of Lionel Bart and the pseudo-Elvis of Tommy Steele. It is true that at first they played nothing much more than pseudo-rhythm and blues, but in short order they had incorporated their own sensibilities into that rough music and had made something vital and homegrown.

No one had expected England to take the world's lead in popular music. Since the demise of Gilbert and Sullivan, few of the country's popular songs had been worth much. For most of the century London had been embarrassingly dependent on the Broadway shows it received secondhand. Sometimes the Broadway writers did compose new music specifically for a British production but on such occasions they were liable to use London as a dumping ground for their second best material (Gershwin's *Primrose*, for example). Britain, conversely, had for most of the century been unable to export any of its pop musicians to America. Local stars such as Cliff Richard had minimal impact on the U.S. market, despite the efforts of their backers and publicists. The Beatles changed all of that — but they themselves sang with American accents.

Liverpool had been like the Lower East Side — a sudden burst of music in dismal surroundings. Other songwriting communities in the 1950s and 1960s developed along more businesslike lines — around small companies run by enterprising father figures. Cosimo Matassa, owner and chief engineer of J&M Studios in New Orleans, recorded and, in some cases, discovered many of the best songwriters living in and around the New Orleans area. In the early and mid-1950s Fats Domino recorded some of his finest compositions under Matassa, as did Little Richard and Charlie Price. Sun Records in Memphis, owned and operated by Sam Phillips, was a magnet for such local writers as Carl Perkins and Jerry Lee Lewis. Up north in Chicago, Chess Records, run by Leonard and Phillip Chess, performed a similar function for Muddy Waters, Chuck Berry and Bo Diddley.

These studios were independent and out-of-the-way regional affairs, each with its own identifiable sound. At A&M, for instance, Matassa, because of the unique and primitive acoustics of his studio, created a sound which later writers, no matter how sophisticated their gear, found impossible to duplicate. Sun Records singlehandedly created rockabilly when it fused the singing of whites such as Elvis Presley with the rhythm and blues numbers of Big Bill Broonzy, Junior Parker and others.

At the height of their success, these studios were not part of any establishment. They attracted and promoted songwriters for whom the more traditional outlets, such as Broadway and Hollywood, were impenetrable. Yet, they were company affairs, run by moguls of a kind. They were not the loose and disorganized street life centers of the Lower East Side of or Liverpool. Nor were they the self-conscious warrens of like-minded and politically active talent such as Greenwich Village and the Haight/Ashbury. They were a halfway point between the beatnik/hippy mentality and those great monoliths, Broadway and Hollywood.

One of these independent companies rose head and shoulders above the rest. It began in a warehouse, back-of-the-store manner but it eventually pushed a piece of the establishment aside to make room for itself. This was Motown, founded in 1959 by Berry Gordy, Jr. Gordy was born in Detroit in 1930 and was raised in its slums. The son of a plasterer, he quit school in the eleventh grade to become a professional boxer, then a record store owner. But it was as a songwriter that he first achieved some success. In 1957 Brunswick Records bought his song "Reet Petite" which led to other sales and, before too long, he was able to quit his job as a chrome-trimmer for Lincoln-Mercury and found Motown (which had initially been christened "Hitsville USA").

Motown's first million-seller was "Shop Around," penned in 1960 by 19-year-old Smokey Robinson. Four years later the company was selling twelve million records a year, employing 100 performers and providing executive desks for ten of Gordy's relatives. It was all one big family. Marvin Gaye married Gordy's sister Anna, a Marvelette married a Contour and yearly Christmas parties were family as well as company affairs. Nearly everyone at Motown was a native of Detroit (although there were exceptions: Jimmy Webb, a white songwriter from Oklahoma, worked briefly for Motown in the mid-'60s), and a good percentage of the population of Detroit wished they could become part of the company.

Gordy chose writers whose appeal would cut across racial and songwriting categories. Though the music was written and performed by blacks, and though it was based on gospel and rhythm and blues, it contained the kind of harmonic novelty and melodic sweetness favored by whites. At J&M, Sun and Chess there had been much less of this Tin Pan Alley-style calculation and craft. The writers associated with those labels were intuitive and impulsive, as one might expect from artists who were primarily performers. At Motown there was more control; in a way, Gordy was a benevolent dictator. Those who wrote for him wrote within the bounds of what came to be a readily identifiable Motown style, one which critic Jon Landau separated into the following elements: simply structured songs based on repetition, sophisticated melodies and harmonies, and relentless four-beat-to-the-bar rhythms. Performed by top-notch studio musicians, sung by groups whose roots lay in gospel music, and mixed toward the treble for best effect on A.M. radios, Motown recordings were often overwhelming.

Gordy picked young writers who would grow with and into this style. Smokey Robinson and most of his group, the Miracles, were still teenagers when Gordy plucked them from a Detroit high school. Robinson was the lead singer and songwriter for the group but at Motown he also wrote and produced for others, including Mary Wells and the Temptations. In the 1960s he produced many of Motown's hits, including "My Guy," "My Girl," "You've Really Got a Hold on Me," "The Tracks of My Tears," "Ooo, Baby Baby," and such inventively titled songs as "The Hunter Gets Captured by the Game" and "I Second That Emotion."

Stevie Wonder was another of Gordy's discoveries. Born a month premature and blind in 1950, Wonder grew up in Detroit, the third of six children, each fathered by a different man. He was only ten when he joined Motown — and he was just thirteen when he recorded his first hit song, "Fingertips, Part 2" (there never was, apparently, a "Fingertips, Part 1"), which topped the charts in 1963. A string of hits followed — "Uptight (Everything's Alright)," "I Was Made to Love Her," "My Cherie Amour" — until Wonder abandoned the Motown style in the 1970s.

Other Motown songwriters preferred to remain in the background, writing and producing for singer groups. Norman Whitfield, composer of "I Heard It Through the Grapevine," "War," "You're My Everything," "Cloud Nine" and many others, was one. But a far more extensive and glorious batch of hit tunes was written by Lamont Dozier, Brian Holland and Eddie Holland (the Hollands were brothers), all born and raised in Detroit. Dozier had played in local groups and had later worked anonymously as a Motown writer/producer until Gordy teamed him with the Hollands. In 1963 the three of them wrote "Heat Wave," a huge hit for Martha and the Vandellas and, in the next four years, they wrote 28 top-20 pop hits, including "Baby Love," "Come See About Me," "Stop in the Name of Love," "Back in My Arms Again," "You

Keep Me Hanging On," "Reflections," and "Reach Out I'll Be There."

It is not clear just who in HDH did what. Each probably had a hand in music, lyrics and production, but Dozier appears to have been the principal composer, Eddie Holland the main lyricist. Prior to teaming up, Eddie Holland had been a singer with a few hit records to his credit; after the trio disbanded in the late '60s, Dozier embarked on a singing career. But during their heyday at Motown, working mainly with the Supremes and the Four Tops, they stayed behind the scenes. From inside the unpretentious clapboard houses of Motown's West Grand Boulevard lot, they turned out an extraordinary number of fine songs between 1963 and 1967.

In the mid-1960s another songwriting community sprang up spontaneously, unrelated to any commercial enterprise. This was the Haight/Ashbury district of San Francisco. Their most obvious antecedent was Greenwich Village and they shared much of the Village ethos — both its political and social values. They were also like the Village in that they were primarily out-of-towners, an ingathering from across the nation. One contingent, including Janis Joplin, Doug Sahm and Steve Miller, was from Texas. Members of the Jefferson Airplane came from Cincinnati (Marty Balin), Chicago (Grace Slick), New York (Spencer Dryden) and Washington, D.C. (Jack Casady and Jorma Kaukonen). A few of the musicians were actually native to the area: Jerry Garcia, lead guitarist for the Grateful Dead, was born in San Francisco; John Fogerty of Creedence Clearwater Revival was from Berkeley and Country Joe McDonald was born to the south, in El Monte, California. But they were the exceptions.

Musically, the Haight/Ashbury could not have been more unlike the Village. These were not purists. Folk, blues, bluegrass, rhythm and blues, rock and roll and most of the imaginable variants of pop were acceptable to them, as if it would have been as wrong and reactionary to discriminate in that way as it was to do so on the basis of race. There were other differences as well. In the Village the art of songwriting had been subordinate to the importance of maintaining folk and political purity. In the Haight the songwriters' art was subordinate to another kind of communal ideal: that of playing in a band. These were groups which saw themselves as part of a still larger group: that spiritually mobile and politically radical tribe which, in the mid-1960s, came together not through geography but through music. Still, they had a healthy respect for fine songwriting. They themselves went about the job more professionally than had their Village counterparts and, when faced with tunesmiths of genius, they tended to fall to their knees. Had Dylan come to the Haight in 1966 or 1967 he would have seemed like a god — not because of his lifestyle or because of his political views, though they certainly played a part, but because he was the best songwriter in the country at the time. Dylan never did make it to San Francisco during that era but one of the Beatles did. In 1967 George Harrison took a stroll up Haight Street toward Golden Gate Park and an idolatrous crowd collected in his wake. He was strumming his guitar but he might just as well have been playing the pan pipes for the effect that he created. A more formal act of deference occurred two years later when local San Franciscan bands such as the Grateful Dead and the Jefferson Airplane were billed below England's Rolling Stones at the Altamont concert. The Stones were not nearly as close to the spirit of the times as either of those bands but Jagger and Richards were kowtowed to because they were superior songwriters.

Like the Village, the Haight was a musical community which had come together not with ambitions of fame or fortune (those attributes took the Jefferson Airplane by surprise, just as they had taken Dylan by surprise) but out of the simple desire to be together. In this way they conformed to a larger pattern. Songwriters seem to arise in clumps, like mushrooms. Rare is the great tunesmith who comes like a hermit out of the back woods (even Cole Porter shared his home state of Indiana with Hoagy Carmichael). Nowadays, with popular music in the doldrums and with the world becoming more and more of a global village, one anxiously awaits the next songwriting community, knowing that it may be too late in the game for something so quixotic and parochial.

Chapter Two

PARTNERSHIPS

Bob Dylan arrived on the American music scene within a few weeks of the Kennedy inaugural. The Beatles arrived within a few weeks of the Kennedy assassination. For Dylan, politics was the new dimension, a new world rising. For the Beatles, politics was already an old dimension. Yet they had something of the quality of the Kennedys: their haircuts were reminiscent but more extreme versions of John Kennedy's unruly mop. Their sense of the absurd matched that of the late President, but they had more fun with it. Kennedy had been lively. The Beatles were exhilarating.

The Kennedys instinctively respected art. But, for them, art was another realm of officialdom; it came to the White House wearing a black tie. The Beatles, naturally and ebulliently, *were* what art is. They were a fresher, funnier, younger and more ethereal version of the Kennedys. They were what one sensed the Kennedys might have been had they not been so serious about themselves, so driven and so immobilized by the cliches of the world.

But the great similarity between the life-affirming Beatles and the Kennedys who, despite their zest, had come to symbolize death, was the fact that each quartet had a collective psyche. What had struck a responsive chord in young Americans about the Kennedys was that here had been four brothers who would always rise above fraternal squabbling to come to the defense of one another. In real life they were what brothers seldom are but what one is taught that they ought to be. But here too the Beatles did better. They were friends who had grown into brothers. That is the stuff of myth: of the Knights of the Round Table and the Three Musketeers and Robin Hood — except that, unlike all of those fellows, the Beatles were real and, even more important, they were not warriors.

This brotherly love played a large role in their music-making. It is the quality that sets their music apart not only from every other recording and performing act of the 1960s, but apart from every other songwriting partnership in this century. Even on those cuts in which only one or two of them played (and there are many, beginning with

"Yesterday" and on through "The Ballad of John and Yoko") those Beatles who did come to the studio seemed to sense and bend to the others' presence. "There were really five of us in the studio," Ringo has said, "the four of us plus magic."

When the group disbanded one waited to see what kind of solo works they would put out. McCartney was first with his spring 1970 *McCartney* album. It was a stunning disappointment. It was shaky-kneed. Many of the songs were fragmentary, betraying the author's uncertainty. Others were loose and ragged, displaying none of the cinched-in tightness of "Lady Madonna" or "Get Back." That winter came the first solo albums by Lennon and Harrison (that is, song collections, since both men, while still Beatles, had produced such works of *musique concrète* as *Two Virgins* and *Electronic Sound*). Both were well made and well received, and yet, something was missing. On *John Lennon/Plastic Ono Band* Lennon had not taken the time to perfect his songs, only his tone of voice. Harrison's *All Things Must Pass* was not, at second glance, the cornucopia it had initially seemed to be. Ringo, not a songwriter, had recorded *Sentimental Journey*, consisting of pallid arrangements of standards from the 1930s and 1940s. In short, these works were something that the group albums had never been: they were fallible. Something very curious was happening but it was hard to define at the time. It was not that the music was all that bad. Fine examples of songwriting are to be found on each of those first solo efforts. "Maybe I'm Amazed" on McCartney's first; "Dear Boy," "Uncle Albert/Admiral Halsey" and "The Back Seat of My Car" on *Ram*, his second; "Mother" on Lennon's first; "Imagine," "Jealous Guy" and "Give Me Some Truth" on his second; Harrison's "My Sweet Lord," "Apple Scruffs," "Beware of Darkness" and "All Things Must Pass" are all first-rate songs which do not suffer in comparison to what the three men had been turning out in the previous year or two when, as Beatles, they had been at the peak of their powers. An album of those songs as performed by the group would have made an impressive addition to the Beatles' catalogue. But missing from them was the old élan.

Missing too was that second Beatle trademark: abundance. The Beatles loved to give bonuses, from their generous fourteen-song English LPs (until *Sgt. Pepper* they did not control the American packaging of their recordings) to the comic book in *Magical Mystery Tour* and the goodies in the *White Album*. But the best bonuses were always to be found in the music. Many songs did not end before sprouting an altogether new idea or melody, not heard before on the record. The mantra-like ending of "Hey Jude" and the sudden, truncated tune at the end of "The Ballad of John and Yoko" are two examples. Sometimes the songs ended with a minute's worth of instrumental or electronic tinkering. These bonuses gave an impression of inexhaustible overabundance that, for fans, carried over into the Beatles' private lives. To see a photo of Lennon and McCartney was to have a feeling of munificence. To imagine them strapping on their guitars gave one the same sense of potential energy as one had seeing Muhammed Ali getting into the ring. Together, the Beatles always gave off that feeling of excessiveness. But their excesses were wit, good nature, talent, understatement, the love of fun and an inability to abide the nonsense of traditional show biz and politics. Such abundance reached a truly dizzying point in the psychedelic period. Their music became so extraordinary that otherwise rational people actually believed that their power might move the world in ways barred to political heroes. They had become the world's most exclusive club. By then the Kennedys numbered in the dozens. One could even hope to become a Kennedy by marriage. Not so with the Beatles. The world would get only four of them.

In 1970-71 it was hard for critics to clearly state the difference between their group and solo efforts. For the most part, the commentators dwelt on the political and ethical contents of the lyrics. McCartney in particular came in for abuse. His lyrics were clearly halfhearted. Harrison and Lennon were praised: their words were more earnest and urgent. But deep down, reviewers and fans alike knew that the words had little to do with the deterioration in quality. The Beatles had often taken the line of least resistance as far as words were concerned. They frequently threw up their hands and kept a dummy lyric like "Get Back."

What really was missing from these records and from all the solo works that followed was the presence, whether ghostly or real, of other Beatles in the studio. That gone, it was inevitable that all the organs of Beatle music would become vestigial and dry up. Promising melodies could now be sabotaged by halfhearted release sections and by production values which, though never sloppy, always seemed to be short of the respect that the Beatles, when together, gave to the characteristics of individual instruments. On a Beatles record every instrument always sang clearly and elegantly in its own distinctive voice. Every guitar line seemed to be a definitive one for the instrument. The bottleneck guitar in "For You Blue," the harpsichord in "Because," even the comb and tissue paper in "Lovely Rita" were instruments speaking authoritatively in their own voices. They were never allowed to melt into acceptable but inconsequential blends.

But in those first days of solo Beatles all this was difficult to put into words. The songs did not sound as good and yet, upon careful inspection, it was hard to say why. The talent was still there, that was obvious. For confused fans the best course seemed to be to wait until the glow of the group had faded in order to allow one to impartially judge the individual efforts. But months passed, then years and the glow did not fade. One could return to those group efforts, thirteen albums released in eight years, and become hypnotized all over again. It was there — even in such musical slapstick as the Christmas records and "You Know My Name" and in bootlegged recordings of their rehearsals. A peculiar kind of bonding had taken place, not only among the four musicians but between them and the public as well.

The show writers of a generation earlier had never depended on any such bonds for the success of their artistry. Even the Gershwins, who really were siblings, never stopped collaborating with others. Ira did not become George's full-fledged partner until 1924, five years after George's first Broadway show. And, as late as 1936, a year before George's death, Ira was writing lyrics for Harold Arlen, Vernon Duke and others. Other partnerships were much less faithful. Jerome Kern worked successfully with Guy Bolton and P.G. Wodehouse in the 1910s, producing a renowned series of chamber musicals at the Princess Theatre. He later formed a successful partnership with Oscar Hammerstein II, which resulted in *Show Boat, The Cat and the Fiddle* and other Broadway musicals. Then, in Hollywood, he wrote some of his finest songs with Dorothy Fields, Johnny Mercer and Ira Gershwin. Harold Arlen had three long-running partnerships: first with Ted Koehler with whom he wrote a series of standards for Harlem's Cotton Club, then with E.Y. Harburg with whom he wrote *The Wizard of Oz* and other memorable scores, and later with Johnny Mercer. (Mercer's collaborators included, besides Arlen, Harry Warren, Jimmy Van Heusen, Richard Whiting, Walter Donaldson, Kern, Arthur Schwartz, Henry Mancini and William Hartman Woodin — a one-time U.S. Secretary of the Treasury.) Irving Berlin and Cole Porter, of course, needed to go no further than their own mirrors, for both wrote their own lyrics. Of The Six, Richard Rodgers was the only one to form the kind of close-knit partnerships that the rock writers of a later generation would get into. In the forty-year period between 1920 and 1960 he had only two of them: Lorenz Hart and Oscar Hammerstein II. Hart never wrote with anyone else, but Hammerstein continued to work with Kern, even after teaming up with Rodgers.

These partnerships were not marriages. When they ended, the careers involved did not end or even slacken. Moreover, the public hardly cared about who was writing with whom. In the 1960s, however, the breakup of partnerships seemed to affect the public almost as much as it did the partners themselves. A new code of fidelity had been created. A strange new set of expectations was formed. The public wanted the Beatles to be together. If they could not write and record together, well, it would be nice just to see them palling around once again. To a lesser degree they felt this way toward Simon and Garfunkel, Crosby, Stills, Nash and Young and others. Something new was going on. This generation of writers was also this generation's performers and, because they did double duty, they took on a double burden.

Many reasons have been given for the Beatles' break-up: musical differences, political differences and business differences are often cited. As for musical differences, a lot has been written *ex post facto* about who provided the group with which musical elements. In the 1970s it became common for reviewers to point out that Lennon had been the hardliner of the group — both in his commitment to rock and roll and to blunt self-expression. McCartney, on the other hand, was seen in retrospect as the balladeer. Overlooked was the fact that in addition to having written "Yesterday" and "Michelle," he was also the creator of "She's a Woman," "Back in the USSR," "Get Back" and "I'm Down." John Lennon, on the other hand, contributed such wistful entries as "If I Fell," "Julia," "Sun King," "Don't Let Me Down," "Nowhere Man," "Good Night" and "Across the Universe."

As for political differences, it is true that Lennon, influenced by Yoko Ono, spent his last months as a Beatle playing the fool to create publicity for his peace campaign. The fact that he posed nude for an album cover is said to have profoundly embarrassed the other Beatles. However, Lennon had always been the wild card of the group — he was the one who had ruffled feathers in 1966 by saying that the Beatles were more popular than Jesus. And, as far back as the Hamburg days of 1960--62, he was the one who set the foursome's leather-jacketed, insolent and insulting tone. His unorthodoxy was nothing new to Paul, George and Ringo. In that respect they had long been under his spell. Nor was there any indication that the other Beatles disagreed with Lennon over political issues. They were all against the war in Vietnam, against all war in fact and they were all unable to abide racism. Instinctively, they recoiled from the great breeding grounds of hypocrisy and phoniness in politics, business and the entertainment establishment. It is worth noting that none of them has ever turned into a show biz personality. On the infrequent occasions that they have turned up on television interviews and talk shows they have always been unwilling or unable to project the egotistical sincerity so common in such forums. None of the four has ever been able to take himself seriously on that low level.

Finally, there are the business disagreements. Most marriages, it is said, disintegrate over money. But this was never really the case with the Beatles. None of the four ever seemed to have his eyes on the others' wealth. At issue here were questions of contractual

The Beatles in 1964. For the first time in history, great music was being written by a committee.

obligations and business management. After the death of Brian Epstein in 1967 they began managing themselves, setting up the utopian but misguided Apple Corps in the process. In 1969 the time came to sort out the financial mess that that company, run by cronies and sapped by hangers-on, had gotten into. McCartney wanted to bring in his new father-in-law, Lee Eastman. Lennon was in favor of Allen Klein who had formerly counseled the Rolling Stones. For several years McCartney had been *de facto* leader of the group but when the chips were down, Lennon still had more power over Harrison and Starr and he convinced them that Klein was the one. Much has been made of this conflict but it does not seem to have represented any profound division. Lennon preferred Klein because the latter had arisen from the working class. He saw McCartney's touting of Eastman as another indication that Paul was developing social pretensions. But just a few years later all four ex-Beatles were suing Klein for one reason or another.

In truth, there was nothing all that decisive or clean about the break-up. It was like pulling taffy apart. The Beatles themselves would say, simply, "We grew up, that's all," a line which, to the show writers of a generation past, would have been all but incomprehensible. When else in popular or any music has art (especially evolutionary art, such as the Beatles were engaged in) been abandoned because the artist "grew up"? But because they were nearing the age of thirty, a self-imposed whammy, each seemed to undergo a psychological change which undermined his creative efforts. None of the six great show writers had produced the most significant portion of his output by the age of thirty — not even Gershwin, who died at the age of thirty-eight. But the Beatles' *Abbey Road*, their last work as a group and the last unassailably great work for any of them, was finished in the summer of 1969, when none of them had yet turned thirty.

It has already been noted that Richard Rodgers, like McCartney and Lennon, and more than any of the other show writers, was dependent on his partners. The first, Lorenz Hart, was probably the most gifted lyric writer in American theatrical history. A descendant of the poet Heinrich Heine (or so he claimed), Hart had made a meagre living translating German plays until he and Rodgers made it big with the Theater Guild's production of the semi-amateur *Garrick Gaieties* of 1925. From then until 1942 the phrase "Rodgers and Hart" became synonymous with effortless and eloquent songwriting. A high percentage of Rodgers' tunes in those days had a youthful unself-consciousness; they were born young and, like all youngsters, had a natural and nubile appeal. Hart's lyrics, though much more self-consciously wrought than Rodgers' tunes, could sometimes, through the back door of humor, be more touching than the more

37

Richard Rodgers and Lorenz Hart circa 1925.

direct and maudlin efforts of others.

The relationship between Rodgers and Hart was one of deep friendship and mutual respect. But, unlike Lennon and McCartney (and Harrison and Starr), who were so much alike, Rodgers and Hart were two extremes. Rodgers was of moderate height, handsome, sober and happily married. He was dedicated to both the business and artistic ends of the theater. Hart was tiny, a toper and a homosexual. He was derelict in business matters and he was always late for appointments. Sometimes he never showed up at all. Toward the end, Rodgers had to act more like a nanny than a partner. Though he clearly loved Hart as a friend and as an artist, and though Hart's work remained as fresh and as charming as ever, Rodgers knew by the early 1940s that the partnership had become untenable. Cautiously, he sent out feelers to prospective collaborators. First he went to Ira Gershwin. But the latter, after his brother's death, was gradually lapsing into retirement and was uninterested. Next he approached Oscar Hammerstein II. Rodgers had in mind a new project, an adaptation of Lynn Riggs' *Green Grow the Lilacs*. Hammerstein knew and liked the play and, not having had a success on Broadway in ten years, was more than happy with the prospect of working with so successful and imaginative a composer as Rodgers. Hart gave the new team his blessing (he was to die a few months thereafter) and the resulting work, *Oklahoma!*, launched not only a new partnership but the golden age of the American musical theater. Rodgers and Hammerstein were to become so phenomenally successful that, by 1950, their production company was grossing more than fifteen million dollars a year.

Like Hart, Hammerstein was descended from famous people. His grandfather and namesake had been a notable impresario and his father, William Hammerstein, had managed the Victoria Theatre in New York. Oscar Hammerstein II had been a classmate of Hart's at Columbia and, like Hart, was several years Rodgers' senior. But that is where the similarities between the two lyricists ended. Unlike Hart, Hammerstein was a big man and a sentimental one too. His lyrics turned to philosophy more than they did to wit (though in *Oklahoma!* he wrote some of his funniest lines, conscious as he was of having taken Hart's place). He was hardworking, wholesome, and optimistic. He was not a creature of the city as Hart had been; he was of the country — there was something bucolic in his soul — and he brought this element out in Rodgers, whose music now ceased to be urban and became more and more, if not countrified, then suburban.

Hart had written his words to completed Rodgers tunes. But with Hammerstein the words came first. Rodgers was therefore setting poetry to music and was thus more inclined to write outside the

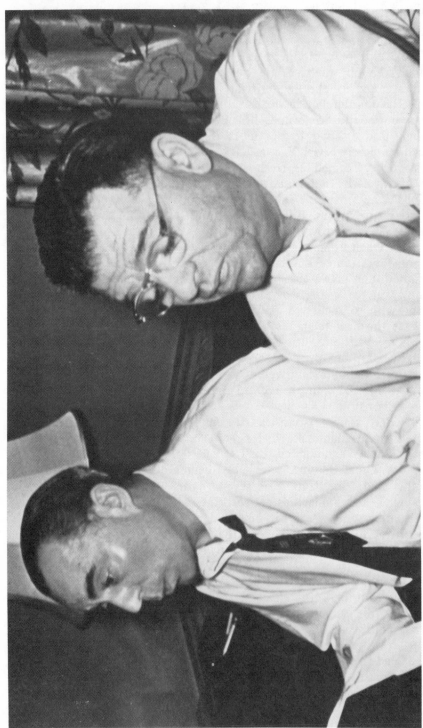

Richard Rodgers and Oscar Hammerstein II working on "The King and I" in 1951.

traditional thirty-two bar pattern so as to be able to accommodate Hammerstein's thoughts. The shape of the music became more complex but, rhythmically and harmonically, the music had been more adventurous when he had written with Hart. It was developing something akin to middle-age spread. Perhaps this aging process was partly due to the fact that Rodgers was now in his forties. But it was also a consequence of his having teamed up with Hammerstein — a man who seems to have been born old, at least insofar as the musical theater goes. A veteran of operettas such as *The Desert Song*, having written the world-weary "Ol' Man River" (with Kern) at the age of thirty-two, Hammerstein was a lot soberer, both literally and figuratively, than Hart. As an example, "Some Enchanted Evening" is an older song than a Rodgers and Hart counterpart, say, "Where or When." The best songs of Rodgers and Hammerstein were clearly equal to the best of Rodgers and Hart, but, like Hammerstein, they were born older.

Paradoxically, Rodgers and Hammerstein brought more excitement to Broadway than Rodgers and Hart ever had. Phenomenal expectations arose when their new musicals approached the boards. Pre-opening ticket sales usually amounted to more than a million dollars. There was nothing like this again in pop songwriting until Beatle albums began appearing in the mid-'60s. In the words of that later era, Rodgers and Hammerstein musicals "shipped platinum."

Why was this so? For the same reason that the Beatles' works were so eagerly awaited. People knew that they were in for a new and, at the same time, an easily assimilated experience. As the Beatles would be doing in the future, Rodgers and Hammerstein were, with the utmost care and professionalism, always breaking new ground. Their first show, *Oklahoma!*, was, as has been said, a landmark in American musical theater history. "No girls, no gags, no chance," declared one reviewer after a preview performance in New Haven. But that was the point. This was the first musical play untouched by any of the vestiges of either musical comedy or of operetta. It remained on Broadway for five years and nine months, garnering seven million dollars at the box office, not to mention the millions earned by touring companies, recordings, sheet music and the motion picture. The show was so enormously successful that theatergoers awaited the team's next Broadway opus with palpitating hearts. *Carousel*, produced in 1945 and adapted from Ferenc Molnar's *Liliom*, did not let them down. It was an even finer achievement than *Oklahoma!* Here the team attempted and succeeded at outright tragedy and Rodgers broadened his range with such disparate works as a sea-chantie ("Blow-High-Blow-Low"), a hymn ("You'll Never Walk Alone") and a long, multi-thematic aria ("Soliloquy").

41

They were less successful with their next effort, *Allegro*, which was produced in 1947. For this play Hammerstein wrote an original story about the life of a physician caught between his humanitarian ideals and the lure of easy profits. To tell this story his and Rodgers' theatrical experiments grew bolder. There was no formal scenery; instead, patterns were projected onto a screen. A Greek chorus was used to unify scenes taking place across a span of thirty years. And Rodgers continued to stretch himself, writing choral and instrumental numbers in addition to the usual popular songs. Unfortunately, the results were unsatisfactory, partly because directing chores were divided among Rodgers, Hammerstein and choreographer Agnes de Mille, partly because, as Rodgers later admitted, the show was "too preachy," and mostly because the score was devoid of catchy tunes. But *Allegro*, having taken chances, did not burst the Rodgers and Hammerstein bubble. Their Broadway openings still made for great expectations. And their next effort, *South Pacific*, more than satisfied. It grossed $2.5 million in its first year and ran for 1,925 performances, second only to *Oklahoma!* In addition, it won the Pulitzer Prize.

In the 1950s the works of Rodgers and Hammerstein were uneven. The high point was *The King and I*. Produced in 1951, it is perhaps the most perfect of their plays. Then came a series of lesser works: *Me and Juliet* in 1953 (an original story about backstage antics during the production of a play), *Pipe Dream* in 1955 (an unsuccessful adaptation of John Steinbeck's novel *Sweet Thursday*), *Cinderella* in 1957 (a television production), *Flower Drum Song* in 1958 (a moderately successful adaptation of C.Y. Lee's novel about life in San Francisco's Chinatown) and then *The Sound of Music* in 1959, which was another huge success.

When Hammerstein died in 1960 the team had been together seventeen years and in that time they had dominated Broadway. Despite the decline of their output in the 1950s, they were magic until the end. Rodgers, in teaming with Hammerstein, had, in a phrase that Paul McCartney was to use regarding his success with Wings, "reached for the pie and come up with the cherry twice."

Rodgers and Hammerstein were similar in temperament, in work attitudes, ideals and philosophy and, yet, they never became close friends. Hammerstein was certainly no shrinking violet but he let Rodgers dominate. It was Rodgers, for instance, who decided not to give director Joshua Logan any royalties for having helped write the libretto to *South Pacific*, even though Hammerstein had promised Logan otherwise. Logan received credit for these efforts but in a typeface smaller than that used for Rodgers and Hammerstein. Rodgers also had the habit of reserving for himself the larger compartments on trains, as well as the entire front row at rehearsals, and he was even known to hog space while autographing pictures of Hammerstein and himself. It is commonly supposed that Hammerstein gave in on these details so as to keep the partnership on an even keel. Then again, Rodgers may have been nettled in similar ways by his lyricist.

Rarely was there an artistic disagreement between the two. But Hammerstein was sometimes irked not only by the speed with which Rodgers worked (he wrote the score of *Oklahoma!* in six days, "Oh What a Beautiful Morning" in eight minutes and he clocked in with the song "Bali-Ha'i" in five minutes; Hammerstein, on the other hand, could spend weeks on a single lyric and days over one rhyme) but, on occasion, by Rodgers' matter-of-fact response to his hard-wrought lines. The wait seemed interminable for Rodgers' reaction to his lyric "Hello Young Lovers" and then it was only, "Oh, I got that lyric. It works fine."

Just before he died, Hammerstein asked his friend and protégé Stephen Sondheim, "What do you think of Dick?" When Sondheim asked the reason for the question Hammerstein said that he did not know Rodgers all that well. Rodgers seems to have been just as puzzled by Hammerstein. In 1975, fifteen years after the latter's death, he said, "I was very fond of him — very fond of him — and I never did find out whether he liked me or not."

Rodgers had a reputation for being an uncommonly placid, businesslike, sane man. "Without eccentricities of any kind," was how Winthrop Sargeant described him in *The New Yorker*. But this was far from the truth. Like most men, he had his inconsistencies. On the one hand, he would work hard to avoid the label "genius." When asked about his reputation for phenomenally fast melody writing he would groan and reply that it was only the act of writing the tune down that took five minutes. Weeks, possibly months had gone into mulling over the character, the situation and the atmosphere to which the tune would have to address itself. However, he had also been heard to say, "It's easier to write a tune than to bend over and tie your shoelaces." In the same way, he would sometimes denigrate the idea that his work had lasting value. "I'm just a commercial theater kid," he would say. "I don't write for posterity." But even as he said these words he was consciously striving to create shows that were more than ephemeral — that would be revived again and again.

It was true that he had an iron grip on himself in front of others. But in the late 1950s he had to be hospitalized for a nervous breakdown. Of all things, he had developed a drinking problem. The malady left as suddenly and mysteriously as it had come and it was probably related to the fact that he had suffered a bout with cancer of the jaw. Still, Rodgers was certainly at least the equal of

Hammerstein in emotionalism. Some of his music — especially the scores for *Carousel* and *The King and I* — are that rare thing for Broadway compositions: deeply felt. And it is said that after writing a good melody he would be literally covered with goose-bumps.

After Hammerstein died in 1960 and until the Stephen Sondheim shows of the late '60s and early '70s, Broadway lost its evolutionary momentum. All of pop music, in fact, went into the doldrums until 1964, when the Beatles arrived. That arrival is inevitably depicted as a musical replacement for Elvis Presley, not Rodgers and Hammerstein. But this is because the histories of theater songs and studio songs have, as if by mutual consent, been kept segregated. Presley, whose rebelliousness had been quashed by a stretch in the army and whose music was, year by year, becoming watered down to the level of his imitators, did leave a gap that sooner or later had to be filled. And the Beatles did fill it. In this respect they were part of a line that extended back to Frank Sinatra in the '40s, Bing Crosby in the '30s, Rudy Vallee in the '20s and Al Jolson in the '10s. They were, in part, another manifestation of that twentieth century peculiarity, the singer-god. But now, with the hindsight of another generation, the Beatles are remembered best as songwriters. And, as such, they have nothing in common with Sinatra or Presley. As innovative songwriters the mantle they inherited was that of Rodgers and Hammerstein.

This really is not all that far-fetched when one considers the parallels between Rodgers and McCartney (despite Rodgers' expressed antipathy to rock music). Both men were not only first-rate melodists — they were also capable of writing melodies which packed an emotional wallop. Both were also extremely versatile. McCartney has written successfully in any number of forms, from country ("Rocky Raccoon," "Country Dreamer") to ballads ("Yesterday," "Here, There and Everywhere") to rockers ("She's a Woman") to medleys (side two of *Abbey Road*, "Band on the Run") and on and on. For his part, Rodgers was able to come up with everything from a soft shoe for Maurice Chevalier ("Mimi") to an ersatz Austrian landler ("Edelweis") to a Souza-like rouser ("Guadalcanal March"). One has the sense that no matter what the assignment, both, while in their primes, would have come up with something at least interesting and probably memorable.

Rodgers and McCartney were both born diplomats and cool-headed negotiators. It was McCartney who wrote the "Dear Sir or Madam" letters touting the group in the days before Brian Epstein. And he was the one who took over public relations for the Beatles after Epstein's death. In the same way, Rodgers provided most of the common sense of Rodgers and Hart. Rodgers and McCartney were both good businessmen. Rodgers' career in this regard really took off after he ended his relationship with Hart. He and Hammerstein not only wrote their own shows, they also served as producers of a series of successful shows and plays written by others. The most famous of these was *Annie Get Your Gun* with music by Irving Berlin, but there were many others, including straight, non-musical dramas. At their height, Rodgers and Hammerstein were as much a conglomerate as they were a songwriting team.

Like Rodgers, who became a successful businessman after he left Hart, McCartney developed his business acumen after he left the Beatles. Then, once rid of the Apple fiasco, he invested his money wisely: some of it in the song catalogues of other writers, one of whom, Buddy Holly, had been his childhood hero. Currently, McCartney holds the still-profitable copyrights to hundreds of tunes written by others.

Both men were steady, hard workers who could never stay away long from their respective media: the stage and the recording studio. After Brian Epstein's death it was McCartney who cajoled the other Beatles into and through most of their remaining projects and, after the break-up, he was by far the most prolific of the four. Rodgers, for his part, worked steadily in the theater for forty-five years, was associated with forty shows and probably wrote a greater quantity of memorable show music than anyone in history. A few weeks after his cancer operation in 1957 he was back in the theater attending rehearsals for *Flower Drum Song*. In the 1970s, a heart attack and another bout with cancer that left him without the use of his vocal chords could not deter him from writing the music for three separate productions.

They also shared a certain amount of idealism. Rodgers' was on a lower flame but it burned longer. Throughout his career he fought closed-mindedness, bigotry and racism. McCartney, for his part, was one of the spearheads of that generation which tried to do it all at once: root out every ill in a spectacular revolution of the human heart. When this did not come to pass he pulled in his feelers and, like others his age, tried to tidy himself up.

There are two ways, however, in which these men, though so much alike, were still very different and these factors go a long way in accounting for the difference in the length of their creative primes.

First of all, there is the nature of their partnerships. As has been seen, both needed to work with partners. Rodgers went it alone only once, albeit successfully, in the 1962 production of *No Strings* (actually, he had by then written both words and music for songs that were used in the movie remake of *State Fair*). But he chose not to repeat that experience, preferring instead to work with a series of new lyricists even though none of them proved very satisfactory. A proposed linkage with Allan Jay Lerner (who had written *My Fair*

Lady and *Camelot* with Frederick Loewe, recently retired) did not get off the ground. An alliance with Stephen Sondheim produced only one show, *Do I Hear a Waltz?*, which was not a success; neither was the partnership. Then came failures with Sheldon Harnick (*Rex*) and Martin Charnin (*Two By Two* and *I Remember Mama*).

Paul McCartney, after breaking with John Lennon, did not seek another partner. The working relationship between Lennon and himself had been very different from what Rodgers had had with his partners. Both McCartney and Lennon were quite capable of doing whole songs themselves. Each of them could compose music as well as lyrics and, in addition, each was able to effectively sing his own songs and arrange the accompaniment too. In none of the show writers' partnerships was there a case where these lines were crossed — where each writer was responsible for both music and lyrics. In the theater each partner plied his separate craft, sometimes in close collaboration, sweating out bars and phrases in all-night sessions, and sometimes from a distance. Harold Arlen and Truman Capote completed a substantial portion of their score for *House of Flowers* before they ever met. With Capote in Europe and Arlen in Beverly Hills, songs were written via transatlantic phone.

But the mutually versatile Lennon and McCartney were a new kind of songwriting team — though for quite some time after they appeared on the scene, observers tried to think of them in the old mold. It was generally thought that McCartney wrote the music and Lennon the words (an assumption based in part on Lennon's two published books). It seemed only logical that one was the composer and the other the lyricist and neither man seemed particularly anxious to set the record straight. It was only after the *Sgt. Pepper* recording in 1967, when they began to develop individual writing styles, that their working habits became clearer. Basically, each was a songwriter in the Irving Berlin or Cole Porter sense. Each wrote complete songs, music and lyrics. But each was always there to help the other with any musical or lyrical problem and the Lennon/McCartney moniker was attached to all of their individual or joint compositions.

The paradox was that while they were each as self-sufficient as a Berlin or a Porter, both had also learned to be dependent on a partner to smooth out the rough edges, to provide criticism and to be a spur to innovation and perfection. They were separate but intertwined. As Beatles, the fate of their creations was tied up not only in one another as songwriters but as performers too. Such a close and total collaboration produced many more opportunities for strained relations than did the more traditional kind of partnership. There was always the possibility that suspicions would develop — that one would play less enthusiastically while recording the song of the other or that one would even try in a subtle way to sabotage the recording of the other's song. In one of his last interviews, Lennon complained of exactly that:

> The Beatles didn't make a good record of "Across the Universe" . . . I thought Paul subconsciously tried to destroy my great songs. We would play experimental games with my great pieces, like "Strawberry Fields," which I always felt was badly recorded . . . . We would spend hours doing every little detail cleaning up Paul's songs, but when it came time to mine — especially a great song like "Strawberry Fields" or "Across the Universe" — somehow an atmosphere of looseness and experimentation would come up.

Considering the potential for such suspicions it is remarkable that their partnership lasted as long as it did. Perhaps the presence of Harrison, who as a songwriter was something of an apprentice to both men, and of Starr, a lesser ego whose humor served to drain tension from the group, enabled Lennon and McCartney to postpone jealousy as long as they did. But a relationship like theirs, one without clear lines of demarcation, is one that, from hindsight at least, was bound to explode.

In the 1960s there was only one other songwriting team very much like them. That was Mick Jagger and Keith Richards of the Rolling Stones. To this day it has not been made clear which of the two is responsible for what vis-à-vis words and music. The impression is that Jagger is mostly responsible for the lyrics while Richards is mostly responsible for the music, though in some songs it seems that Jagger has been both composer and lyricist. But the interconnectedness of these men is not nearly so complete as it was between Lennon and McCartney. As performers, the division is easily apparent. Jagger is occasionally seen with a guitar strapped to his chest but he has never vied with Richards, a superb guitarist, in this respect. Similarly, Richards has often sung harmony to Jagger's lead vocal and has even sung lead himself on occasion but he has never threatened Jagger's primacy in that area. As for the others in the group, they have always been a backup for the principal duo. Even Brian Jones, the founder of the band, was never a composer or a lyricist in his own right. The Stones have weathered the years as well as changes in personnel and they threaten to go on forever. It may have been possible for them to do this because there are such distinctions between Jagger's and Richards' crafts.

Another reason might be that the Rolling Stones today are basically what they were fifteen years ago. Despite a few perfunctory and imitative experiments in the mid-60s, they have been a static force. The Beatles, on the other hand, were true innovators — something very rare among popular songwriters. Their music became more complex harmonically, rhythmically, in its arrangement and orchestration. As for lyrics, these became whimsical, idiosyncratic and, occasionally, heartfelt. And, like Rodgers and Hammerstein, the Beatles tinkered with the vehicle itself. In their case this was the long-playing record. They tried to create albums in which each part was somehow related to the whole. Though their attempts in this regard were more haphazard than ebullient fans gave them credit for, it is also true that *Rubber Soul* did have a unifying musical characteristic in its use of acoustic instruments as well as in more thoughtful and personal lyrics. *Sgt. Pepper* did have the vague aegis of a mock stage show. The second side of *Abbey Road* was an attempt to organize songs and song fragments into a medley unified by recurring instrumental motifs.

This points to the second reason for the fact that Rodgers' creative prime was longer than McCartney's. Songwriters do not write pure music — they are not symphonists. They must use words. When songs are not attached to shows, these words are liable to be the same ones over and over again, variations of boy/girl and June/moon. Had Rodgers been a pop songwriter unattached to the theater, he would have lost his anchor. It has been seen that he and Hammerstein were not very good at making up their own stories. The two shows that they wrote from Hammerstein's original scripts were failures (*Allegro* and *Me and Juliet*). They got the best results when they sought out material that was worth adapting. All of their great shows were based on books or plays or films that had already been produced. For the Beatles there was no precedent in rock and roll for doing something like that — and they always followed at least that one rule: every recording they made was firmly embedded in rock precedent. It is probable that they considered stories only in the context of movies and, at that, mainly exploitation films such as those made by Elvis and even their own film *Help!*, which they regarded as somewhat senseless. But when they tried to think up a plot of their own, as in *Magical Mystery Tour*, things turned out even worse. The Beatles were no better at making up plots than were Rodgers and Hammerstein (or, for that matter, than was William Shakespeare) but they were uninterested in going the adaptation route. Rodgers had been able to draw inspiration by putting himself in the place of characters such as Maria von Trapp or Emile de Becque. He had also been faced with the challenge of writing for the specific talents of the singers who played those parts: Mary Martin and Ezio Pinza. The Beatles were less fortunate. The closest they came to this was when John and Paul tailored an occasional song for

Ringo. Then they wrote for his whimsical off-key voice in the way that Rodgers wrote simple yet affecting tunes for the weak-voiced Gertrude Lawrence in *The King and I.*

Unable to test their imaginations by writing from inside fictional characters (another avenue might have been to set the poetry of others to music and, in fact, McCartney followed this route when he set the nursery rhymes "Golden Slumbers" and, later, "Mary Had a Little Lamb" to his own tunes) they could only search within themselves for new material. This is what they did until their options were reduced to two: self-revelation and nonsense. Almost all of the songs written by Lennon, McCartney and Harrison in the late '60s and early '70s fell into these two categories. Confessions, polemics and sermons are a limited source of song lyrics. So is the nonsense or novelty number. They were stuck. They had come to artistic maturity dependent upon fellow members of the band and yet, on their own, each, being a jack-of-all-trades, did not seem to need any help. They were fully as talented as the greatest of their songwriting forebears and yet their songs could be written for only one character and one voice. After the break-up, that voice sang in a studio that had always been stark but which now seemed especially bare, seeing as how their friends were gone.

Chapter Three

POP ORCHESTRATION

Only lately has the public come to expect its pop songwriters to expand their horizons, Beethoven-style. Like good cobblers, the show composers were expected to stick to their lasts and produce hit songs. If they occasionally felt other ambitions it was not because anyone was egging them on. Far from it. People knew and respected names like Kern, Berlin and Porter but few followed their careers and still fewer took note of their musical progress. Only when scandal touched them was the public particularly interested and, with the exception of Irving Berlin's romance with Ellin Mackey, there was not much of that.

As public figures they were in a kind of limbo. They were not serious threats to Gable and Garbo as celebrities; nor were they taken seriously by music critics. They did not expect to be. Instinctively, the theater writers respected the difference between "songwriters" and "composers." They understood that a composer follows through on the implications of his ideas — develops them and makes the most of them — while a songwriter presents his ideas in their pure, natal state. And, just as there was little room for development within a song, so was there little for progress between one song and another. The show writers were not expected to work in a continuum, producing music that advanced beyond or elaborated on or even took much notice of what they had written before. Their careers were discussed in terms of their hits, not their art, and few wondered what unpredictable directions their talent — genius — would take.

With the exception of Richard Rodgers, it was a rare thing for any of The Six to commit himself to or even contemplate a truly ambitious project involving his native Broadway. Whenever they felt their musical talents straining at the self-imposed limits of popular songwriting, their thoughts turned instead to the concert hall. Every one of them had a brush with this kind of ambition. In the first few years after World War I, Irving Berlin toyed with the idea of writing an American opera. But he was woefully lacking in even the meagerest musical training. Not only did he have no formal education, he was not even self-taught. He relied on his custom-made piano, the famous old oak "Buick" with its key-changing lever, or on his musical secretaries or on a dictaphone. Nevertheless, he seems to have allowed himself some fancy thoughts in the early days. He told one interviewer, "I hope that some day I might write an operatic score in jazz," and, for his 1914 show *Watch Your Step*, he produced a long recitative called "Opera Burlesque" in which Giuseppe Verdi chides tunesmiths like Berlin himself for their lack of ambition. On January 3, 1924, an article in the *New York Tribune* announced that he was writing a syncopated tone poem for Paul Whiteman's upcoming February 12 concert, memorable now for the premiere of Gershwin's *Rhapsody in Blue*. Berlin, however, produced no such work and it seems that, with the advent of Gershwin's concert career, he became content to write hits and leave loftier ambitions to others.

Unlike Berlin, Jerome Kern was a trained musician. He studied piano and harmony at the New York College of Music and was instructed by private teachers in Heidelberg. He was familiar with the instruments of the orchestra and as a young man in London he orchestrated tunes for English stage plays. Nearly forty years later he took up scoring again, transcribing his songs for string quartet (with the assistance of Charles Miller) and producing two full-fledged symphonic works. The first, in 1941, was a suite from *Show Boat* called *Scenario*. The second, written the following year, was called *Mark Twain: A Portrait for Orchestra*. This was one of a series of patriotic works, including Copland's *Lincoln Portrait*, which were commissioned by Andre Kostelonetz during World War II. Despite the care that he took in both the composition and instrumentation of *Scenario* and *Mark Twain*, neither work caught on and hardly anyone has heard or heard of them.

Cole Porter's musical training was even more thorough than Kern's. After World War I Porter studied counterpoint, orchestration and harmony at the Schola Cantorium in Paris with the Impressionist composer Vincent d'Indy. But his only concert work, as has already been noted, was less than a success. This was the ballet *Within the Quota*, whose mild jazz was orchestrated by a Frenchman, Charles Koechlin. Porter never again wrote music in any form other than the popular song.

Harold Arlen's first published composition was not a song but a piano solo called "Minor Gaff." His early career really was more that of a jazz musician than a songwriter and, like most jazzmen, he picked up his musical education not through formal study but by listening to and playing with others. He worked with a number of bands as a crooner, a pianist and an arranger before stumbling onto his first hit tune, "Get Happy," and from then on he stuck to

52

songwriting, although every now and then he would write a piano piece or, occasionally, something more ambitious. In the 1930s he composed *Mood in Six Minutes*, a concert work orchestrated by Robert Russell Bennett. In 1939 he wrote "American Minuet" for Meredith Wilson's orchestra (it is not clear who orchestrated this piece). In 1940 there was *Americanegro Suite* — a work consisting of six concert songs (lyrics by Ted Koehler) for chorus and piano. Then, in the late 1950s, Arlen added new songs plus recitatives to his 1946 show, *St. Louis Woman*, to create *Free and Easy* (orchestrated by Samuel Matlowsky), intended as a companion piece for *Porgy and Bess*. But none of these works has entered the repertoire.

Richard Rodgers also produced his share of orchestral curiosities. He had studied harmony, counterpoint, musical theory and composition at the Institute of Musical Art (now the Juilliard School of Music) and, except for Gershwin, was the most successful of The Six in writing lasting instrumental works. The first of these was *Slaughter on 10th Avenue*, a ballet that was part of the 1936 musical, *On Your Toes*. In the same year he wrote *All Points West*, a concert piece for solo baritone and symphony orchestra (lyrics by Larry Hart). In 1939 the Ballet Russe de Monte Carlo produced Rodgers' *Ghost Town* (it was part of the same trend toward Western-style ballets that inspired *Billy the Kid* and *Rodeo* by Aaron Copland) and six years later the musical *Carousel* dispensed with a traditional overture and instead used a waltz suite that Rodgers had originally written for Paul Whiteman's orchestra. In 1952 he wrote the music for the twenty-six episode television documentary, *Victory at Sea*, consisting of thirteen hours of his musical themes as arranged and orchestrated by Robert Russell Bennett. In 1960 he wrote another television score, *Winston Churchill — The Valiant Years*, again arranged by Bennett.

But the only writer among The Six who wrote concert works that were more than novelties and who consciously developed his craft in symphonic terms was George Gershwin. Unlike Porter and Rodgers, Gershwin never studied music in a formal setting. Instead, his musical education consisted of lessons from a series of teachers, including Charles Hambitzer, Edward Kilenyi, Sr., and Rubin Goldmark. By the age of nineteen he was on his own, although in his thirties he sought the tutelage of Joseph Schillinger, a man who believed that he had discovered the mathematical laws behind musical composition. Gershwin's highbrow output was slight: four works for piano and orchestra (*Rhapsody in Blue, Concerto in F, Second Rhapsody, I Got Rhythm Variations*), two for orchestra alone (*An American in Paris, Cuban Overture*), one for piano solo (*Three Preludes*), and a single opera, (*Porgy and Bess*). There are also a few miscellanies: an early one-act opera (*Blue Monday*), an even earlier one-movement string quartet (*Lullabye*), piano transcriptions of eighteen songs (*George Gershwin's Songbook*), an "art song" ("In the Mandarin's Orchid Garden"), a work for violin and piano ("Short Story") and a few others. But that is the extent of it. His death at the age of thirty-eight had a lot to do with the brevity of this list. However, Mozart and Schubert, composers with gigantic catalogues, also died young. In a sense, Gershwin was like his peers. Songs and shows came first; the larger works were sneaked in between them and, as a highbrow composer, he was almost a dilettante.

But not quite — for these are not the works of a dabbler. Every one of them, even those which failed to enter the permanent concert repertoire, are greater than the song pastiches that filled the concert efforts of Kern and Rodgers. This was so partly because of Gershwin's greater ambition. But it was also because he, as an accomplished pianist, was used to expressing himself in non-vocal, instrumental ideas. Nearly all of his composing was done at the piano. There, simultaneously with the melodies, would be born accompaniments, harmonies and counterpoint — all welded into a complete and idiosyncratic language. The other songwriters wrote vocal lines enhanced by harmony. But Gershwin's song tunes were born with their harmony and of necessity they had to be extraordinary — otherwise, they could easily have sounded like transcriptions of intrumental pieces. Even so, one can clearly see the pianistic origin of many of them, particularly the early songs, such as "Fascinating Rhythm," "Sweet and Low Down," "Someone to Watch Over Me" and "The Man I Love." All of those are made up of the type of repeating patterns which come so readily to a keyboard composer.

The foursquare sheet music of the day prohibited much in the way of piano commentary. Therefore, for pianistic inventions which could not be made into songs, Gershwin had no other outlet than his concert pieces. In the first half of his career — that is, in the 1920s — these were his most compelling ideas. They expressed the same personality as the songs did, but provided a much more complete picture of it. That was why the public had no trouble following him into the concert hall. And it was in the concert hall that they got the sense of him as an extraordinary and an evolving talent. The premiere of his first concert work, the *Rhapsody in Blue*, set up an anticipation over Gershwin's future which was further whetted by his next efforts, the piano *Concerto in F* and the tone poem *An American in Paris*. He was growing — not so much in the Beethoven sense since the sensibility or "philosophy" behind each of his works was always basically the same. But he was learning to express his personality via the highbrow composer's art. He was learning not only to state and disguise his themes but to develop them; Gershwin-watchers noted with satisfaction that his compositions were becoming less and less a matter of disjointed episodes and more like well-plotted plays. The themes never metamorphosed very far but they arrived, did their tricks and went according to a satisfactory plan. Another, less tangible factor, was the earnestness of his assault on the concert hall. Americans could not help rooting for him — he was the home team. He was "our Georgie" — immensely gifted, mostly self-taught — and he represented us in his musical social climbing. It did not take much sophistication to see the imperfections in his concert music. Gershwin himself saw them. Yet, only fools would look down at what he was doing — for his music, though easily comprehended, was nevertheless something new in the world.

For Gershwin there was no more crucial step to be taken in scaling the academic walls than that most exalted and mysterious of the composer's arts: orchestration. He had not orchestrated the *Rhapsody in Blue*. That was done by Ferde Grofé who, at the time, was the arranger for Paul Whiteman's band. But from the *Concerto in F* on, Gershwin was responsible for every note in all of his orchestrated works (although he was content to let others score his Broadway shows). He understood that an inability to orchestrate would mean that his larger works would not be entirely his own and that if such were the case, they would be much less exciting.

This points up an odd fact about the works of the show composers. Their legacy, those hundreds of memorable songs, does not exist in any finished, definite form. In fact, the songs of Gershwin and other Broadway composers present something of an ontological problem. Where do you go for the composer's version? Where do you go for the original? Each song came into the world without definitive clothing. Even the printed sheet music was usually someone else's handiwork. Gershwin understood this limbo and that is probably why he made those solo piano transcriptions for eighteen of his songs. But these arrangements are certainly not the basis upon which the songs were or are known. In the final analysis, there is no way to get one's hands on a score of Gershwin's "They Can't Take That Away from Me" or of Arlen's "My Shining Hour" or of Porter's "Anything Goes" that has been produced in its entirety by the composer. Every version is somebody else's arrangement. That being the case, one can never be sure how much of the composer's hand is in the harmony, much less the orchestration.

The show composers were aware that their songs existed only in this disembodied manner and maybe this is why they said over and over again that they were just tunesmiths, writing for the most ephemeral of markets. Nevertheless, immortality would sometimes beckon, resulting in their occasional, oddball forays into the concert hall. But they always needed that shadowy collaborator, the arranger, the orchestrator. "I suppose I could learn to orchestrate,"

Richard Rodgers told one interviewer, "study up on the range of the oboe and that kind of thing . . . but what's the use? Robert Russell Bennett orchestrates much better than I could . . . it would be nothing but ego on my part." The point, however, is that orchestration is the most prominent and recognizable symptom of serious composition; it is a signpost indicating that musical ideas are being developed and carried to fruition.

In 1928, at a party in honor of the premiere of *An American in Paris*, Gershwin was given a humidor covered with the signatures of his friends. The presentation was made by Otto Kahn, a financier and patron of the arts, who used the occasion to make a little speech in which he wished the young composer "an experience — not too prolonged — of that driving storm and stress of the emotions" which might "deepen" his work. There was then and there still exists in the highbrow world a consensus that Gershwin's concert works are "light" music and that they go better on a pops program than on the agenda of a major orchestra's regular season. His orchestral works are usually heard in all-Gershwin programs, most often in the summer and in a relaxed shirt-sleeved atmosphere, frequently under the stars (a tradition he started himself with summer concerts in New York's outdoor Lewisohn Stadium). To critics of the day, Gershwin's chief musical characteristic was his sentimental melodicism and many words have been written about the obsessive gaiety of what he wrote. At the same time, one of the instantly recognizable traits of his music is something very different. It is certainly not despair and not even melancholy and it is not well-served by the word "blues." It has the quality of dark mahogany. In the first half of his career it was to be found in a few songs ("The Man I Love" is one) but mostly in his instrumental works. In the early 1930s this quality seemed to disappear, which might account for the fact that, for the first time in his life, Gershwin suffered a series of real failures. After the 1931 Pulitzer Prize-winning *Of Thee I Sing*, he wrote two successive flops: *Let 'Em Eat Cake* and *Pardon My English*. He was not faring much better in the concert hall; none of his orchestral works in the 1930s entered the repertoire. In 1934, however, he started work on *Porgy and Bess* and it was here that everything came together. It was in this work that the umber, mahogany quality reached its full maturity.

Is "Summertime" a sad or a happy song? Until this piece of music every one of Gershwin's songs was either a ballad or a rhythm number, the twin categories of popular music, categories which still obtain to this day. But "Summertime," "A Woman Is a Sometime Thing," "It Ain't Necessarily So," "There's a Boat That's Leaving Soon for New York" and others land in neither slot. This may be due in part to the lyrics. Read separately, the words do have images that are both positive and negative, pessimistic and funny. And, in setting these words to music (until *Porgy and Bess* he had always written the tunes first), Gershwin wrote rhythms that were both bright and nervous. The harmonies, often in measures which alternated between major and minor tonalities, contain a sense of foreboding. The music is never lugubrious but there is melancholy in it, more melancholy than is in the words.

In all of the argument over whether *Porgy and Bess* is really an opera and whether these pieces are songs or arias, commentators have always missed this point: *Porgy and Bess* gave Gershwin his first opportunity to fully flex his composer's muscles while writing for the voice. In a sense, he had been holding back with all of his earlier commercial songs. Not that they were half-hearted efforts. "Liza," "I Got Rhythm" and their companions are nothing if not full-tilt. "Someone to Watch Over Me," "How Long Has This Been Going On" and "But Not for Me" are as heartfelt as pop songs can be. Yet, he *was* holding back — the songs allowed him to use only a few sentences worth of what was, in fact, a full language. In *Porgy and Bess* he was able to exercise that language — now developed, mature and inspired by a libretto — and use it for the first time for the human voice. This was why it was so important to Gershwin that *Porgy and Bess* be regarded as an opera. It could not have been written had he not so regarded it. In his mind it was not a musical comedy or even a musical play (a form to come later with *Carousel* and *West Side Story*). In his mind, because of the fact that he was writing every note in it (it took him nine months to orchestrate the piece), it was an opera. It was he who put so much stress on this classification and it is probably because he wanted it so badly that so many critics have begrudged him the word. The history of music criticism has a silly streak and this is an instance.

Confusion about *Porgy and Bess*'s categorization has traditionally resulted from the fact that is is full of songs. And that is true — it is a work that offers little bel canto. Moreover, the songs of *Porgy and Bess* are clearly related to those written for other Broadway shows. "Summertime" can certainly be compared to Kern's "Look for the Silver Lining" for the shape and the simplicity of its melody (but not harmony — the harmony of "Summertime" is from another world) and both melodies are very effective when sung with no accompaniment at all. The two songs, like their composers, share a common ethnic background. Nevertheless, "Summertime," because it involved the exercise of Gershwin's melodic, harmonic and orchestral resources, is opera, no matter how close its kinship to Kern's song. Opera, after all, uses the same elements as all other kinds of music, including pop — its audience is drawn from the same species of primate. But in the case of *Porgy and Bess*, the distinction "opera"

George Gershwin orchestrating "Porgy and Bess" in Palm Beach, Florida, February 1935.

is important. It, like all operas, is a work for the dramatic stage in which the musical element is overwhelmingly predominant.

Having premiered to mixed reviews, *Porgy and Bess* disappeared after a short run. Gershwin then spent an aimless six months. He wrote a nondescript song, "The King of Swing," travelled to Mexico in a futile search for inspiration (his 1932 trip to Havana had inspired the *Cuban Overture*) and then, not having earned his usual solid income recently, he turned to Hollywood. It was there that he spent the last year of his life. He produced no more highbrow works, only twenty-five songs. All of them are of a very high quality and a few of them rank as the finest ever written by an American: "They Can't Take That Away from Me," "A Foggy Day," "Our Love Is Here to Stay," "They All Laughed" — and their harmonic language is, if anything, more subtle than that of *Porgy and Bess*. Subtlety was necessary because the Hollywood studios were concerned that Gershwin, with his "artistic" inclinations, could no longer write hits of the "Lady Be Good" variety.

The miracle of these songs is that, while they were hits, they were also well beyond "Lady Be Good" and "Clap Yo' Hands." In consideration of his audience, Gershwin had to be wary of minor keys (just as Mozart had to use them sparingly). But he was able to achieve some touching effects through a harmonic legerdemain that was far more sophisticated than anything being written in pop music at the time. The pedal point B-flat beneath the coda of "They Can't Take That Away from Me," the F-eleventh chord on the word "suddenly" in "A Foggy Day," the gentle melody of his last song, "Love Is Here To Stay," which, at one point, descends slowly like a falling leaf — are unexpectedly emotional. He was enough of an expert now to achieve such effects within the confines of thirty-two bar songs and without resorting to the more overt technique of melodrama, as used in such contemporary works as "Night and Day," "Dancing in the Dark," and "Let's Face the Music and Dance."

But being back in the pop field, Gershwin was unable to control the arrangement and orchestration of his works. It was a fact of life that had never seemed to bother him before. But this time it did annoy him. His concern over the treatment given "They Can't Take That Away from Me" brought him to the recording studio where, with some concern, he audited the session. That song was apparently quite special to him. He was so unhappy with the way some of the music for that film, *Shall We Dance*, was being arranged, that he himself scored its "Walking the Dog" sequence (later retitled "Promenade") for a group of chamber players. It was his reaction to Hollywood's traditionally overblown orchestration. For the next film, *A Damsel in Distress*, he took matters further by scoring two mock-madrigals for chorus, so as to preempt their being sung by the stars of the film. He died before the next movie, *The Gold-wyn Follies*, was completed but it was clear that by that time he was itching to regain control of his scores. Among the projects he was considering were a string quartet (he had become friendly with Arnold Schoenberg in Hollywood and had subsidized a private recording of the latter's quartets), a ballet and another opera.

With the death of Gershwin, orchestration again became an art wholly separate and distinct from tunesmithing in popular music. As sophisticated as Broadway musicals were to become, they were always scored by someone other than the composer. Even Leonard Bernstein, who is both a conductor and a symphonist, has allowed others to orchestrate his Broadway efforts. It was not until the 1960s that this state of affairs began to change in popular music. But it did not happen on Broadway.

It began with a new breed, the singing songwriter, who inspired what critic Jon Landau calls "the search for the author" in pop music. Alabama-born Hank Williams was one of the first. His songs were simple (rarely did they broach more than tonic-dominant harmony) but they were good. They were so good that, unlike the songs of such country music forebears as Jimmie Rodgers and Hank Snow, they managed to cross the once sturdy membrane dividing country and mainstream pop. Through recordings by Tony Bennett and Jo Stafford these songs were accepted in the more general market.

In the 1950s Williams was followed by other talented singer/songwriters such as Chuck Berry and Buddy Holly. These were men who controlled every aspect of their songs: music, lyrics, performance and arrangements too. The settings were rudimentary. Williams had worked with a group of musicians called The Drifting Cowboys and his songs were inevitably played on an acoustic guitar, pedal steel guitar, bass and, occasionally, a violin or a piano. Buddy Holly's band was even more Spartan than Williams': guitar, bass and drums. But this music, unlike the music of the show composers, was born on the very instruments which eventually would disseminate it. It was thought up in terms of those instruments.

In the 1960s, with access to the modern recording studio, the singer/songwriters began to experiment with instrumentation, thus becoming arrangers — or, as the new parlance had it, producers. Brian Wilson and Phil Spector (a writer but not a singer) were the most prominent in this regard. They followed in the footsteps of Williams and Holly — not so much as to the style of their compositions but because their music was created with its instrumentation in mind. Now, in the studio, this included not only the traditional strings and percussion but a new category: electronic effects. They were easing their way, naturally and guilelessly, into the halls of the avant-garde, the domain of such highbrow composers as Varèse and Stockhausen. But it was still pop music, that lower-browed cousin of theater music. The songs were raw and unpretentious and they were three minutes long.

Then came the Beatles. Like Irving Berlin, they could not read a note of music. But unlike Berlin (and like Gershwin) they were accomplished instrumentalists. Their melodies were from the beginning created amongst instrumental ideas — fills, leads and, to an extent, the novel sounds of an occasional, unexpected instrument: a harmonica, a tambourine, a piano, an electronic studio trick. Moreover, the Beatles, as a singing group, were capable of vocal counterpoint, as well as two- and three-part vocal harmonies. Within that foursome there had always been the seed of a full, if novel orchestra. Given a modern recording studio like the EMI lab at Abbey Road, plus the technical and worldly direction of a musician/engineer such as George Martin, what they accomplished begins to seem comprehensible. They were budding songwriters who were, concomitantly, budding arrangers. For the first time in pop music it became impossible to say which had come first: the songs or the arrangement. Very often, both were identical, created at one and the same instant. Thus, when the Beatles' musical horizons began to expand, these elements expanded together. Far more than had ever been the case with Gershwin, the compositions of the Beatles began of and with their ultimate orchestrations. Listening to their recordings in chronological order, one can clearly see it happening. Their first period, one of a huge backbeat and a single melodic line, ended with the 1965 album *Rubber Soul*, which ushered in a period when the arrangement, the performance and the songs themselves all became more understated, more self-conscious. Part of the composition of "Michelle," for instance, was its guitar solo, which was a separate but related melodic line. Next came *Revolver*, an eclectic album in which each song seemed to live in its own orchestral world. "Yellow Submarine," a daffy novelty record, is, as performed by the Beatles, not merely a song but a true composition. John Lennon blowing bubbles through a straw is, somehow, as important to the whole as the rudimentary harmony strummed on McCartney's guitar. Other songs on the album, notably "Eleanor Rigby" and "She Said, She Said," also could be seen as ingeniously orchestrated compositions. Without thinking about it much, the Beatles had accomplished a synthesis that had heretofore always seemed impossible in pop music. They had crossed the magic barrier into orchestration. Their next album, 1967's *Sgt. Pepper's Lonely Hearts Club Band*, was hailed by critics as the first pop concept album. But the concept really was a slim one: a performance by a mythical, ill-defined band about a similarly ill-defined subject. To that end the Beatles added the sounds of an audience: coughing, laughter. Otherwise, the only real attempt at unity came with a reprise of the title tune just before the conclusion of the album. Nevertheless, this LP was a giant step towards the solution of the ontological problem of pop orchestration, bridging the gap between the limbo of Broadway theater song arrangements and the organic orchestrations of highbrow musical literature. Actually, *Sgt. Pepper* went the highbrow world a step farther. Not only were the songs and arrangements inseparable. The performance had become fixed too. It was not a work which, like *Porgy and Bess* or *Aida*, would ever need to be recreated. This unlikely amalgam of Tin Pan Alley, rhythm and blues, Edgar Varèse and Spike Jones was performed once and for all and that performance remains fixed. It is as solidly highbrow as any classical song cycle. But it does not need a printed score.

The Beatles had become composers in the highbrow sense, since the main difference between an art song and a pop song is not the number of high or difficult notes but the extent of the composer's control over the song's elements. When the melody is unthinkable without the setting provided by the composer then you have a highbrow composition. The Beatles were the first pop songwriters to fully encompass and take advantage of this fact and they did so with greater breadth and imagination than anyone else, before or since. Of the show writers, only Gershwin provided definitive vocal settings for his songs, and then only in *Porgy and Bess*, his opera — whose orchestration, though adequate, was not innovative. With the Beatles, however, the idea of the musical setting underwent a radiant and radical expansion — to the point where art song mastery was finally attained in the context of pop songwriting.

Because of the Beatles, orchestration became the experimental component of the pop composer's art while harmony, which had lagged behind since the days of Hank Williams, was all but lost as a field for exploration. The studio writers were never to even remotely approach the harmonic sophistication of the theater writers. Not only that, they were to pave the way for an age in which orchestration would dominate not just harmony, but the very inner sanctum of the pop song — melody. But that would be a problem for the 1970s, not the '60s when melody was still, as always, the prime ingredient in pop. The '60s audience still expected melody but it had developed a taste for melodies that were part and parcel of daring orchestral textures.

Orchestration in popular music, after so long a dormancy, had suddenly become an important part of the songwriter's arsenal — only now, instead of a sheet of twelve-stave music paper, orchestrators faced four- , eight- and sixteen-track recording consoles. That being the case, it is ironic that, next to the Beatles, the songwriter whose instrumental thinking was the most original and exciting was a man who took little or no interest in multi-tracking. This was Bob Dylan who, as has been seen, had experimented with a variety of styles before settling on the self-authored folk song, as practiced by Woody Guthrie. He was a singer/songwriter like Hank Williams, thinking up his own accompaniments. But, unlike Williams, Dylan was a one-man band and, as such, there was not much arranging for him to do. He was further hemmed in by the folk movement's antipathy to most musical instruments. Therefore, his songs did not change musically at first, only lyrically. Early political songs gave way to more personal lyrics: love songs which, instead of sentimentality, used sarcasm — not the tongue-in-cheek sarcasm of a Larry Hart or an Ira Gershwin but the genuine article, such as one might encounter in a street argument. But when the Beatles came to America Dylan decided that he too wanted to work with a band and, from that point on, the excitement generated by his music was directly linked to changes in his instrumentation. The lyrics continued to evolve — the sarcastic love songs gave way to Blakeian visions and hallucinatory images. But the truth is that, published as poetry, Dylan's lyrics would never have gone very far. He was always primarily a musician and his career was inevitably rekindled by changes in his musical style. In 1965 he gave up his solo act to play with such blues-based rock and roll musicians as Mike Bloomfield and Al Kooper. The sound that they and others created on Dylan's three hard rock albums (*Bringing It All Back Home, Highway 61 Revisited* and *Blonde on Blonde*) is one of the most extraordinary in pop music.

Dylan was always too jumpy and too nervous to concoct impeccable arrangements. By the time of *Sgt. Pepper*, the Beatles were spending months at a time in the studio, laboring over their compositions, wringing every possibility out of George Martin's four-track console. Dylan, on the other hand, would walk into a studio, play his songs once for the attending musicians and then tell the engineer to get the tape rolling (he had walked out of his first studio session when, playing harmonica for Harry Belafonte's *Midnight Special* album in 1961, he had been annoyed by the latter's painstaking perfectionism). Dylan did not systemically work out his arrangements. Instead, he carefully picked those musicians who would, given his material, create the sound that he had in mind. What the Beatles had in orchestral complexity, therefore, he attained through the novelty and the purity of his sound.

Until 1970 Dylan and the Beatles kept up with one another. Dylan created a succession of sounds, all of them pure, original and authentic. In 1965 he had adopted their electrical amplification while they, in turn, had made use of some of his acoustic guitar stylings. At the height of their baroque psychedelic phase he offered *John Wesley Harding* which featured the simplest and most subdued instrumentation: guitar, bass, drums and piano. It was not a new sound but it was an unexpected one and, given Dylan's expert song-writing and his novel use of lyrics as parables, it single-handedly ended pop psychedelia. This was 1968 and, as it turned out, both Dylan and the Beatles had only one more new direction up their sleeves. For the Beatles, it was a return to arrangements which could be played by the foursome without too much assistance from studio gadgetry or outside musicians. This did not mean a return to pre-*Rubber Soul* days. The songs were at least as sophisticated as they had been the year before, in 1967. But electronic and symphonic effects were now largely replaced by the Beatles' own instrumental abilities. As players, they had matured to an astounding degree.

The last ace up Dylan's sleeve was one of his original loves, country music. The instrumentation of *Nashville Skyline* (which, ironically, contains his most hand-crafted, Tin Pan Alley songs) was as pure in its way as the sounds on *Blonde on Blonde* and *John Wesley Harding* had been. From then on, none of Dylan's albums would have that kind of purity. Each of them, for instrumentation, would draw on a potpourri of his past accomplishments, sometimes ineffectively so. There is no question that his songwriting became uneven at this point, though the best songs of the '70s ("Watching the River Flow," "If Not for You," "Never Say Goodbye," "You're a Big Girl Now") equaled his best of the 1960s. But most lacking in his music were the unique instrumental combinations that had been present on his albums from 1965 through 1969.

The best of the present day pop orchestrators now fall into one of two categories. In the first are writers who, following in the footsteps of Hank Williams, Chuck Berry, Buddy Holly, Dylan and the Beatles, take responsibility for the way their songs are arranged. Their ranks include Paul Simon, Randy Newman, Joni Mitchell, Elton John, Billy Joel, Bruce Springsteen and Stevie Wonder.

The second type of pop orchestrator is the record producer. Working in cave-like recording studios, they shape and color songs written by the musicians and bands who come to them, and they trace their lineage back to such folk as Robert Russell Bennett, Hershey Kay and Ferde Grofé, who were the middlemen between the show writers and the public, especially on Broadway. George Martin, Jerry Wexler, Arif Mardin and Richard Perry are a few of the current stars in this field and it is their perspective that has begun to dominate. Many of the studio writers have stopped composing idiomatically for particular instruments, becoming content instead to write their songs first and then gloss them with acceptable arrangements — arrangements which have begun to have a ready-made, suit-off-the-rack quality. Because this is so and because the studio writers have refused to delve into non-orchestral musical elements such as harmony, they have gotten themselves into ontological problems that are much worse than those faced by the theater writers. Their new music, lacking melodic, harmonic, rhythmic and orchestral identity, has begun to suffer the fate of Gertrude Stein's Oakland — "there is no there there."

Chapter Four

THE SONGWRITER AS PERFORMER

Every so often, pop music rids itself of hard-won insight and sophistication. This was true at the end of the 19th century when songs with simple melodies and even simpler harmonies gained favor over the relatively complex compositions of operetta makers. In those days, American popular music was going backwards, oblivious not just to Offenbach, Sullivan and Léhar but to the symphonic composers who were adventurously exploring the fertile post-Wagner harmonic terrain. In the first decade of this century Debussy and Ravel were at work in France, Mahler and Schoenberg in Germany, Scriabin in Russia and Ives in the United States. But American songwriters were moving in the opposite direction. In a sense, they were cleansing themselves of a European burden. While light music of European origin was still being written in America by such knowledgeable composers as Victor Herbert, the trend was against them. The tree of pop harmony was being pruned back and the new shoots were simple, more basic and more susceptible to new influences such as early blues and jazz.

Fresh new harmonies then arose from these American sounds. Kern made use of them in the 1910s and he led the way to Gershwin, whose last songs were as harmonically complex as popular music has even become. After Gershwin's death in 1937 the level of harmonic invention in popular songs remained high, but it had already reached its peak. Still, the songs written in the 1940s for Broadway and Hollywood were eminently sophisticated. Even in a show such as *St. Louis Woman*, in which Harold Arlen wanted to simulate the pop music of a simpler time, the songs took into account all that had been learned in the harmonically adventurous period that began with Kern.

At mid-century, however, pop music went back to the basics all over again. This was because it had become estranged from the youngest segment of its audience. At fault was a combination of factors, including a new tendency on Broadway to avoid slang. In earlier days one left the theater singing phrases like "I Like the Likes of You." But show tunes now were liable to be about Venice or edelweiss or Anatevka. Another problem was that theater music and jazz both became more cerebral. The theater writers were now composing music that illuminated the psyches of the fictional characters who populated their stage plays. Jazz had forsaken the dance band for the worlds of Miles Davis and Thelonius Monk, cutting its tether to the kind of melody and rhythm that had once been the source of its appeal. Many young songwriters were unimpressed by all this intellect, just as show composers had once shuddered at the uncommerciality of Ravel and Mahler.

But the most important single factor in pop's mid-century change was the discovery made by white teenagers, through the phenomenon of Elvis Presley, of music made by blacks which had formerly been called rhythm and blues and which now became rock and roll. This music was to the Broadway tradition what ragtime had been to European operetta. It wiped the slate clean.

It had taken a while for ragtime to really enter the bloodstream of pop and, when it did, it lost much of its zip — but its presence had a lot to do with the indigenousness and sophistication of American pop songs of the period between 1910 and 1950. The same thing happened with rock and roll. After the first blossoming in the mid-1950s (in the recordings of those years, such as the ones produced by Sam Phillips of Sun Records, one finds music of much more wit and daring than any Broadway devotee would ever have admitted at the time), early rock lost much of its spunk. In rock and roll lore this is traditionally blamed on Presley's draft notice, though it probably had more to do with the public's fancy for entertainers with movie star good looks. In that arena Buddy Holly, Carl Perkins and Jerry Lee Lewis could not compete. Black writers such as Chuck Berry and Little Richard were, for racial reasons, out of the running altogether. But Pat Boone, Frankie Avalon and Fabian did fill the bill. And, with their coming, it became apparent that rock and roll was liable to lose its essence when the writer and the performer were not one and the same. It is true that Presley never wrote a song. But in the early days the songs he sang were created around him. Those who wrote for Presley in that period moved mentally to his gyrations. But, Presley aside, all the other great rockers of the 1950s were both writers and performers.

The music dictated that this be so, for in this music rhythm predominated. It was not an easily reproducible beat that was simple to recreate in one's mind, like a waltz. This was an elusive rhythm that could appear in many guises — fast, slow, march-like or based on rocking dotted notes — but it was always instantly recognizable when it was real and just as easily dismissed when it was not. Writers could best obtain the beat by performing the music — by latching on to it, as if it was always around, always there, unseen and waiting. It could come by like a train, pluck the performer up and sweep him along like a mail pouch. Only when this rhythm was found, when one fell into its "groove" on a guitar or a piano or, better yet, in a band with a solid bass/drummer combination — could a melody be coaxed out of it. That had been the way of the blues, though blues melodies were too predictable to satisfy the public's real and insatiable demand for melodic novelty. Rock and roll did create memorable melody, but melody was an attribute which refused to appear unless the rhythmic ambience was correct.

In 1964, after an aimless half-decade, this true rhythm or beat was brought back into rock and roll by the Beatles. They had been devoted to the records of Presley, Holly and Berry and they were able to extract memorable melodies from genuine rock rhythms. Between 1964 and 1970 the Beatles went on to distinguish themselves as songwriters, approaching, as no rock writers before or since, the sophisticated heights of Broadway. But in every one of their songs, from the ballads to the rockers to the novelty numbers and to those which, like "Strawberry Fields" and "I Am the Walrus," defy classification, the beat is there and it always rings true. In a song like "Help!" for instance, the melody escapes monotony — even though it is basically a single repetitious note — because it takes a successful if bumpy ride on the rhythm around it. In a ballad such as "Julia," where the principal strain is again a single note, the rhythm helps brings about the success of the song.

The age of the performing songwriter was therefore created by the nature of rock and roll. Rock songwriters were best off as players in a band, where they were engulfed by a beat that inspired melodies. More than any other group, the Rolling Stones fashioned their composing style to accommodate this fact of life. Unlike the Beatles, they were performers before they were writers; only after some years as a rhythm and blues band did they begin writing their own material. But when they did, the music kept close to that first beat, afraid to go very far, like a child around its mother's skirts. Their greatest up-tempo songs — "Jumping Jack Flash," "Brown Sugar," "Street Fighting Man," "Happy" — are all fashioned from a similar, exuberant rhythm, apparently the one most favored by guitarist/composer Keith Richards. Their ballads, on the other hand, do tend to stray into the easier and less stringent rhythms of folk music. Compare the definite rhythmic emphasis of such Beatle songs as "Eleanor Rigby," "The Fool on the Hill" and "Hey Jude" with the less emphatic rhythms of "Lady Jane," "Angie" and "Wild Horses." The Stones may have written so few ballads for precisely that reason — they found themselves wandering off the mark. Instinctively they understood that if they even once lost contact with that first big beat they might lose it forever. The Beatles understood this too (at least as a group) but they were more confident of their ability to allow the lifeline to get longer and longer. Having been both performers and composers from the beginning, their self-confidence was large in both areas, but probably greater in the latter. Their creations influenced their playing more than the other way around. For the Stones, the opposite was true. They were more self-confident as performers and their creative potential was held in check by their performing style. Still, like the Beatles, they were able to get worthy melodies out of the beat and they realized, whether instinctively or consciously, that as long as the beat came naturally, everything would probably be all right.

Can the beat slip out of one's grasp? One might not think it possible, for a band ought to be able to maintain it by listening closely to past recordings. In a sense, the Beatles did this. Before recording sessions they would warm up by performing 1950s rock and roll — the songs that had inspired them in the first place. They would also, according to reports, replay their most recent records so as to know what direction they had been heading in at the time of the last session. But none of them continued to do this after the break-up. In the 1970s each, to a greater or a lesser extent, expressed an aversion to what they had accomplished together in the '60s (or, at least, to thinking about it) and they all avoided Beatle music during their solo recording sessions. That may have accounted for some of the aimlessness which so swiftly plagued all of their solo careers.

The same thing happened to the Stones after their 1972 double album, *Exile on Main Street*. On 1974's *It's Only Rock 'n Roll* the title song is only one of several which reach for and fail to find the old mesmerizing beat, a problem which would plague every subsequent album. They have tried to shake off this jinx by going on the road and, before expectant audiences, they have sometimes been successful at finding the spirit of their first incarnation. Performance is still the spur for their creative juices, just as it was at the beginning of their career. It dominates them.

As much as the Beatles or the Stones, Bob Dylan has genius as a performer, whether it is before a live audience or in a recording studio. He is a great singer — greater than Jagger and at least as good as Lennon or McCartney. Of all the composer/performers of the 1960s, only Dylan and Lennon were able to consistently sing from and to the heart and Dylan, despite his conversion to Christianity, has always made good use of the Wailing Wall strain in his voice. But it is as a composer that Dylan first achieved renown and his creative discoveries have always had a huge influence on his performing style, sometimes bending it in an all but unrecognizable way.

Unlike the Beatles and the Stones, Dylan did not begin his career — at least his professional career — as a rock and roller, and it was not until his fifth year as a professional, 1965, that, playing on electrically amplified instruments with musicians who were influenced by urban Chicago-style blues, his music developed a backbeat. When it came, however, the beat was a revelation — more insistent than that of the Beatles, more snide than that of the Stones. It was a star-crossed sound. In it was the presentiment of early death, James Dean style. Appropriately enough, it ended like James Dean, in a road accident. Dylan survived but that manic, hyper beat did not. Probably he left it rather than the other way around, for his new and still artistically valid songs called for subdued and countrified settings. But Dylan has since wanted it back, only to find futility in chasing it — even though he continues to work with rhythm and blues-oriented musicians. His beat was once the greatest, as well as the most personal of the 1960s songwriter/performers. Now he has lost it both as a songwriter and as a performer. Neither side of the coin sparkles for him these days.

Songwriters who write for their own performing styles live a precarious creative existence. It has been seen that the beat can elude their grasp. But there are other dangers as well. For a performer/songwriter, there is always the chance that the idiosyncracies of one's playing or singing style will have a negative influence on one's creative thought. Rock composers have been particulary vulnerable to this. Lennon as a singer would end phrases with a kind of cantillation that became one of his signatures (it can be heard in "All I've Got to Do" on the word "do" in the title phrase) and this always threatened to distort and even dictate the direction and shape of his melodies. McCartney, as a solo artist, found it hard to resist overdubbing "oohs" and "woos" which inevitably sapped his songs of vitality. Harrison's tendency was toward atrophy — both in his singing and in his guitar playing. When Lennon and McCartney had been with him in the studio his voice had managed to keep a certain amount of its early rock and roll fervor (he is the one who sang on the Beatles' version of Chuck Berry's "Roll Over Beethoven"), but as a soloist his singing became less outgoing, shier, as did his guitar playing and, consequently, his songs. The Rolling Stones also suffered from this phenomenon, mainly on account of Mick Jagger. It was not so much that Jagger's voice lacked range and nuance, although that was a factor; it was because, as a singer, he adopted a tone of menace and braggadocio that was self-limiting.

There was a time when songs by Dylan and the Beatles were being successfully sung by any number of singers and groups. "Blowin' in the Wind" and "Yesterday" have by now been recorded as often as "Blue Moon" and "Night and Day." Moreover, both Dylan and the Lennon and McCartney team would sometimes give away tunes that they themselves did not intend to perform. Mary Hopkin had a hit with "Goodbye," a Lennon and McCartney number that was never recorded by the Beatles. Joan Baez did well with "Farewell Angelina," a song written but never recorded by Dylan. But, as time went on, many songs by these and other studio writers became too idiosyncratic to be used by other singers. It is hard to imagine anyone but Lennon singing "Oh Yoko" or "Hold On John" and only Dylan could do "Wedding Song" and "Sara." With Jagger, there was a different problem: by the 1970s many of his songs were not as much written as they were performed; that is, Jagger's vocal style, his purring and his growling, became a substitute for independently conceived melody lines. Jagger's songs did not exist apart from his voice and they therefore had no independent existence *as* songs. It was no wonder then that, as time went on, fewer and fewer cover versions were made of his works or of those written by the other studio writers — for they had developed ontological problems of their own.

This sort of difficulty was not faced by the show composers because none of them was a professional performer. Berlin and Arlen had begun their careers as singers but they had both given up vocalizing upon becoming successful writers. Gershwin, as has been noted, was an accomplished pianist and he often performed his concert works with symphony orchestras (for a time too he hosted his own radio program, on which he would perform his latest tunes as well as those of other composers), but performing to him was never more than a sideline. None of the theater writers was greatly influenced, much less tyrannized, by the exigencies of performing. Yet, they were influenced — and strongly so — by the fact that they composed at the keyboard. For, in using a piano, one sees a melodic pattern — and this ability to visualize a melody, to see it as well as hear it, helped them recognize a tune's latent musical potential. Almost all of the studio writers used guitars, not pianos (the exceptions were Carole King and Lamont Dozier) and, because this was so, their musical perceptions were very different from those of the theater writers. Since it is difficult to play melodies and harmonies simultaneously on a guitar, they would often compose their tunes by singing, while they sought appropriate harmony by strumming chords. So it was that their melodies were simpler than those of the show writers. Having only aural memories (Paul Simon and Carole King were the only ones who could read and write music), they were more liable to eschew revisions and stick with a tune as it first appeared.

Pianos made an even greater difference in the way these two generations approached harmony. It is much easier to explore harmonic relationships at a keyboard than it is to do so at a fretboard.

72

Piano composers who have some knowledge of theory (and theory too makes more sense at a keyboard) are often anxious to go on harmonic excursions. With a guitar, however, chordal relationships are less obvious and, unless one makes a systematic study of jazz or classical guitar, it is likely that complex harmonic patterns will be forever out of reach. This was so with most of the studio writers (with the exceptions of King and Dozier, who were pianists, and of Simon, who, though a guitarist, made a conscious effort to increase his harmonic vocabulary). Their harmonies were simpler and more predictable than those of the show composers. This is not to say that there was no harmonic novelty in songs by the Beatles, Dylan and the Stones. Because these writers did not know how chords are related to one another in the tonal system, they would sometimes throw in a chord that was outside of the key they were working in. Such harmonic interlopers made sounds that, while not exactly shocking, were still unexpected. In "I Am the Walrus," for instance, Lennon, though he was writing in the key of A (whose chords are A, B-minor, C-sharp-minor, D, E, F-sharp-minor and G-sharp-diminished), came up with the following progression: A, D, F, G, A, F, B, C. This was the way the studio writers' harmonic experiments were carried out. The chords themselves were never very complex — usually they were simple triads — but sometimes, by ignoring relationships that they did not know existed, they created interesting, even exciting harmony. The trouble was that there were limits to this hit-or-miss style of exploration. There were no limits to the more logical harmonic excursions of the show writers.

In the theater writers' generation, composing and performing were two segregated activities. And, because this was so, the theater writers always found themselves rising to an occasion. Sometimes the occasion was a show whose plotline or characters required songs to be tailor-made to fit exacting specifications. Sometimes the occasion was the demanding presence of a certain star for whom a songwriter was working. In either case, these were healthy, salutary demands. Of course, relations between composers and performers could be tense. Richard Rodgers found himself in one uncomfortable situation after another until, as the producer of his own shows, he was able to hire whomever he pleased. In the 1930s he had worked in Hollywood and then again on Broadway with George M. Cohan. Both times Cohan's stage role had been that of the President of the United States and it seems to have made him even more cocky than usual. Being the composer of a few hits himself, Cohan had turned his nose up at Rodgers and Hart's scores for both projects.

Another unpleasant episode occurred while working on the film *Love Me Tonight*. After Rodgers and Hart played "Mimi" and other songs from their score for the star, Maurice Chevalier, the latter snubbed them. As Rodgers tells it in his autobiography, *Musical Stages*:

> Paramount had assigned us to a cell-like cubicle on the first floor of one of their buildings. It couldn't be dignified by being called an office; if we went over to the tiny window and stuck our noses right up against the glass, we could see a patch of about six inches of sky. One day we heard a knock on the door and there, with eyes twinkling and teeth gleaming, stood Maurice Chevalier. Everything he wore was blue — blue jacket, blue sport shirt, blue scarf, blue slacks, blue shoes — which accentuated the incredible blueness of his eyes. He greeted Larry and me as if we were old friends, told us how happy he was that we were writing the songs for his picture, and asked if we would mind playing some of them. With Chevalier practically sitting on my lap in our cramped quarters, I played the music and Larry and I took turns singing the words. Chevalier sat silent throughout, his usually expressive face without a trace of either approval or disapproval, and when we'd finished he simply rose and left without saying a word. We were stunned. The only conclusion we could reach was that he didn't like what he'd heard. Now what? Should we start all over again? And what about our reputation once it got around that Chevalier, the screen's leading musical star, had turned thumbs down?

As it turned out, there was no need to worry. Despite his inexplicable behavior, Chevalier had loved the songs. But the incident does go to show that relationships between show composers and performers were not always comfortable. The balance of power was sometimes with the composer but just as often the performer held sway. Nevertheless, these relationships were almost always synergetic. Nowhere is this more clearly demonstrated than in the careers of two great favorites of the theater writers, Fred Astaire and Ethel Merman.

A box score of the tunes that Astaire introduced shows that he inspired more great songs than anyone in the century:

Year	Song	Composer/Lyricist
1924	Lady Be Good	Gershwin/Gershwin
1924	Fascinating Rhythm	Gershwin/Gershwin
1927	Funny Face	Gershwin/Gershwin
1927	'S Wonderful	Gershwin/Gershwin
1927	How Long Has This Been Going On?	Gershwin/Gershwin

1931	Dancing in the Dark	Schwartz/Dietz
1932	Night and Day	Porter
1933	The Carioca	Youmans/Kahn/ Eliscu
1935	Top Hat, White Tie and Tails	Berlin
1935	Cheek to Cheek	Berlin
1935	Isn't This a Lovely Day?	Berlin
1935	I Won't Dance	Kern/Harbach
1935	Lovely to Look At	Kern/Harbach
1936	Let's Face the Music and Dance	Berlin
1936	The Way You Look Tonight	Kern/Fields
1936	Pick Yourself Up	Kern/Fields
1936	A Fine Romance	Kern/Fields
1937	I've Got Beginner's Luck	Gershwin/Gershwin
1937	Let's Call the Whole Thing Off	Gershwin/Gershwin
1937	They All Laughed	Gershwin/Gershwin
1937	They Can't Take That Away from Me	Gershwin/Gershwin
1937	A Foggy Day	Gershwin/Gershwin
1937	Things Are Looking Up	Gershwin/Gershwin
1937	Nice Work If You Can Get It	Gershwin/Gershwin
1938	Change Partners	Berlin
1940	I Concentrate on You	Porter
1940	Dearly Beloved	Kern/Mercer
1943	One for My Baby	Arlen/Mercer
1943	My Shining Hour	Arlen/Mercer
1948	Steppin' Out	Berlin
1955	Something's Gotta Give	Mercer

The show composers loved him. "You can't work with Fred without knowing you're working for him," said Berlin. "I'd never have written *Top Hat* without him. He makes you feel secure." Berlin would constantly consult with Astaire as the songs were written in order to get the latter's opinion and to see if the tunes were danceable. Astaire was a songwriter himself and so was well able to discuss, understand and criticize the material he was handed. The Gershwins also wrote with Astaire's enunciation and dancing style specifically in mind.

The first song that Cole Porter ever wrote expressly for a performer was "Night and Day," which he handed to Astaire in 1932. Porter's writing technique was well suited to this kind of tailoring for, being both composer and lyricist, he could indulge in a peculiar method of song construction. He would begin with the rhythm of the song (although sometimes he already had a title) and to that he would then add the words. Only later would he get around to the music. (The idea for the chorus of "Night and Day" is said to have come to Porter when he heard a mezzuin in prayer; its verse — "the beat beat beat" — is said to have been inspired by the dropping of rain on Mrs. Vincent Astor's porch.)

Porter wrote many songs for Astaire. Unfortunately, a lot of them came in the early 1940s, a fallow period for the composer, whose heyday had been the mid-'30s. In those days his songs had most often been written for Ethel Merman. She was second only to Astaire as an inspiration to many of the great show composers. And, as unlikely as Astaire's voice was, that of La Merman (as Porter dubbed her) was even more so. Unsubtle would perhaps be too subtle a word to describe it. Brassy and strident (it is possible to believe that fire engines pull to the curb when *she* goes by), it nevertheless was like catnip to Porter who loved to have her in his shows. She was in five of them between 1935 and 1943. For the first, *Anything Goes*, he submitted his songs not only for her approval, but for the approval of her mother and father. And it was in this show that Porter paid Merman his highest compliment. He actually rewrote a song — "Blow, Gabriel, Blow" — for her. This is something he had always fought against, as did most of the show writers. If a singer did not like a song he would sooner withdraw it and save it for the future, writing a new one in the meantime, than tinker with what he had already done.

For the 1936 show *Red, Hot & Blue* Porter studied Merman's voice so as to better write for it. (He liked to study up for a project. He was meticulous about making *Can Can* an accurate representation of 19th century French dance hall music and he took a course from jazz impresario Norman Granz as preparation for the song "Now You Has Jazz" in *High Society*.) From his study of Merman, he concluded that her best notes were A-flat, B-flat and C and so he wrote lyrics with important words on those notes. "Down in the Depths" was an example of this from *Red, Hot and Blue*, as was "De-Lovely," which Merman sang with Bob Hope. For *DuBarry Was a Lady* in 1939 he wrote "Friendship," "Well, Did You Evah!" and "But in the Morning, No!" for her. Porter's last show for Merman was 1943's *Something for the Boys*. It was not a success and the professional association ended, though they remained close friends for the rest of his life.

Merman was also closely associated with Gershwin and Berlin. She did only one show for the former, 1930's *Girl Crazy* — but it was her first and one of his greatest. When Gershwin first played the score of *Girl Crazy* for her he asked the twenty-year-old singer if there was anything about the songs she would like to have changed — and these songs included "I Got Rhythm." Maybe it was a rhetorical question, maybe not. But it is certain that Gershwin was another one of her great admirers.

Her association with Berlin came at the end of his career. She starred in two of his last and best shows: *Annie Get Your Gun* and *Call Me Madam*. For the latter, Merman was given a song she did not particularly like, one with the unlucky title of "Mr. Monotony." The composer had salvaged it from the 1949 flop *Miss Liberty*. Like Gershwin and Porter, Berlin took Merman's opinions very seriously. He replaced Mr. Monotony" with a better song, "You're Just in Love." It, like a much earlier Berlin tune, "Play a Simple Melody," was another example of this musically illiterate composer's ability to handle two-part counterpoint.

These two demands, then — the show and the performer — were the only ones made on the show composers. But both offered challenges which allowed them to rise to the occasion. Rodgers' challenge, while working on *Love Me Tonight*, had been to write a happy Frenchified ditty for the vaudevillian talent of Chevalier — and he had come up with "Mimi." In *Annie Get Your Gun* Irving Berlin, constrained by requirements of character and plot, had written "hillbilly" numbers such as "Anything You Can Do" and "You Can't Get a Man With a Gun."

But the rock and roll songwriters of the '60s were under no such constraints. They were their own Astaires and Mermans; they were their own subjects too. True, they were allowed to write about anything that occurred to them. But without the prodding of other singers and without the stimulus of a plot, such license, though heady at first, was liable to lead them to early burn-outs. Dylan was the first to take advantage of the new freedom, trying his hand at coffee-house poetry in "Mr. Tambourine Man," "Gates of Eden" and other songs. But his imagination became ingrown; rarely was he sparked from the outside by the predicaments of real or fictional characters (aside from his early efforts, in which he balladized the tribulations of Hollis Brown and Medgar Evers). One of Gershwin's finest melodies, "Bess You Is My Woman," was inspired by the love of a cripple for a harlot — something surely beyond the ken of his day-to-day experience. But the studio writers, having recourse only to such stimuli as they could find in their surroundings — which had by then shrunk to that very narrow band of the human spectrum called the Jet Set — became more abstract, more obscure and more self-indulgently silly.

When a song's lyric is not *about* something — when there is no subject — then the music can all too easily follow suit and try to get by without any real or motivating idea. Of course, this problem was not unique to the studio writers. But in the days when performers and songwriters were separate creatures a tune was liable to be tossed aside if it did not measure up. Long before any audience or any critic ever got a chance to judge it, it had to face the scrutiny of the performer and the producer and the director and the financial backers. If it could get past all of them there was still the out-of-town tryout in Boston or New Haven, where preliminary audiences and critics gave it the once-over. But no one has the authority or the nerve to tell Bob Dylan or Carole King or Mick Jagger to throw out a song. No modern day Astaires or Mermans are on hand to speak their minds to them or to other studio writers of stature.

Chapter Five

LYRICS

It has been seen that the studio writers were fine musicians and composers — not as harmonically adventurous as the theater writers but more adept orchestrally. How then do they stack up as lyricists? Did any of them write anything as intricate as Larry Hart's "Johnny One Note"?

> Poor Johnny One Note
> Got in Aida
> Indeed a
> Great chance to be brave
>
> He took his one note
> Howled like the North Wind
> Brought forth wind
> That made critics rave
> While Verdi turned 'round in his grave!

Or as serene as Hammerstein's "Hello, Young Lovers"?

> When I think of Tom
> I think about a night
> When the earth smelled of summer
> And the sky was streaked with white
> And the soft mist of England
> Was sleeping on a hill
> I remember this
> And I always will.
>
> There are new lovers now
> On the same silent hill
> Looking on the same blue sea
> And I know Tom and I
> Are a part of them all
> And they're all a part of Tom and me.

Isn't it possible that the studio writers were instinctive composers who, being too proud or preoccupied to employ professional lyricists, insisted on doing the job themselves — and who, lacking the talent to conceive of and follow through on lyrics such as the masterpieces cited above, covered up their shortcomings by obscure and self-indulgent verse?

Perhaps. But an opposite argument can be made. Did any of the theater writers ever capture the mood of an entire generation as Dylan did in "Like a Rolling Stone"? Did any of them express bottled up sexual energy and frustration as well as Mick Jagger did in "Satisfaction"? Did any of them let their minds move into other realms as John Lennon did in "Strawberry Fields"? And did any of them ever speak as directly and intimately as Carole King did in "You've Got a Friend"? What one generation of lyricists lacked, the other one had and what one had the other lacked — or so the argument might go. But it was not so simple. In substituting orchestral thinking for harmonic thinking there was a kind of equivalence. The music of both generations was equally well-made. But in their lyrics the studio writers replaced craftsmanship with self-indulgence, which was something else again — even if that indulgence resulted in an expanded range.

As craftsmen the theater lyricists were far more professional than their rock and roll successors. They worked with the precision of haiku writers and, like Japanese poets, were severely restricted as to space, tone of voice and subject matter. Space often as not amounted to thirty-two bars of music — an exceedingly limited canvas. Tone of voice was usually tongue-in-cheek, though every now and then they permitted themselves an unveiled directness. Subject matter, at least until the mid-1940s when the demands of plot and character gave them more leeway, was almost invariably romance.

Very often it turned out that the best way to fulfill these three requirements was to take a current catch-phrase and develop it into a short essay on romantic love. There are many examples of this kind of thing, including "I Didn't Know What Time It Was," "Right as the Rain," "I Can't Get Started," "Get Out of Town," and "Let's Call the Whole Thing Off." Sometimes these theater lyricists invented their own catch-phrases, such as "Embraceable You" and "I've Got You Under My Skin" but, even so, their working method was the same. They began with a title phrase and then built a lyric around it. The phrase "I've Got Beginner's Luck," for example, was ideal for this method since gambling and romance are a natural analogy. Once Ira Gershwin had this title, the direction of the song was inevitable and only its outcome remained to be decided. His solution was to show that this particular romance, unlike a first lucky gambling streak, was sure to be a lasting one ("I'm lucky through and through/For the first time that I'm in love I'm in love with you").

Gershwin and other lyricists who wrote to already completed melodies — Hart and Dorothy Fields, for example — worked under the strictest kinds of constraints. But it is quite possible that that is the way they liked it. The more stringent the rules, the more one knew just what had to be done. Robert Frost once suggested that writing poetry without attention to meter and rhyme was like playing tennis without a net. It is possible that Gershwin and Hart, had they been forced to come up with a lyric without the prodding of an already-written tune, would have felt as if the basis of their game — their net — had been taken away from them.

The studio writers, on the other hand, were only too happy to play without a net. Though they too liked to begin with colloquial phrases, they were less willing to do the exacting and meticulous work that was needed to develop them. Doing so required discipline and, since they were already exerting prodigious amounts of discipline in the composition of their music, they were not very anxious to double the load by doing the same amount of work on their lyrics. Instead, they granted themselves a type of poetic license which emphasized imagination over logic. In "All You Need Is Love," for example, Lennon began as songwriters have traditionally begun, with a potent catch-phrase that readily lent itself to development. Had he been of the theater writers' generation the logical direction of "All You Need Is Love" would have been in the "penniless but happy" vein of "I Can't Give You Anything But Love, Baby," "I Got Plenty of Nothin'," "I Got the Sun in the Morning" and even the Beatles' own "Can't Buy Me Love." But Lennon did not choose to take "All You Need Is Love" in that direction. His goal was not to write another song about romantic love, but one about the brotherhood of man (the song was written for a live telecast to be transmitted around the world). Yet, typically, he balked after choosing his theme and he refused to follow through. The finished lyric did not talk about brotherhood or peace. Instead, it was, aside from the title phrase, a series of oddball platitudes ("There's nothing you can do that can't be done/Nothing you can sing that can't be sung") which, when closely inspected, evaporated into amusing meaninglessness. Lennon let the title phrase speak for the whole song, reserving the rest of the lyric for the kind of wordplay that he loved so well. The amazing thing was that this did not detract from the impact of the song. Of the many millions who heard it, it is doubtful that any failed to enjoy it or catch its intent because they felt cheated by Lennon's refusal to follow through on the title.

Obviously, the studio writers were not vying with the theater writers for brilliantly executed follow-throughs on germinal song ideas. Doing so had no appeal to them whatsoever, for they were less finicky about the tools of their trade than were the theater lyricists. It did not matter much to them if their rhymes were poor or approximate ("Johnny's in the basement/Mixing up the medicine/I'm on the pavement/Thinking about the government"). It did not matter to them if their songs seemed to wander off course in midstream (as the Beatles did in "Girl," a romantic number which took a sudden, proletarian detour with the line, "and a man must break his back to earn his day of leisure"). It did not even matter to them when their songs *had* no discernible subject (as was the case with the Stones' "Get Off My Cloud"). In fact, as time went on and as they discovered that their music could be successful even if their lyrics lacked precision — even if they lacked meaning — they began to indulge themselves even more, writing and then using what the theater writers would have dismissed as dummy lyrics. By the latter 1960s the studio writers, with unprecedented nerve, were publishing lines which were obviously the first ones that had popped into their heads — something they would not have dared to do earlier in their careers. For example, Paul McCartney's first title for "Yesterday" was "Scrambled Egg." But there was never any chance that that song, written in 1965, was going to end up with that name. Had it been written in 1969, however, he might not have troubled himself to come up with anything better than "Scrambled Egg" for he was by then the author of "She Came in Through the Bathroom Window" — a true dummy lyric if there ever was one.

The theater writers loved clarity but the studio writers loved and sometimes wallowed in gibberish. Jagger, Lennon, Dylan and Simon all delighted in nonsensical wordplay, picking up the banner (if not the precision) that had been dropped by the authors of "Maresy Doats." It is not hard to believe that one of the main reasons that they went in this direction was that it was easy. It was easy to be obscure, for the puzzled listener could never be certain that incomprehensibility was not, in fact, an advanced sort of brilliance; nor could listeners be sure that their inability to understand this brilliance was not, in fact, due to their own limitations. At the same time, it was more than obvious that, however flaky and inexact the words, the music being produced by these writers was carefully and professionally written. Since obscurity was something new in pop lyrics, it was only reasonable to assume that its sudden appearance had a purpose. And since the writers who indulged in it were so obviously talented and diligent in their music, it was hard to believe that their lyrics, though they seemed to be meaningless, really were meaningless. So it was that the public failed to see that there was an "emperor's new clothes" quality about much of what was being written. For example, knowing nods were given to Paul Simon's

"Mrs. Robinson" when it came out in 1968 as part of the score to the motion picture *The Graduate*. The song seemed to be making unyielding if indirect commentaries on a lot of topics, including sex ("most of all you've got to hide it from the kids") and lost ideals ("where have you gone Joe DiMaggio?"). What people did not know was that at the time Simon wrote the song all he knew about *The Graduate* was that one of its characters was a certain ill-defined but unsavory Mrs. Robinson. Under these circumstances the best that he could come up with was an aimless lyric about a woman of that name filled, for lack of any concrete information about her, with random phrases and with nonsensical "coo-coo-ca-choo's" (a tribute, perhaps, to the "goo-goo-g'joobs" of Lennon's "I Am the Walrus"), "ho ho hos" and the like.

A generation earlier the theater writers had often found themselves in similar quandaries, especially in Hollywood where they were regularly told to come up with a score before a script had been written. They usually solved the problem by writing songs that were so general as to be applicable to any reasonably romantic character or situation. But Simon, eschewing that route, set about describing and at the same time avoiding his Mrs. Robinson. It was a sign of the times that not one peep of criticism greeted the song. In fact, people acted as if there were really nothing all that unusual about it. Why had the name of Joe DiMaggio been suddenly brought up — what did *he* have to do with the song or the movie? No one much cared. What was intended by the phrase "Jesus loves you more than you will know" and what was it doing in this song? No one asked any questions about that either. Young people were allured by this kind of lyric writing *just because* it was incomprehensible — for the intangibility of some of "Mrs. Robinson"'s lines was appealing to a generation that did not like things to be too pat, that was happy when the Beatles broke geographical boundaries by introducing the music and the philosophy of India and that was happy too when new political realms were broached. One could not be sure, but song lyrics like "Mrs. Robinson," "I Am the Walrus," and "Sad-Eyed Lady of the Lowlands" seemed to be breaking ground on all of those fronts.

This new style of lyric writing was therefore not only accepted but taken seriously by an admiring, indulging public. By the end of the 1960s a great number of masters and doctoral theses had been written about the meaning of rock lyrics, with particular emphasis on Dylan, who, having produced such inscrutable lines as

> I've walked and I've crawled on six crooked highways
> I've stepped in the middle of seven sad forests
> I've been out in front of a dozen dead oceans
> I've been ten thousand miles in the mouth of a graveyard

became, like William Blake, an invaluable resource for the exegesis-minded student. Because Dylan, the Beatles, the Stones, Simon and others were writing in the first person, as themselves, and not in the once-removed format of the theater writers, because their words had an enticing and poetic way of fading into and then out of lucidity, because some of their lines were truly beautiful (Dylan's "She Belongs to Me," for example) and, most of all, because the music was so fresh and vital — they were the first pop lyricists ever to inspire serious criticism. First a cadre, then a legion of annotators and explicators arose who, writing for newly established journals such as *Crawdaddy, Creem* and *Rolling Stone*, had a great impact on the youthful pop music audience. Ever on the prowl for significance and for meaning, they spent long hours sifting through lines that had often been dashed off in drugged or drunken stupors. Then, in reporting the results of their analytical diggings, these critics set new records for hyperbole. Of Dylan's *Bringing It All Back Home* Jon Landau wrote:

> We get the ultimate dialectic. Dylan himself has become polarized [by] an aesthetically brilliant attempt to transcend the limitation of the self-created myth.

Writing about Mick Jagger's lines in "Sympathy for the Devil," John Kreidel explained that the Stones' vocalist

> never forces you to drink acid in water — like California — like most hip philosophers. He just leads you to water. He is the modern Pontius Pilate. He says we are innocent even if we are formally guilty. By going on record that we are innocent, we can fight bureaucracy even if bureaucracy behaves against our will to become cretins. Christ didn't believe in this way of doing it, but then Christ didn't survive.

It was not uncommon to find, in reading a review of a new album, that the music was hardly mentioned at all. In a way, this was understandable in that, next to sex, music is the most difficult activity to describe in words. It was also understandable when one considered that these new critics were actually just as impulsive, just as ecstatic and just as young as the songwriters themselves. But the irony was that now, when the pop composer had at long last been given his due as an author, it was not for his music but for his words — even though those words were often a kind of by-product.

Nevertheless, no one can deny that the rock critics were pioneers. Never before had the careers of songwriters been analyzed for anything other than the number and the durability of their hits. Of the six great theater writers, only George Gershwin had received any serious musical criticism and then only for his concert works, not his songs. In fact, he and the others had to wait until the 1972 publication of Alec Wilder's book *American Popular Song* to receive their due as authors. But this was not the case with the studio writers who, within a few years of their initial success, were being taken very seriously.

Now, with the perspective of passed time and with mounting evidence of their fallibility, it is difficult to recall just *how* seriously they were once regarded. But in the '60s, admiration and gratitude toward these composers expanded in a geometrical fashion − a phenomenon that becomes more understandable when one considers how much talent they had. The Big Three of the decade − the Beatles, the Rolling Stones and Bob Dylan − were not just tunesmiths but versatile musicians. As singers, Lennon, McCartney and Dylan did not and do not suffer in comparison to other great pop singers of the century. The same can be said for McCartney, Harrison and Keith Richards as instrumentalists: no mere guitar whackers, they were innovative and, on occasion, unparalleled in their playing, mastering many styles and inventing a few of their own. As music writers, they had the energy and ability to seek out diverse influences − from classical western to classical eastern to blues to folk to country − and to use them in their own work without turning that work into a hodgepodge. As lyricists they were bold and honest, if not meticulous, writing words which could encapsulate the feelings of an entire generation. And one must also remember that they were the source of much new fashion, from haircuts to clothing to pop art and to less tangible vogues such as the stance taken by one generation toward its elders and toward authority in general. They were also physically attractive in an unbanal, non-glamorous, often mesmerizing way − recognizable in every photo but never quite the same and, therefore, always fascinating and original. In short, these men possessed such abundant gifts as to seem almost supernatural. Mere versatility was taken for granted. It became rare for anyone to limit himself to just one job − even the Beatles' drummer sang on occasion − and by the end of the decade this jack-of-all-trades trend had gone so far that it was not unusual to find an LP on which one person had written the music and the words, had played on some or all of the instruments, and had even designed the album cover. In the old days, when a composer took up sketching and photography, he was content to think of them as hobbies. Gershwin, for instance, was an accomplished painter but it is hard to imagine him insisting on doing the sets for one of his shows. The '60s writers, on the other hand, were never ashamed of the word "amateur." Sometimes they seemed to revel in that appellation, for they saw the word "professional" as a synonym for "conservative." To use a mundane analogy, these songwriters were like beautiful cars — music was the engine but there were lots of extras too. It was no wonder then that they became idols.

At the same time, there was an assumption on the part of the average worshipper that he and his hero stood shoulder to shoulder. Though placed on Olympus, these writers — the Big Three — spoke not some arcane Elysian language but words that the whole generation understood and had in common. They were not supernatural but, on the contrary, were exceptionally natural. They were what people could and ought to be if they gave themselves the chance.

It is impossible to calculate the pleasure that these music and image makers gave to an entire generation. It is also hard to know how much clandestine depression they caused. After all, what good did it do to become a dock worker or a doctor when it was obvious that human potential was fully realized only by songwriters? No one knows how many anonymous egos were whittled down in the process of elevating these songwriters, but there is the record of how their peers, lesser songwriters, were affected. One, Phil Ochs, having spent most of his adult life in the shadow of Dylan, with whom he had begun as an equal in the Greenwich Village days, ultimately killed himself. Others, who confined themselves to simple resentment, were probably happy to witness the decline and fall of these Olympians in the 1970s.

Rock critics had an instinctive feel for the sociological trappings that attended the studio writers, which was another reason that they spent much more time analyzing lyrics than music. They were especially interested in the political content of these lyrics because they assumed that, just as this generation of songwriters was the first in the history of pop to choose real poetry over trivial light verse, so it was the first to have a courageous and a coherent political viewpoint. But the new critics were forgetting — or perhaps they never knew — that the 1930s had been the era of the political musical on Broadway with the Gershwins' *Of Thee I Sing* and *Let 'Em Eat Cake* (they had written an anti-war musical, *Strike Up the Band*, as early as 1927), Arlen and Harburg's *Hooray for What?* and Marc Blitzstein's *The Cradle Will Rock*. One need not be a scholar of the theater to know that the great theater composers had opposed war and racism. But politics was never a priority with them. When their songs dealt directly with issues of the day, they did so as palliatives. A few numbers, like "Ten Cents a Dance" and "Brother Can You Spare a Dime," directly addressed the Depression but most, like "I Can't Give You Anything But Love, Baby," poked gentle fun at it. Later, with a new world war on the horizon, they took the same tack: "Dictators would be better off if they zoom-zoomed now and then," wrote Ira Gershwin in "Slap That Bass," while Irving Berlin advised people to "Face the Music and Dance."

In the 1960s the studio writers appeared to be less circumspect. They seemed to be in the heart of the battle. Dylan had begun his career with songs that directly challenged war and racism while, by mid-decade, the Beatles had made their beliefs plain: first by crediting their musical origins to black musicians, whom they clearly idolized, and then by using the word "love" in many of their songs as a synonym not for sexual desire but for brotherhood. The Stones, for their part, spoke openly about revolution, and Jagger at one point declared that, had he been a Frenchman, he would have been on the barricades during the political uprisings of 1968. Still, if one reads through the lyrics that these men wrote in the mid-to-late 1960s, it becomes clear that their political attitudes, though sometimes implied, were rarely if ever stated directly. Dylan did not utter a political thought in the 1960s after the assassination of President Kennedy. As for the Beatles, their only direct political statement during that time came in the 1968 song "Revolution," in which Lennon waffled on the subject of his own participation in any political upheaval, saying at one point to count him in and at another to count him out. Tackling the same topic in "Street-Fighting Man," Jagger also landed on both sides of the fence, voicing his support for the revolutionists while, at the same time, notifying them that he would probably have to sit out the fight. Although the studio writers were freer to state their political beliefs than the theater writers had been (for they sold their albums directly to an audience that existed all over the world, while the earlier writers had to sell tickets to Broadway theaters, which were filled up by a more selective, less proletarian group) they chose not to do so. Working at a time of worldwide political change — a change that pitted their generation, which they spearheaded, against their parents' — they were at least as coy politically as the theater writers had been. They mostly confined themselves to nose-thumbing: the Stones wanted to put a picture of a toilet on the cover of *Beggar's Banquet*; the Beatles wanted to show dismembered baby dolls on the cover of *Yesterday and Today* and so on. One always knew where they stood vis-à-vis the generation gap because they looked like radicals (or, more accurately, the radicals looked like them). But one would never have known of the existence of such issues as the Vietnam War and Civil Rights by their lyrics alone. Sometimes there was a song from which a political message could be extracted — the Beatles' "All Together Now," for instance ("black, white, green, red, can I take my friend to bed?"), Dylan's "Maggie's Farm" (the story of a hired hand who refuses to work any longer for a family of lunatics) and Paul Simon's coupling of "Silent Night" with a recording of war reportage on the

"7 O'Clock News." But, for the most part, the studio writers pussy-footed about politics. After Dylan backed off in 1963, not one of them wholeheartedly entered the fray until 1969 when Lennon began three years of activism with "Give Peace a Chance."

It cannot be denied that their bold rejection of tradition made these studio writers a remarkable phenomenon. But if their poetry was flawed and if their politics were shaky, what was their claim to distinction as lyricists? How did they stack up against the likes of Cole Porter and Larry Hart? Judged on the basis of how they handled the tools of their trade, the answer has to be: not so good. As rhymsters they were not in the same league as the theater lyricists. In "I Get a Kick Out of You," for instance, Porter came up with nine rhymes in the space of 28 syllables — each one adding to the song's momentum:

> Flying too high
> With some guy in the sky
> Is my idea of nothing to do
> But I get a kick out of you.

In none of their songs do any of the studio lyricists approach this level of artistry. On those rare occasions when they gave it a go the result was much less effective — as in the Beatles' "It's Only Love" where, unable to think of as many words as was required by the melody, they simply repeated one:

> I get high when I see you go by
> My oh my
> When you sigh *my my* inside just dries

Nor were they very good at thinking their lyrics through to make each one complete and of a piece. Had "You're a Big Girl Now" been written by Hart and not by Dylan, for instance, the song would have stuck to the premise of its title; that is, it would have been about a woman who, having come into her own, has been able to do very well without her former lover. But Dylan, not content to play Hart's game, does not develop this theme for very long. Soon he is focusing not on the newly won independence of the "big girl" but, instead, on his own self-pity. Nevertheless, the words to this song, because of their controlled intensity, do stand up as real poetry. And, as such, they illuminate a fundamental truth about the lyrics of the studio writers. Once one accepts their hit or miss quality — the fact that there is a persistent unevenness (not only from song to song but within individual songs) — then there is much beauty to be found. They were not looking for the kind of iron-clad logic that is present in the lyrics of the theater writers. But they did want and they got individual lines that were worth remembering. This generation of lyricists believed that song lyrics did not have to be great in their entirety — they only had to have one or two well-turned phrases. Mick Jagger's memorable declaration that wild horses could not take him from the side of his lover (in "Wild Horses") and Paul Simon's metaphor for a loyal friend in the title phrase of "Bridge Over Troubled Water," are two examples of lyrics in which a single line is meant to carry a whole song. There was an emotional directness in these writers that had been missing in the earlier generation. Hart, Porter and Ira Gershwin had all been almost obsessively dedicated to the tongue-in-cheek tone of voice. Even in so emotional a song as "My Funny Valentine," Hart still found it necessary to throw in some sarcasm. But a generation later, the studio writers rose to a similar intensity with lines that were utterly simple and unveiled (Carole King's "You've Got a Friend" and John Lennon's "Jealous Guy" are two examples of this). And it ought to be noted that these studio writers *were* capable, on occasion, of combining humor and feeling with something approaching Hart's mastery. The gentle metaphysics of Lennon and McCartney in "Penny Lane":

> Behind the shelter in the middle of the roundabout
> A pretty nurse is selling poppies from a tray
> And tho' she feels as if she's in a play
> She is anyway

and the wounded but funny sensuality of Dylan's "Buckets of Rain":

> Like your smile and your fingertips
> Like the way that you move your hips
> I like the cool way you look at me
> Everything about you is bringing me misery

are two instances of the masterful use of this sort of directness and intensity. But there was another side to the coin, one that did not bode well for the studio lyricists — or at least for their productive longevity. All of their lines were drawn from the same well. All came from inside the writer himself and without any of the filters enjoyed by the theater lyricists. Chief among those filters was the ability to speak through another's voice — a character on a stage or on a screen or on a bandstand. For the '60s lyricists, the intensity that was needed to reach inside one's self again and again, without the stimulating screen of those other points of view, combined too with the constraints of being not just famous, not just a celebrity, but an

89

oracle and an avatar, added up to a ton of pressure. You could end up taking yourself too seriously or not seriously enough. Without that great asset of the theater lyricist — distance (and the cool-headed craftsmanship that went with it) — this new generation, though amazingly talented, was at a real disadvantage.

Chapter Six

PRODUCTIVE LONGEVITY

George Gershwin: 25 Last Songs

One might argue that popular songwriting is an ephemeral task by definition, that pop composers only write for the moment and that they are nothing more than faddists. But the melodies of Stephen Foster and Jerome Kern seem to have been as genuinely touched by eternity as those of Mozart and Chopin. They have stood the test of time. Obviously, the mental craft that went into their construction is less sustained than what went into a Mozart piano concerto or a Chopin ballade but the essential goodness and rightness of each is the same. It would be foolish to say that one will outlive the other.

Why, then, did the careers of so many great popular songwriters run out of steam? Or, conversely, why do the careers of so many highbrow composers have so much forward momentum? Perhaps the answer lies in two factors which are almost always present in the careers of the highbrow composers and which seem to be prerequisites for productive longevity. One is that a composer keep faith with the original source of his inspiration. Beethoven, for instance, even in his late and highly idiosyncratic string quartets, maintained the essence of what he had inherited from Mozart and Haydn. Arnold Schoenberg, whose break with the past was probably even more spectacular, kept strong and definite ties to the music of Beethoven and Brahms. As for popular composers they have almost always, by instinct or by public pressure, adhered to this rule. Until very recently, there has been almost no room for self-indulgence on their part and whatever experimentation they did — Gershwin's and Kern's harmonic excursions, for example — was accomplished almost by stealth, so as not to unduly topple the expectations of their audience.

The second factor is where highbrow composers tend to outdo their pop counterparts. This is the continuing development of richer, more complex ideas. Illustrations of this are plentiful, the most obvious being Beethoven's symphonies, which became increasingly

Harold Arlen and Ira Gershwin in 1936. The photo is by George Gershwin.

elaborate in design and intent. Of course, Beethoven turned to the simpler combinations of chamber ensembles in his last years. But his later music, even though pure and streamlined, was highly evolved. This was not the case with the last works of Porter, Rodgers or Berlin. Compare Porter's final songs, written in 1958 for the television production of *Aladdin*, to what he wrote in 1934 for *Anything Goes*; or Rodgers' work for *Two By Two* (1970) to *Carousel* (1945); or Berlin's score for *Mr. President* (1962) to the one for *As Thousands Cheer* (1933). The simplicity of the later material is of an altogether different stripe then the seeming simplicity of Beethoven's last works. It has a bare-bones quality that has nothing to do with economy but which, instead, has a lot to do with fatigue and sentimentality.

No great highbrow composer, except for reasons of mental or mortal illness, has ever suffered a decline in his creative powers. On the contrary, the highbrows usually wrote their finest works at the end of their careers — at the end of their lives, that is, for the lives and their careers were one and the same. Wagner and Verdi, the two most notable 19th century theater composers, produced very great works at the conclusion of long lives. Wagner was nearly 70 at the Bayreuth premiere of *Parsifal*. Verdi, after several years of inactivity, came back at the age of 74 with *Otello* and then, at 80, wrote what is probably his greatest work, *Falstaff*.

One must remember, however, that none of The Six enjoyed a healthy, robust old age. By the time of *Aladdin*, Porter was suffering and had suffered physical and mental agonies which would have done in many men half his age. Rodgers wrote *Two By Two* shortly after a severe heart attack (just as he had written *Flower Drum Song* 12 years earlier after a bout with cancer). Berlin wrote *Mr. President* after a decade of physical and mental misery. Arlen, suffering from hepatitis, underwent a series of blood transfusions while writing *House of Flowers* in 1954. As for Kern and Gershwin, the former did not live beyond middle age and the latter did not get past his youth. But despite ill health and despite the field they were in — one which has always been most hospitable to extreme youth — these men more than held their own over the years. They could still write hits while in their 60s — as Porter showed with "I Love Paris" and "True Love," Berlin with "You're Just in Love" and "It's a Lovely Day Today" and Rodgers with "The Sweetest Sounds" and "Do I Hear a Waltz." (Arlen was the only one who, having been granted a seventh decade, failed to write any standards during the course of it.) What was missing from their music was not the occasional hit, the odd moment of glory. Missing was the second half of the covenant for productive longevity: the continuous striving for richness and complexity. To have that, an artist must have an inner momentum.

Each of his works must stretch the boundaries of the one that preceded it. This has been very rare in popular music. Prior to rock and roll, a pop composer could develop intellectually only if he had a sense of himself as part of some other artistic tradition, as Gershwin did vis-à-vis the concert hall. Gershwin, because he saw himself as part of the highbrow continuum and because he had the ability to think instrumentally, was the member of The Six who was best able to achieve those two requirements of productive longevity.

"Longevity" might seem to be an odd term to apply to the work of a man who died at the age of 38. But Gershwin died at the very height of his powers — powers which not only showed no sign of decline but which were clearly expanding in the way that highbrow composers' powers have traditionally expanded. There can be no doubt that he saw himself differently than the other five saw themselves. According to his brother Ira he looked on his talent "with almost mystical wonder." Friends liked to tell the story of the day he asked DuBose Heyward's wife to listen to something he had just written. He was relaxing at the Heywards' home in Charleston, South Carolina, before returning to his beach house on Folly Island, where he was making use of the locale for his work on *Porgy and Bess*. Mrs. Heyward was half out the front door, on her way to an appointment, and she asked Gershwin if the presentation could wait. To this he replied, "Dorothy, listen to the greatest music ever composed in America!"

There was nothing idle or small-minded in this boast; there was only exhilaration. For it was while composing *Porgy* that Gershwin saw for the first time how huge his talent really was. In writing that opera he was overwhelmed by the certainty that he had produced America's *Carmen* — and it was because he had this sense of himself that he was of the highbrow more than of the traditional pop composer's mold.

In 1936, with the opera under his belt, he had to reassure the Hollywood movie studios that he would not go arty on them, that he could and would still "write hits." It was humiliating in a way but deep down Gershwin might have been pleased by their attitude. Despite their yahooism, the executives at RKO were taking him seriously as a composer — a sentiment that was far from unanimous at the time and one that is hardly unanimous even now. There are those who still believe that he distinguished himself — that he *was* himself — only in his popular songs and not in his concert works. In his book *The Joy of Music* Leonard Bernstein contends that Gershwin, though a born songwriter, was something of a stumblebum in the concert hall; that it was not until his pop and highbrow careers joined up triumphantly in the opera house that he "found himself" as a serious composer. While there is some truth in this — Gershwin certainly was a natural songwriter and *Porgy and Bess* was surely his apotheosis — it wrongly leaves the impression that his songs were more worthy than his concert pieces. The truth is that, prior to *Porgy*, his symphonic works were much more extraordinary than his theater songs. This is the case insofar as every musical element is concerned: melody, rhythmic invention, harmony, orchestration, even form and structure. That Gershwin was far more prolific as a songwriter than he was as a symphonic composer has also been offered as proof that songs were his natural medium. But this is not so cut and dried when one considers the number of *worthy* efforts in each category. Prior to *Porgy*, Gershwin had written six orchestral works plus a suite of preludes for piano — all memorable. In the same period he had written only about 20 unassailably great songs:

> Swanee (1919)
> I'll Build a Stairway to Paradise (1922)
> Somebody Loves Me (1924)
> Fascinating Rhythm (1924)
> Oh, Lady Be Good (1924)
> The Man I Love (1924)
> Someone to Watch Over Me (1926)
> 'S Wonderful (1927)
> I've Got a Crush on You (1927)
> How Long Has This Been Going On? (1928)
> Liza (1929)
> Strike Up the Band (1930)
> Bidin' My Time (1930)
> Embraceable You (1930)
> I Got Rhythm (1930)
> But Not for Me (1930)
> Of Thee I Sing (1931)
> Who Cares (1931)
> Love Is Sweeping the Country (1931)
> Mine (1933)

There are a few borderline cases such as "Do It Again" and "My One and Only," but the songs on this list are the ones written between 1919 and 1933 that we remember today. In the first fifteen years of his professional life and prior to the final three years of his natural life, Gershwin had therefore averaged about 1.5 great songs per year. It was a highly respectable ratio, especially when one remembers that many writers had a single hit and nothing more. Nevertheless, it is an unnerving one for Gershwin devotees who picture their hero churning out classic after classic during the years of the Jazz Age. Even more unsettling is the fact that it was in only a couple from this handful that his harmonic sensibility asserted itself in anything like the way it did in the *Concerto in F* or in *An American in Paris*. Though such songs as "Swanee" and "I'll Build a Stairway to Paradise" had not been without harmonic interest (the former for its switch from the key of F-minor in the verse to F-major in the chorus; the latter for its verse, which leaps from key to key before settling into C), there was in them little of Gershwin's patented harmonic language. "The Man I Love" was the first of his songs to show a preoccupation with subtle harmonic effects and then two years passed before another of his songs, "Someone to Watch Over Me," did the same thing. These are the only two Gershwin tunes up to that point which, via harmonic legerdemain, tug subtly on the emotions. On the other hand, his concert works of those years do this fairly consistently (examples can be found on nearly any page of any one of them but one might pay special attention to the second movement of the piano concerto).

In 1930, with a Broadway show called *Girl Crazy*, this disparity began to change. From that show came "I Got Rhythm," "Bidin' My Time," "But Not for Me" and, most significantly, "Embraceable You." The latter is so singable that most listeners are only subliminally aware of its harmonic structure. But emotionally they know that the initial musical phrase ("Embrace me"), though at first firmly buttressed by the tonic, is, when repeated over a diminished chord ("my sweet em--"), on shakier ground — the bottom has been pulled out and poignancy has been created. That is the way Gershwin liked it. As a songwriter, he did not have the option open to a highbrow contemporary like Ravel, who could produce an exotic sound for its own sake. Gershwin's harmonic doings had to be extremely subtle, almost sneaky. But, as is made obvious by "Embraceable You," he thrived on this limitation. And, from that point on, his harmonies lie under his tunes like a wondrous waterworks.

In the 21 months of life left him after the October 1935 premiere of *Porgy*, Gershwin's output consisted almost entirely of popular songs (the exception is a suite for orchestra culled from *Porgy and Bess* and entitled *Catfish Row*). There are twenty-five of them (if one includes "Walking the Dog," a tune used as background music in the film *Shall We Dance*; it was later published as a piano piece and retitled "Promenade"). The first, "King of Swing," was written for a Radio City Music Hall revue by Gershwin and Albert Stillman (Ira was on vacation) and it was a failure. Six others were not used or published in his lifetime ("Hi-Ho," "Wake Up, Brother and Dance," "Put Me to the Test," "Sing of Spring," "Pay Some Attention to Me" and "It's Just Another Rhumba"). Of the 17 remaining, fully 15 are masterpieces (the exceptions being "Stiff Upper Lip" and "I Love to Rhyme"):

By Strauss
(I've Got) Beginner's Luck
Let's Call the Whole Thing Off
Shall We Dance
Slap That Bass
They All Laughed
They Can't Take That Away from Me
A Foggy Day
I Can't Be Bothered Now
The Jolly Tar and the Milk Maid
Nice Work If You Can Get It
Things Are Looking Up
I Was Doing All Right
Love Walked In
Love Is Here to Stay

In other words, Gershwin's "classic ratio" had risen dramatically since the 1920s, when he had been turning out about one and a half per year. In the last three and one half years of his life (early 1934 to July of 1937), the scores for *Porgy and Bess, Shall We Dance, A Damsel in Distress* and *The Goldwyn Follies* contained at least thirty songs that are still played and enjoyed constantly all over the world. This, despite the relative complexity of their form and harmony ("Bess You Is My Woman," for examples, is a far cry from 32 bars — it takes a full nine pages of vocal score to unfold). In these works he managed to keep in touch with the core of his early style and inspiration while his art deepened and gained freedom from earlier constraining rules. Other than "The King of Swing," there is not one clinker in the lot of all of his published songs in this period. And even among the unpublished ones, this high standard seems to have held. "Just Another Rhumba," unused in *The Goldwyn Follies* and finally published in 1959, is first-rate, as are "Sing of Spring" (recently recorded by The Gregg Smith Singers and pianist Oresta Cybriwsky on Turnabout) and "Hi-Ho" (a recording is available on Mark 56 Records: the singer is Ira Gershwin; the pianist, Harold Arlen).

George and Ira wrote their first post-*Porgy* song, "By Strauss," for a Vincente Minnelli Broadway revue called *The Show Is On*. It is an excellent parody of the waltz kings, father and son, and its introduction, or verse, is a preview not only of this song's refrain but of the exceptional verses which Gershwin would write for every one of his final songs. He had always taken great care with verses — those to "Fascinating Rhythm," "But Not for Me" and "Lady Be Good" are particular standouts. They were a way of showing the world that he had ideas to burn (the verses of the other show writers, especially

97

those of Berlin and Porter, are often minimal). But now his verses would be consistently as interesting as the refrains themselves. "By Strauss" also shows Gershwin's great gift for mimicry. Previously, he had parodied the patriotic march in "Strike Up the Band" and he had made fun of campaign songs with "Wintergreen for President." In the coming months he would apply this talent to the English madrigal as well with "The Jolly Tar and the Milk Maid."

After "By Strauss" Gershwin settled down to work for the movies, writing songs that fall into three distinct categories. First are the novelty items: "Slap That Bass" is something of a throwback to the days of "Swanee," when jazz was new, though it is harmonically more complex, especially in its verse. "The Jolly Tar and the Milk Maid" and "Sing of Spring" are, as has been said, parodies of the English madrigal style. They and "By Strauss" are both atypical and unexpected Gershwin music.

A second category, the largest grouping, is made up of eight light-hearted, unaggressive up-tempo songs, every one of them in the key of G: "(I've Got) Beginner's Luck," "Let's Call the Whole Thing Off," "They All Laughed," "I Can't Be Bothered Now," "Nice Work If You Can Get It," "Things Are Looking Up," "I Love to Rhyme," and "I Was Doing All Right." The verses of three of these songs ("Beginner's Luck," "Let's Call the Whole Thing Off," and "Things Are Looking Up") are a sub-family, all being in the key of D. These songs are different in outlook from those that Gershwin had been writing before *Porgy and Bess*. A sea change had taken place. They are less hard-driving, more forgiving and, like "By Strauss," they have self-awareness. They are also full of the kind of witty and emotional harmony that, prior to *Porgy*, had been easier to find in his concert works than in his songs. Typical of the bunch is "I Can't Be Bothered Now," whose catchy, lilting tune evolves into an even more lilting release, made especially tender because the singer begins it on an F-natural, a note which is not only outside the key of G, but which is outside the notes in the supporting harmony of C. It is a double dissonance which somehow falls lightly and tenderly upon the ear.

The third and final group consists of songs in flat keys, either F-major or E-flat major. They have the good nature of the eight G-major songs but they rise to special heights. They avoid melodrama — they are not like "Ol' Man River" or "In the Still of the Night" — but they have a kind of covert spirituality. "They Can't Take That Away from Me" might well be the finest song that Gershwin ever wrote. It began when, toying with the victory motto from Beethoven's *Fifth Symphony*, he played three E-flats and a G instead of three Gs and an E-flat (in a similar vein, John Lennon came up with "Because" by inverting the opening chords of Beethoven's

"Moonlight Sonata"). Its verse is very fine, presaging with poignant dissonances in its final bars the emotion that will come in the refrain, especially in the final four measures where the words "No! They can't take that away from me" are sung to simple chords over a B-flat pedal point, producing an exalted effect, like a religious chorale. The lyrics of this song perfectly express the music: tongue in cheek, almost flippant, yet they do not entirely hide the urgency of the title phrase.

"A Foggy Day" is another one of Gershwin's last, supreme works. According to Ira Gershwin it was written very quickly:

> One night I was in the living room, reading. About 1 a.m. George returned from a party . . . took off his dinner jacket, sat down at the piano . . . 'How about some work? Got any ideas?' 'Well, there's one spot we might do something about a fog . . . how about *a foggy day in London* or maybe *foggy day in London Town*?' 'Sounds good . . . I like it better with *town*' and he was off immediately on the melody. We finished the refrain, words and music, in less than an hour. ('Do, Do, Do' is the only other . . . in so short a time.) Next day the song still sounded good so we started on a verse . . . All I had to say was: 'George, how about an Irish verse?' and he sensed instantly the degree of wistful loneliness I meant. Generally, whatever mood I thought was required, he, through his instinct and inventiveness, could bring my hazy musical vision into focus.

The song itself is a pure example of the way Gershwin used harmony to adjust the heartstrings without slipping into melodrama or bathos. On the third word of the refrain ("A foggy *day*") he has already switched from his initial major tonality to a minor sixth chord. He swings back to major four syllables later ("in London *town*") but then chips away at it by flatting the ninth of the chord. He does this kind of thing with great deftness throughout the song. The minor seventh on the third syllable of the next phrase ("had me *low*") is quickly altered, becoming a more disquieting minor sixth. Five bars later there is another slight shift into the minor (from a major seventh to a minor sixth) on the word "alarm." As with "They Can't Take That Away from Me," the most potent harmonic magic occurs at the end of the song. Alec Wilder has described the three notes of melody on the word "suddenly" as "truly chilling," which is true. But at the very end, as in "They Can't Take That Away from Me," the song resolves into a simple, childlike chorale.

The other two songs in this grouping are Gershwin's last: "Love Walked In" and "Love Is Here to Stay." Both are much more

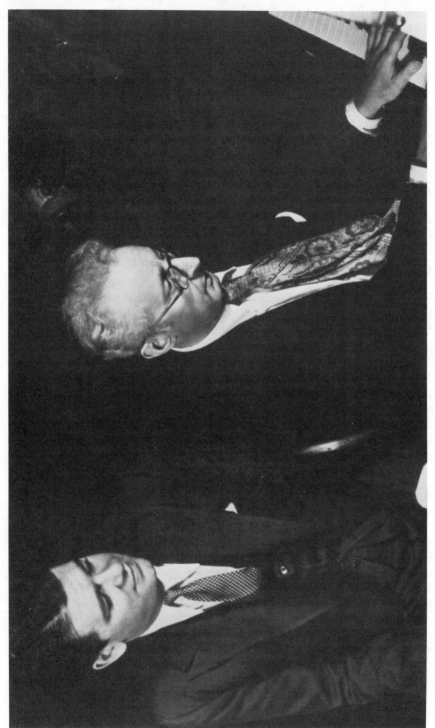

Oscar Hammerstein II and Jerome Kern.

straightforward harmonically than "They Can't Take That Away from Me" or "A Foggy Day" but each contains the heartfelt quality that, in his songs, had come to fruition in *Porgy and Bess*. The verse of "Love Is Here to Stay," good as it is, must be credited to Vernon Duke, who finished the music for *The Goldwyn Follies* after his friend's death. As for the refrain, since Gershwin had not written it down, it had to be reconstructed by another friend, Oscar Levant, who had heard the composer play it. This song is about timelessness, appropriately enough.

These last songs show that Gershwin had met the two requirements for productive longevity. He kept faith with the source of his early inspiration and yet his work became more intricate, more purposeful and more delicate. "Death can be kind and it can be just," Vernon Duke wrote, "but it had no business taking our George, who was in the full flower of his fine youth and who was unquestionably doing his best work."

Jerome Kern: Beautiful Pranks

Kern was an avid and knowledgeable collector of beautiful things — old silver, antiques, rare books (in 1929 he sold his book collection for $2 million) and he became an expert in every subject that caught his interest — real estate, architecture, interior decorating, racing, poker and baseball (it is said that he bought a car one day when he couldn't flag a cab to the Polo Grounds). He was also an inveterate prankster and jokemaker. When the lethargic Ira Gershwin was less than prompt about writing words for the melody to "Long Ago and Far Away," Kern sent him a dummy lyric that began, "Watching Alice pee . . . " And there was Kern's temperance oration, with which he was always ready to startle new acquaintances and which he on one occasion delivered to pedestrians from the balcony of his suite at the Beverly-Wilshire Hotel. As his position in the American musical theater became more eminent and secure, Kern let those two elements of his personality, perfectionism and playfulness, seep more deeply into his work. His songs became complex and full of surprises.

So it was that he, like Gershwin, remained true to the source of his initial inspiration (elegant theater songs) while he consistently built upon that foundation so as to create a more intricate kind of beauty. He was not, however, nearly so multi-faceted as Gershwin. Kern had little of the latter's rhythmic prowess — he was hard-pressed to write a really good rouser — and almost all of his best songs were ballads. Nor was his audience prepared, as Gershwin's was, to expect the unimaginable. Consequently, he generated less excitement than did the younger man. (Their friendship had a rocky beginning: when Gershwin refused to take Kern's advice regarding the composition of his first Broadway score, *La La Lucille*, Kern stopped speaking to him for two years.) But he continued to grow and develop throughout his career. Like Gershwin, he brought a friskiness to his music. He took an impish delight in the manipulation of his musical material.

Kern was only three years older than Irving Berlin but he was born into a much older musical world. Where Berlin's boyhood was spent on the streets, earning his own living, inhaling all the slang and raunch of music in the Bowery, Kern grew up in prosperity, adoring and adored by his parents (he was the last of nine male siblings, only three of whom survived), listening to the operetta tunes that his mother played on the piano. He published a tune of his own at the age of 17, a piano piece called *At the Casino*. Then, after lessons at the New York College of Music and further study in Heidelberg, he was hired to write the opening numbers for a series of London musicals (the best songs in those shows were always reserved for the later acts). By 1904 he was back in New York, working as a song plugger for the Shapiro-Remick Company. In 1905 he obtained an interview with Max Dreyfus, head of Harms Music House. Dreyfus would later publish Gershwin and Rodgers but Kern was his first big catch. Hired as a song-plugger at $12 per week, Kern quickly produced his first hit, "How'd You Like to Spoon with Me?," which was used in a play called *The Earl and the Girl*.

By 1910 his yearly income was in five figures. Yet, it was not until 1914, when he was 29, that he wrote the first of the songs for which he is now remembered. This was "They Didn't Believe Me," a hit from a play called *The Girl from Utah*. In the same year Kern was introduced to Guy Bolton, a stage-struck British architect, and the two men collaborated on a series of shows for the diminutive (300-seat) Princess Theatre — intimate antidotes to the extravaganzas which were then dominating Broadway. These Princess Theatre shows were also unusual in that they tried to avoid the clichés of typical operetta plots, which Bolton once described as follows:

A prince from some neo-Balkan country, disguised, is in love with a poor maiden. She does not know he is a prince; he does not know she is the daughter of an Albanian Croesus . . . There is one situation in every act; the rest is gaps. Comedians fill these gaps with gum scenes, time-table scenes, soda-fountain scenes.

The Bolton-Kern shows substituted ordinary Americans for European noblemen and they contained songs which tended to grow out of the situation on the stage. Because the seating capacity was too small to permit the kind of box office gross which would allow for big-name stars, they had to rely more on the quality of their songs and scripts.

Between 1904, the year of his Broadway debut, and 1918, when the last of his Princess Theatre musicals was produced (P.G. Wodehouse having joined the team), Kern wrote hundreds of songs for the stage. Remarkably, time has cast a thumbs-down verdict on just about all of them. It was not until the 1920s, when Kern was in his mid-30s to mid-40s, that he began to write the standards with which we are familiar today. Oddly enough, this heightened creativity came at the very time that he was again associating himself with old-fashioned, conventional musicals. One, *Sally*, produced by that master of the extravaganza, Florence Ziegfeld, even had a Balkan Grand Duke among its characters. But if Kern had turned his back on theatrical progress and innovation, he had discovered something new and fresh about songwriting. *Sally* featured three classics: "Whippoor-Will," "Wild Rose" and "Look for the Silver Lining." In 1925, working for the first time with Oscar Hammerstein II (they had met at Victor Herbert's funeral the year before), Kern came up with *Sunny*, another hodgepodge of a show, but it included "Who?," also a standard.

In 1927 Kern was again exploring musical comedy's horizons with *Show Boat*, written with Hammerstein and based on Edna Ferber's novel of the same name. The score was probably his greatest. It contained "Bill," "Why Do I Love You," "Make Believe," "Can't Help Loving That Man of Mine," "You Are Love" and "Ol' Man River." Of the latter, Edna Ferber wrote the following (in her autobiography, *A Peculiar Treasure*):

> Jerome Kern appeared at my apartment late one afternoon with a strange look of quiet exultation in his eyes. He sat down at the piano . . . . He played and sang "Ol' Man River." The music mounted, mounted and I give you my word my hair stood on end, the tears came to my eyes, and I breathed like a heroine in a melodrama. This was great music. This was music that would outlast Jerome Kern's day and mine. I have never heard it since without the emotional surge.

After *Show Boat*, Kern never again sought to unify songs, lyrics and libretto into a single work of art. But he was now approaching each of his individual songs in an experimental mood. From 1927 until his death in 1945, almost every year brought forth its crop of Kern classics, each of them singular, each full of adventure and chance-taking; yet none of them was without the pureness of melody which, from his earliest days, had been the hallmark of his work. He was always so true to his initial love of graceful melody that many people — including such close associates as Dreyfus and Hammerstein — were convinced that his style really did not change all that much over the 40 years of his career. To them, "They Didn't Believe Me" of 1914 was not dissimilar to "Nobody Else But Me," Kern's last song, published in 1946. But the equivalence of beauty obscures the fact that the later song was far more complex. It was part of Kern's magic that the public readily accepted this and other tunes of his late period just as it had his simpler hymns in earlier decades.

The main element in Kern's growth was, as it was with Gershwin, harmonic sophistication. But Kern took a very different path in that regard. Where Gershwin had delved into the emotional attributes of altered chords, Kern experimented in modulation (the passing from one key to another). It became something of a game to him to leap as far afield from the home key as possible and then to return to it neatly before the listener was aware that anything untoward had happened. The chords themselves are hardly complex. Kern never went in for the kind of harmonic subtleties that Gershwin demonstrated in "A Foggy Day." It is in the sophistication of his migratory harmony that Kern managed to keep his music fresh and vigorous.

His interest in modulation can be traced back to 1914 and a song called, appropriately enough, "Magic Melody" (just as Gershwin's first experiment in metrics was aptly entitled "Fascinating Rhythm"). But it was not until much later in his career that modulation became a serious and consistent feature of his work. In the 1932 Broadway show *Music in the Air*, written with Hammerstein, there was a tune called "The Song Is You," whose refrain ends on the note E, supported by a C-major chord. In the release this note continues while the harmony changes to E-major — the release thus begins in a new and relatively distant key. Then, at that moment when it leads us back to C from E, it does so preemptorily, with a thrilling jolt (Ravel's *Bolero* makes the same sudden switch at its climax). From the 1933 show, *Roberta*, came "Smoke Gets in Your Eyes," which also changes keys in the release, this time from E-flat to B — the latter being so remote that one is amazed when the return is accomplished in just two bars, via A-flat minor and B-flat seventh chords. The same show included "The Touch of Your Hand," in which Kern, before he ever gets to the refrain, changes key signatures from C-minor to G to C-major. The refrain itself, while simple enough melodically, is suported by highly chromatic harmony — so much so that it reminds one of an extraordinary Gershwin tune, "Blue, Blue, Blue," whose own simple melody is backed by an accompaniment so complex and difficult pianistically as to look like a Rachmaninoff concerto. Oddly enough, the two songs were written in the same year.

Convinced now that he could indulge in this new and exciting game without losing popular appeal, Kern began to take even greater chances. In 1935, for the film version of *Roberta*, he wrote "I Won't Dance" (lyrics by Dorothy Fields and Jimmy McHugh) for Fred Astaire — and in this one he pulled out all the stops. At the release the key jumps from C to A-flat and eight bars later, when one would expect to be heading back to C, Kern suddenly take us into B where the release begins all over again. It is like one of those amusement park rides where, just as you are sighing with relief that it is all over, your car dips into a pool of water. Another song for the film version of *Roberta*, "I Dream Too Much," is also extremely adventurous, this time not only harmonically but rhythmically and structurally as well. It begins simply, a waltz in F, but continually threatens to go elsewhere, to F-sharp or to E. The fact that is is also highly syncopated causes further disorientation, for the *Tempo Di Valse Moderato* marking had led us at first to expect something a little more staid. But the most unusual aspect of this song is its structure. It is in four separate sections, each with its own melodic, rhythmic and harmonic nuances. The final section, the waltz proper, has an exciting forward motion, due to the syncopation of the melody which seems always to be just a step ahead of the chromatic harmony.

In 1936 Kern's score for the Astaire/Rogers film *Swingtime* rivaled what he had written a decade earlier for *Show Boat*. It included "A Fine Romance," "Pick Yourself Up," "The Waltz in Swingtime" and "The Way You Look Tonight." In these songs he lost none of those qualities which had always made him so special — he certainly wrote no melody lovelier or more pure and simple than "The Way You Look Tonight" — but he had reached a point where everything he did was now touched by some pleasure-giving intricacy: the peripatetic harmony of "Pick Yourself Up" (the song is in several successive keys, including F, G and A-flat), the triplets (sometimes chromatic, sometimes diatonic) in "A Fine Romance," the instrumental motif and the release section modulations of "The Way You Look Tonight," and the odd structure of "The Waltz in Swingtime," which is partly sung, but mostly instrumental in nature.

Despite a serious illness in 1937, Kern continued to write superior songs: "You Couldn't Be Cuter" (a rhythm number) and "Just Let Me Look at You" (a ballad), both in 1938, and, in 1939, a fine score for his last Broadway show, *Very Warm for May*. Its best song, "All the Things You Are," was one of Kern's boldest — so bold, in fact, that neither he nor its lyricist, Hammerstein, gave it any chance of popular success. Beginning in the key of F-minor,

Richard Rodgers in 1975.

the melody, in the seventh measure, comes to rest outside that key on an E-natural. The initial phrase is then repeated not in the original key but in C-minor. This time Kern has not even waited until the release before effecting a modulation — perhaps because he has even stranger doings up his sleeve for the middle of the song: it begins in the key of G but finishes up on the note of G-sharp which, enharmonically, is A-flat, leading us back to the original key. Somehow, despite all this chicanery, the song falls naturally upon the ear. Kern was astonished one day when he heard someone on the street whistling it correctly.

In 1940, when he was 55 years old, Kern set Oscar Hammerstein's poem, "The Last Time I Saw Paris," to music. It was interpolated into the film *Lady Be Good* and it won the Academy Award for 1941. He was nominated for the same award the next year for "Dearly Beloved" (written with Johnny Mercer for the film *You Were Never Lovelier*) and again in 1946 for "All Through the Day," written with Hammerstein. While such kudos is not always a good indication of merit, it does show in this case that Kern was producing fine songs until the end of his life. In late 1945 he had returned to New York City from Hollywood in order to attend rehearsals for a revival of *Show Boat* and to discuss the possibility of writing the music for *Annie Get Your Gun*. While taking a walk he collapsed on Park Avenue near 57th Street and was taken to a public ward on Welfare Island. It was where Stephen Foster had died. Kern died some days later, after being transferred to Doctors' Hospital. He was sixty years old.

Richard Rodgers: The Sweetest Sounds

The musical theater had a truly mesmerizing effect on Richard Rodgers. As a boy he was happy only when he had saved up enough money to get into a Broadway matinee. At the age of fifteen he wrote his first musical — a war benefit that was staged by an amateur group — and two years later he enrolled at Columbia with no goal other than to write its varsity shows. His first submission was accepted (Oscar Hammerstein II was one of the student judges) and a second varsity show brought him into contact with Larry Hart. Sparked by the prospect of a career in the theater, Rodgers and Hart left college and began to haunt Broadway, where they managed to interpolate a song ("Any Old Place with You") in a show called *A Lonely Romeo* (it starred Lew Fields, who was half of the comedy team of Weber and Fields and father of lyricist Dorothy Fields). Then, in 1920, two more Rodgers and Hart originals were used in a show called *Poor Little Ritz Girl*. But they were unable to follow up on these initial successes. For the next five years the team could not get any one of its four feet past a Broadway transom. Hart had to go back to translating German plays and Rodgers was about to become an underwear salesman when, in 1925, they were asked to do a semi-amateur show for Broadway's Theatre Guild. The result, *The Garrick Gaieties*, opened at the Garrick Theatre on May 17, and by May 18 the phrase "Rodgers and Hart" was well on its way into the national lexicon.

But success was not enough. From this point on it was Rodgers' goal to uplift musical comedy — to take the pap out of it and turn it into the musical play. At first he and Hart did this by satirizing the weather-worn formulae of revues and operettas. In that first edition of *The Garrick Gaieties*, one of their songs, "Sentimental Me," made fun of overly emotional love ballads while another, "Manhattan" (their first big hit), presented a sophisticate's answer to that simple-minded paeon, "The Sidewalks of New York." This show also lampooned the Canadian mounties of the Rudolf Friml/Oscar Hammerstein operetta *Rose Marie*. Like Rodgers, Hart was anxious to upset the applecart. He was, in Rodgers' words, "violent on the subject of rhyming in songs, feeling that the public was capable of understanding better things than the current monosyllabic juxtaposition of 'slush' and 'mush.' " Rodgers had no such zeal regarding his music *per se*. He was not out to re-invent the popular song or to infuse it with any new brew such as jazz (Rodgers, after Kern, was the least jazzy of The Six). But he was determined that the shows that he, Hart and librettist Herbert Fields (Lew Fields' son) were associated with would bring the musical theater nearer his sacred goal — the integration and interdependence of songs and plot. Slowly and steadily, they moved in that direction. In 1926 there was *Dearest Enemy* which, in telling through words and music how a British general was purposefully detained by an American lady during the Revolutionary War, went beyond the usual Broadway confection of mistaken identities. Their next opus, produced in the same year, was *The Girl Friend*, a show which dispensed with the obligatory opening chorus and told its story in the form of a Freudian dream fantasy — surprising stuff for the 1920s. Rodgers and Hart continued this type of derring-do for the rest of their partnership. In the mid-to-late 1930s, after their unpleasant stay in Hollywood, they wrote *On Your Toes* (the first Broadway musical to advance its plot via an extended ballet), *Jumbo* (the first to take place in a circus arena) and on through *Pal Joey* (the first to feature an anti-hero). In fact, Rodgers and Hart sometimes seemed to enjoy the prospect of doing a show only if it included some new "first" — an attitude which Rodgers later brought to his collaboration with Hammerstein

(*Carousel* was the first in which the hero died; *Allegro* was the first to feature a Greek chorus; *South Pacific* was the first to deal with interracial romance, and so on). It will be noted that in the above discussion, little has been said about Rodgers as a songwriter. It is a tribute to his success that his shows are often discussed as works in their own right and not simply as the packaging for his songs. With a few notable exceptions (*Porgy and Bess, Show Boat*) this can hardly be said of the shows of any of the other members of The Six. In recalling Gershwin's works, for example, one is much more likely to have heard of "A Foggy Day" than *A Damsel in Distress*, the film for which it was written. But Rodgers was happiest when he could put his melodies in service of the plot and characters of the show.

That being the case, one might expect that his songs would have less of a life outside the theater than did those of the other writers. Not so. Rodgers' songs are everywhere — radio, television, nightclubs, elevators — and he probably wrote more hit songs than anyone, including Irving Berlin. He and his lyricists were never so consumed by the needs of their shows as to write songs that would be unintelligible outside the theater. No Broadway score is better integrated than *Carousel* but none of that show's big songs — "If I Loved You," "You'll Never Walk Alone," "June Is Bustin' Out All Over" — refers to the names of the characters or to anything that would puzzle anyone unfamiliar with the plot of the play. This is one of the factors which separates such a show from opera. In *Porgy and Bess*, for instance, Gershwin had no qualms about indelibly marking some of its most important numbers with the proper names of its principals ("Bess You Is My Woman Now," "I Loves You Porgy"). But Rodgers, though willing to let his music do the bidding of the play, was always — even in his most ambitious moments — attuned to the requirements of the wider pop song marketplace.

Though he was always sophisticated and sometimes brilliant in his use of harmony ("I Didn't Know What Time It Was," "You Have Cast Your Shadow on the Sea") and rhythm ("Mountain Greenery," "This Can't Be Love"), it was melody that made up the lion's share of his musical gift. "Pure talent" was how Igor Stravinsky described this kind of ability and it is certain that Rodgers had a vast surplus of it. Analysts have tried to understand his methods, pointing out that many of his melodies are built on arpeggios of tonic and dominant chords ("Oh, What a Beautiful Morning") or the effective use of leading tones ("Bewitched," "I'm in Love with a Wonderful Guy"). But the use of that word, "built," is certainly inaccurate. Rodgers did very little conscious construction. He was very often — more often than most — inspired.

Another factor which helped him both on Broadway and on the radio was the essentially American sound of his music. In this case

"American" is not synonymous with "jazz," for Rodgers was a far less jazzy composer than Gershwin, Arlen or Berlin. But his music was always very American. Unlike Kern who, to his dying day, continued to write Lehár-ish atavisms, Rodgers' songs are consistently indigenous — even when he was writing of Bali H'ai or edelweiss. But his America, especially in his later years, was the heartland, not the city. There is little city-slicker guile in his melodies and their attending harmonies, as opposed to some Arlen and Gershwin songs which are claustrophobically dense. Rodgers' best songs are full of breeziness and open air. An example is "A Wonderful Guy," from *South Pacific*. The chorus of this brisk waltz passes through a long succession of chords, all of them close relatives of one another — Rodgers rarely leapt into the harmonic unknown as did Kern — but because the changes are so frequent and because they almost always come on the downbeat, the piece really moves and dances — you can become winded just by listening to it. This is typical of Rodgers' waltzes (Winthrop Sargeant called them "scherzos"), from "The Most Beautiful Girl in the World" (1935) to "Do I Hear a Waltz" (1965). They are not slow ballads like Berlin's waltzes. They are up-tempo and whirly, like the waltzes of Tchaikovsky, who was also at home and unbuttoned in three-quarter time. In fact, Rodgers could well have written *The Waltz of the Flowers* or the waltz from *Eugene Onegin*; and Tchaikovsky, conversely, could have written the *Carousel Waltz*. In a way, Rodgers was an American version of Tchaikovsky, with all of the gloom and doom removed, for the emotionalism in the work of both men is very similar. Rodgers' melodies, especially those written to Hammerstein's frankly sentimental lyrics, are often very touching (Irving Berlin once said that "You'll Never Walk Alone" was as affecting as the Twenty-Third Psalm). *Carousel* is the show most chock-full of melodies which bring a lump to the throat — "Soliloquy," "What's the Use of Wondering," "If I Loved You" and the above-mentioned hymn. But so do "This Nearly Was Mine" from *South Pacific*, "Hello, Young Lovers" from *The King and I* and the title tune from *The Sound of Music*. There is an implicit religiosity in these and in many of Rodgers and Hammerstein's songs, a quality that had also asserted itself in Rodgers' work with Hart ("Where or When," too, hinted that there was something more out there than meets the eye), but not nearly so often. Not only theatergoers but the public at large responded to the directness of this kind of emotional appeal.

Nevertheless, Rodgers, despite his prowess as a songwriter, was not a musician in the sense that Gershwin and Arlen were musicians. That is, music was never an end in itself with him. Between shows he could forget about composition entirely; nor did he play the piano for his own amusement: he was about as interested in composing music for his own pleasure as Houdini was in performing dangerous escapes away from an audience. A magician needs an audience and Rodgers was not interested in amusing himself. As it turned out, this conviction that "the play's the thing" was the source both of his long reign on Broadway and of his eventual decline and fall. His preoccupation with the Broadway musical as an art form certainly extended the length of his prime — for when the play was a good one he could rise to the occasion. But when the libretto was sub-standard, he was stranded — and that is how his decline began. It did not happen all at once but with hindsight it is clear that the year of *The King and I*, 1951, was the last year of Rodgers' infallibility. Being so much a theater man and so committed to theatrical innovation, his gift was dependent on a good story and on interesting characters. Of all the theater writers he had been the best at choosing libretti. But now, after *The King and I*, this sureness of touch failed. It will be remembered that Rodgers' music for the somewhat pretentious *Allegro* (of 1947) had not been nearly as good as what he had written for *Carousel* (1945) which preceded it, or for *South Pacific* (1949) which followed. Those two shows, having been artfully adapted from stories which had already been successful in other media, brought out his best. *Allegro*, on the other hand, was an original story by Hammerstein and it did not work. After *The King and I* (another adaptation), Hammerstein wrote a second original and equally unsuccessful play, *Me and Juliet* (1953) and for that jumble Rodgers provided one of his least distinguished sets of tunes. The show's only hit, in fact, was "No Other Love," a melody hijacked from *Victory at Sea*. The team then returned to the adaptation route. But by turning John Steinbeck's novel *Sweet Thursday* into *Pipe Dream* (1955), Hammerstein got himself involved in a plot and characters whose seediness did not suit him. Again, the poor libretto failed to spark Rodgers, a pattern which continued to the end of his life. Whenever the vehicle had life, so did Rodgers' songs. This was true of *Flower Drum Song* (1958) and of *The Sound of Music* (1959). But after Hammerstein's death in 1960 Rodgers spent almost two decades looking for a suitable project. He and playwright Samuel Taylor thought up their own story for *No Strings* (1962) but this tale of star-crossed lovers in Paris was hardly any story at all. Poor libretti plagued each succeeding project, from *Do I Hear a Waltz?* (1965) through *I Remember Mama* (1979). The forward momentum on which he had always counted so much was gone.

Rodgers' road as a composer was thus a tricky one. It was hard for him to remain true to the source of his original inspiration when that source, the innovative Broadway show, was, due to a scarcity of good libretti, closed to him. Yet it was impossible to make intricate music when he had little interest in doing so away from Broadway.

Irving Berlin in the 1960s.

After 1951 he continued to write lovely songs but, at best, they only intermittently achieved the heights of earlier days and even then they usually expressed ideas and emotions that he had already explored. For example, there is the very underrated score for *Do I Hear a Waltz?* which, besides the excellent title song, has a lot of Rodgers' old magic. There is "Someone Like You" (a ballad in which he seems to be paying homage to Kern), "What Do We Do? We Fly!" (an excellent comedy number), "Moon in My Window" (with its wonderful release), "We're Gonna Be All Right" (with its youthful Rodgers and Hart feel) and the equally catchy "Here We Are Again." But listening to this score back to back with *Pal Joey* or *Oklahoma!* is like playing Paul McCartney's *Band on the Run* after listening to *Rubber Soul.* Past their primes, the two men occasionally reached the heights they had attained in their youth, but the fullness of youthful creation eluded them (youth here being a relative term; McCartney was 23 at the time of *Rubber Soul* while Rodgers was 41 at the premiere of *Oklahoma!*).

Rodgers had opened 1962's *No Strings* with "The Sweetest Sounds," for which he wrote not only the music but these words:

> The sweetest sounds I'll ever hear
> Are still inside my head
> The kindest words I'll ever know
> Are waiting to be said.

It was the voice of a defiant man who, having had nearly four decades of success, did not see why he could not have four more. When *I Remember Mama* opened at The Majestic Theatre on May 31, 1979, just seven months before his death, Rodgers was still valiantly trying to keep that pledge.

Irving Berlin: Reaching for It

Irving Berlin wrote enough masterpieces to stoke half a dozen successful careers — so many great songs, in fact, that some observers, shying away from the whole of his output, have been content to celebrate only his career as an anthem-writer. To them it was amazing enough that he had come up with "White Christmas" and "Easter Parade" for the religious seasons, "God Bless America" for the nation's unofficial national anthem, "Oh, How I Hate to Get Up in the Morning" and "This Is the Army" for the foot soldier, "A Pretty Girl Is Like a Melody" for the fashion and burlesque industries and "There's No Business Like Show Business" for the narcissists of Broadway and Hollywood. Harold Arlen once complained that, after Berlin, the only holiday still available to a songwriter was Halloween. (That is not true: Berlin tried and failed with a Thanksgiving song called "I've Got Plenty to Be Thankful For" and with a Washington's Birthday song called "I Can't Tell a Lie.")

But he did not spend all of his time writing songs of praise. He was also the master of the swinging up-tempo tune ("Heat Wave," "I Got the Sun in the Morning"), the cheerful ditty ("Let's Have Another Cup of Coffee," "It's a Lovely Day Today"), the sentimental waltz ("Remember," "The Song Is Ended," "The Girl That I Marry"), the sophisticated ballad ("Be Careful, It's My Heart," "Cheek to Cheek"), the dramatic number ("Suppertime," "Let's Face the Music and Dance"), the jazz song ("Puttin' on the Ritz," "Blue Skies") and novelty numbers ("You Can't Get a Man with a Gun," "A Sailor's Not a Sailor 'Til a Sailor's Been Tatooed"). Whatever was going, whatever was in style — that was his domain. Prior to World War I there were ethnic songs ("Dats-a-My-Gal," "Oh, How That German Could Love," "I Wish That You Was My Gal, Molly," "Colored Romeo" and "Goodbye Becky Cohen") and there were mammy/pappy songs ("Was There Ever a Pal Like You?," "I Left My Door Open and My Daddy Walked Out"). During the Great War there were soldier tunes ("Oh, How I Hate to Get Up in the Morning," "Since Katie the Waitress Became an Aviatress") and after it there were mustering out songs ("I've Got My Captain Working for Me Now"). There was a campaign song for Democrat Al Smith in 1924 and another for Republican Dwight Eisenhower in 1952. During World War II Berlin wrote such songs as "When That Man Hitler Is Dead and Gone," "Any Bonds Today," "God Bless the Philippines," "My British Buddy," and "My Russian Buddy." For his last (so far) Broadway show, *Mr. President* (1962), he was up-to-date with a tune called "The Washington Twist." For all anyone knows, he is presently at work on a post-Disco, New Wave item or two.

He wrote so successfully and in so many styles that some suspected him of stealing tunes from other composers, or of buying them outright. One ingenious rumor had it that all of Berlin's songs were actually written by a man who was kept tucked away, presumably underground, like the guard to Jack Benny's vault. It was just hard to believe that a man with next to no literary or musical education, a man who could barely play an instrument and who could not even put music to paper, was the genius behind so many great songs written in so many idioms over so many years. But Berlin did indeed write all of those songs. Like all natural phenomena, his existence was real, if improbable.

His career is all the more remarkable because it had no artistic momentum. Gershwin was pushed forward by his fascination with complex and evocative harmony. Kern's momentum came from his increasingly experimental ballads. Rodgers' came from his involvement with ever more ambitious stage productions. But Berlin had little in the way of internal stimuli. Being something of a weather-vane, he could not rely on inner artistic kinetics. He had to pull every one of his ideas out of thin air. This is what he was talking about when, in January of 1952, he told *The New Yorker*, "I suppose someday there's going to come a time when I reach for it and it isn't there . . . it frightens me." He wrote in so many styles that it was impossible for him to go very far in any one direction. Instead, he simply soaked up and reflected the ambience of each successive era.

Berlin bristled at the idea that his music was a product of his own life's experiences. The only exception, he said, was "When I Lost You," written in 1912 upon the death of his first wife (and it was a huge hit). Nevertheless, some say that his romance with Ellin Mackey was chronicled by the sudden series of love ballads that he wrote in the mid-1920s ("Remember," "All Alone," "What'll I Do") — after all, Berlin gave her the song "Always" to commemorate their marriage. But none of the show writers ever really wrote songs from the 19th century artist's compulsion to express his own soul (even *Porgy and Bess* was written with an eye to the box office, which was why Gershwin had it produced on Broadway and not by The Met). They were much more in the 18th century mold: they wrote for a living, for the audience at hand. They did put themselves into their work but never at the expense of their bank accounts. The '60s writers sometimes contended that theirs was an opposing ethos, that they wrote to express the soul of their generation or their own souls. But marketability was always a huge consideration with them too, even in so iconoclastic a writer as John Lennon. Despite the fact that his arid and severe solo album *Plastic Ono Band* was a critical success, he never went back to art-for-art's-sake because its sales had been far below what he had been used to in his Beatle days. Berlin would never have had anything to do with a *Plastic Ono Band* or a *Porgy and Bess*. More than any other songwriter in this century, he had his finger on the public's pulse. When he retired in the mid-1950s the last thing he wanted to do was seek solitary expression in music.

The 1950s were less than a triumph for all of the four surviving show writers. But they were most unsettling for Berlin. Like Porter and Rodgers, he began the decade at the height of his success. *Annie Get Your Gun* had just completed a three-year run on Broadway and *Miss Liberty*, though a failure as a show, had boasted a good score, including "Paris Wakes Up and Smiles" and "Let's Take an Old-Fashioned Walk." In 1950, at the age of 62, Berlin achieved another solid success with *Call Me Madam*, whose smart score included

"You're Just in Love," "It's a Lovely Day Today," and "The Best Thing for You." Not only did these become instant classics, they also showed all the strengths that one attributes to much younger writers. "Just in Love," for instance, is a tour de force double song — its two melodies are sung separately at first and then in counterpoint — something Berlin had not attempted since "Play a Simple Melody," written in 1914. "It's a Lovely Day Today" also has the bloom of youth about it. It is as sprightly as anything Berlin ever wrote.

Then, for some inexplicable reason, he fell apart. After *Call Me Madam*, Berlin's career all but came to a halt. He continued writing songs until 1954 — a pop tune here and there and a few new songs for motion pictures which mainly featured his earlier work. But for the rest of the decade he wrote no more original scores. Projects were discussed and some nearly came to fruition but he had lost confidence in himself and would back out mid-way or at the last minute. In September of 1951 there were discussions about a Parisian musical (the lyrics to be in French by Albert Willemetz) which would star Maurice Chevalier's protégé, Lady Patachou and, perhaps, Chevalier himself. Nothing came of it. In the fall of 1953 Berlin talked to Joshua Logan about doing a Broadway version of James Michener's *Sayonara* and he went to Hollywood to discuss a new film musical. Nothing came of those projects either. In 1954 he wanted to do another show with Ethel Merman (she had starred in both *Annie Get Your Gun* and *Call Me Madam*) but she refused, preferring to spend more time with her family. A year later, in 1955, he was talking about a new Broadway project called *Youth Parade*, to be produced by and for the Girl and Boy Scouts of America. But this one too died on the vine. Also in 1955, Berlin went through the indignity of a plagiarism suit. A composer named Joseph Smith had made accusations regarding the paternity of "You're Just in Love." Berlin won the suit (after playing his tune to a packed courthouse) but it was at this point that he slipped all the way into retirement.

Retirement was misery. He retreated to his Manhattan townhouse where, suffering from a skin ailment, he avoided sunlight. He shunned his family. Occasionally, he would take late night walks but for the most part he kept himself cooped up, staying awake late into the night, watching television, surrounded by song fragments he was afraid to finish, lest they not measure up. Sometimes he would sing these melodies over the phone to friends who were honest enough to confirm his worst suspicions.

What had happened? That he had been capable of writing notable songs after *Call Me Madam* is shown by "Count Your Blessings Instead of Sheep," written in 1952 and by "Sittin' in the Sun" and "For the Very First Time," both written in 1953. There was no hint of a decline in his powers. Nor is there any reason to suspect that Berlin had balked in the face of rock and roll. He had never been one to throw up his hands at any new musical style. Moreover, rock and roll had not yet touched the Broadway or the Hollywood musical.

It is possible that he decided to retire rather than face the indignity of a slump. On the other hand, he had already successfully weathered at least one dry period. This was during the early years of the Depression when he suffered one failure after another. Timely down-and-out songs such as "Just Begging for Love" did not work and it was not until the success of "Say It Isn't So" in 1932 that he snapped out of it.

But he never did snap out of the doldrums that so suddenly overtook him in the early 1950s, though he "reached for it" one last time with a 1962 Broadway show called *Mr. President*. "One night before I went to sleep," he told *Life* magazine, "I decided that when I woke up in the morning I would start something and finish it. I was tired of pulling out of everything. Tired of letting people down, letting myself down." And, to William Ewald of *The Saturday Evening Post*, he said: "I was using age as an excuse for my fear of failure. I practically talked myself into a wheelchair." The new Irving Berlin musical took in $2.5 million before opening night and it seemed as if Berlin, now 74, was about to duplicate in popular song what the elderly Verdi had accomplished in 1893 with his valedictory opera, *Falstaff*. But it wasn't so. Berlin received worse notices for this show than he had gotten for *Miss Liberty* in 1949. John McCarten of *The New Yorker* was the gentlest of the critics and the best he could say about the music was that it had a "restful beat." Berlin took the results philosophically ("I'd rather be unhappy doing something than really unhappy doing nothing") and, for the next few years, continued to pursue his career, although once again he did so only fitfully. In 1963 he wrote six new songs for another film compendium, *Say It with Music*. The movie was never made although discussions with MGM continued until 1966, by which time Berlin had written additional songs. When *Say It with Music* fell through, Berlin conceived the idea of a 20th anniversary revival of *Annie Get Your Gun* with its original star, Ethel Merman. This project did work out and Berlin added a new song to the score, "An Old Fashioned Wedding." It was another contrapuntal tune in the tradition of "Play a Simple Melody" of 1914 and "You're Just in Love" of 1950 and it was a success. So far, however, it has been Berlin's last published song. He has continued to mull over new ideas — in 1966 he was talking about doing a musical about the East River, for he had grown up beside it in his tenement days and even now he could see it from his townhouse. In the 1970s he would occasionally send a tape

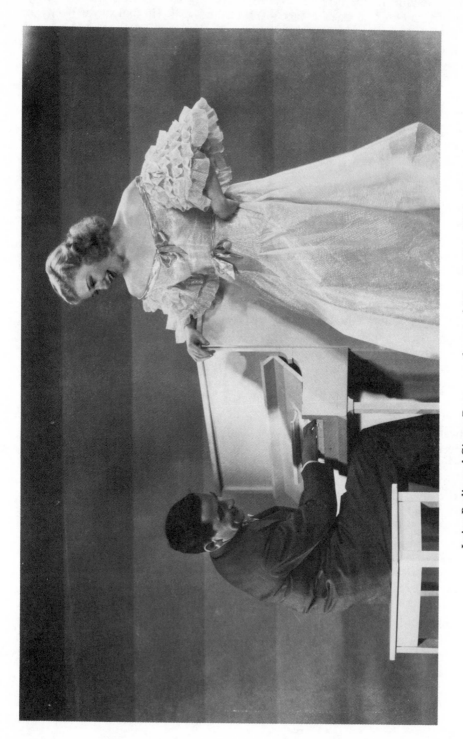

Irving Berlin and Ginger Rogers on the set of "Top Hat" in 1935.

recording of a new song to Fred Astaire or to Bing Crosby. In December of 1972 *Variety* reported that he had completed 75% of the score for a new Music Box Revue and in December of 1974 he told a reporter who inquired into his current doings: "I'm doing what all songwriters do. I'm working at my job. What else is there to do?" In 1978, on his 90th birthday, he was said to be working on another idea for a new Broadway show.

So it was that in his mid-60s Berlin was not unlike the 34-year-old John Lennon who sang, "I'm scared, I'm scared, I'm scared/As the years slip away." But he had held that kind of fear at bay a lot longer than had the former Beatle, his muse having retained its youth and zest for nearly fifty years. Comparing early and late rhythm numbers such as 1919's "Mandy" with 1935's "Top Hat, White Tie and Tails" and then with 1946's "I've Got the Sun in the Morning," one is astounded to see that the energy level has not only been maintained, but increased. In fact, the later songs were much more powerful. "Mandy" is hardly more than a vamp; it contains no release, only an eight-bar motif and a brief coda. "Top Hat, White Tie and Tails," on the other hand, goes wild in the middle, with a sudden, jagged line which, for rhythmic complexity, outdoes Gershwin's "Fascinating Rhythm." It does rhythmically what Kern's releases did harmonically: it goes to the fringes and gets back just in time. But the middle of "I've Got the Sun in the Morning" ("Sunshine gives me a lovely day/Moonlight gives me the Milky Way") is even more joyous. It brims with high spirits and good health.

The consistency of his inventiveness can be pointed out in many other songs. For the 1935 film *Top Hat* Berlin wrote a cheerful tune called "Isn't This a Lovely Day (to be Caught in the Rain?)." Fifteen years later, for *Call Me Madam*, he surpassed it with another song in the same vein called "It's a Lovely Day Today." Both have the same carefree jauntiness. And they both have something else as well — a trait that is present in much of Irving Berlin's work. This is their natural or "discovered" quality. It is as if Berlin had not fabricated them, but had merely found them, as one finds a truffle.

It is impossible to know just what happened to Berlin creatively circa 1954. He himself probably does not know. One can say, however, that once uncertainty hit, he had no central style to fall back on, no core to which he could return and regroup. He had no personal tradition for testing new ideas or for experimentation. That said, one might also note that, by 1954, Berlin had been at the peak of his powers for 43 years, since "Alexander's Ragtime Band," written in 1911. In comparison, Kern's great songs were written over a 32-year span, between "They Didn't Believe Me" in 1914 and "Nobody Else But Me," written in 1945. Cole Porter's were written over 28 years, between "Let's Do It" in 1928 and "True Love" in 1956.

Cole Porter.

Harold Arlen's were done over 24 years, between "Get Happy" in 1930 and "The Man That Got Away" in 1954. Only Richard Rodgers wrote great songs over a comparable span — from "Manhattan" in 1925 to "Do I Hear a Waltz?" in 1965. It is plain to see that staying power was not the least part of the Berlin phenomenon.

Cole Porter: True Grit

It was probably because of its absurdities that Cole Porter loved the theater — the squabbles among backers, directors, writers, producers and that unfathomable creature, the audience (when death threats greeted the cast and writers of *Jubilee* in Boston, only Porter was amused) and the opportunities for outrageous opulence provided by opening nights. He loved the theater but he had no ambition for it. He did not see each production as a chance to advance the state of the art or even of his art. He was a steady-state composer, not an evolutionary one. Gershwin, Kern and Rodgers were all attracted, to greater and lesser degrees, to grand designs. Not Porter.

His was a more traditional artistic temperament than theirs — withdrawn, sardonic, wrapped up in itself — and he was probably well-suited to the kind of puzzle-making and problem solving that goes into the creation of complex pieces of art. Yet he refused to travel down that road. Over the years his songs became less daring, both lyrically and musically, and toward the end they were very simple — a simplicity that was occasionally beautiful, as in "True Love," but which was more often only simpleminded. The spareness of many of those later songs was not calculated. That kind of economy is really just an absence of the energy that complexity and fullness require.

This lack of energy was largely due to a debilitating physical condition brought on by a freak accident in September of 1937. Attending a riding party at the Oyster Bay home of Countess Edith di Zoppola, his skittish horse reared up, fell backward and crushed Porter's legs. While a companion went to get help the composer, convinced that he was not seriously hurt, proceeded to complete the lyric of "You Never Know" — or so he later claimed. That part of the story may or may not be true but there is nothing apocryphal about Porter's courage. Despite almost constant pain and an endless fear of disfigurement and amputation, he continued to work for another twenty years. He went on to write great songs — albeit at a less prodigious rate — and he even topped himself with his greatest Broadway work, *Kiss Me Kate*.

But September of 1937 is an undeniable line of demarcation in Porter's professional life. With the accident came the end of what his friend and editor, Dr. Albert Sirmay, called Porter's "glory years." Those years totalled a mere decade, beginning in 1927 when Porter was already thirty-six years old. He had had to wait a long time for success — much longer than any of the other writers discussed in this book — and then, a brief decade after it came, there was the fateful accident. One can only manufacture theories, most of them unconvincing, to explain why Porter was so late in gaining acceptance on Broadway. Perhaps he had erred in aiming his songs for his own social circle — men and women who were, like himself, wealthy nabobs. But if that is so, how does one account for the popularity of his work of the mid-1930s, which could be even more snooty and precious? Another theory is that until the late 1920s Broadway audiences were too unwashed to appreciate Porter's brand of drollery. But that fails to explain why they took to the words of such sophisticates as Larry Hart, Noel Coward and Ira Gershwin. The truth is that no one can say why it took Porter so long to get started. Even the fact that he had written nothing very memorable prior to the late '20s does not provide an answer because Berlin, Kern and Gershwin were all successful on Broadway before they had written anything very good. It was the same state of affairs in the 1960s when the best work of the Beatles, Dylan and the Stones came *after* they had made it big. Who is to say that their great songs were not inspired by or at least given impetus from such early kudos? And who is to say that the same thing would not have happened to Porter in the 1910s had he received some initial recognition?

Not that his talent was ever entirely ignored. As a sophomore at Yale he was already getting some notice with his songs; a football song, "Bull Dog," is still sung on that campus. In 1915, at the age of 24, he wrote songs which made it to Broadway. Two were interpolated into Kern's *Miss Information* and one was in Romberg's *Hands-Up*. But nothing came of them. The next year he wrote the score for a Broadway show of his own, *See America First*. But it was panned by the critics, one of whom said, "See America first last." At the time Porter was 25 years old — still young, but he was probably aware that Berlin had achieved world renown by that age with "Alexander's Ragtime Band." (Berlin was just three years older than Porter.)

Having failed to make it on Broadway, Porter turned to Europe. In the fall of 1917 he sailed for France and on April 20, 1918, he enlisted in the French Foreign Legion. Just what duty Porter really saw in that capacity is obscured in legend (among songwriters, he was second only to Dylan in making up stories about himself) but, after being mustered out a year later, he continued his musical education in France. Europe was his home base for the next ten years. There he met and married Mrs. Linda Lee Thomas, a wealthy divorcee (her first husband, Ned Thomas, an industrialist, had the distinction of being the first U.S. motorist to kill a pedestrian), who was eight years his senior. She and Porter's society friends, most notably Elsa Maxwell, did all they could to promote his songs. But through most of the '20s Porter's music was known only to connoisseurs — his was like Randy Newman's situation in the 1960s and 1970s. A Porter show called *The Mayfair and Montmartre* failed in London in 1922. A song called "The Ragtime Pipes of Pan" failed when it was used on Broadway that same year. In 1923 his one effort at highbrow composition, the ballet *Within the Quota*, also failed. In 1924 he had another Broadway flop, this one entitled *The Greenwich Village Follies*. Appropriately enough, his next attempt to break into the big time consisted of three songs contributed to a play entitled *Out of Luck*, put on by the Yale Dramatic Association. His career really got off the ground in 1928 with "Let's Do It, Let's Fall in Love," featured in the Broadway show *Paris*, which opened in Irving Berlin's Music Box Theatre (with a strong boost from Berlin himself). Then, juices flowing, Porter went full-speed into his best decade.

Most songwriters have a period when their talent is at its most concentrated and when it burns at its brightest. Gershwin's occurred at the end of his life, between *Porgy and Bess* in 1935 and his death in 1937. Berlin's was between 1932 and 1936 when, in quick succession, he produced the scores for *As Thousands Cheer, Top Hat* and *Follow the Fleet*. In the 1960s there were the examples of Holland-Dozier-Holland and their remarkable output between 1963 and 1967, of the Beatles, whose flame was white hot throughout their recording career together, and Bob Dylan, who was similarly infallible for two years, 1965 and 1966. Porter's greatness was never so inexorable; even at the height of his career he wrote duds. Nor were all of his shows in those years hits (*Jubilee*, for example, was a box office failure in 1935, as was *Red, Hot and Blue* in 1936). But every project that he worked on produced a few true pearls. *Anything Goes* of 1934 was the apex. Out of this show came the title tune as well as "Blow, Gabriel, Blow," "I Get a Kick Out of You," "All Through the Night" and "You're the Top." From *Jubilee* came "Just One of Those Things" and "Begin the Beguine." From the film *Born to Dance* (1936) came "Easy to Love" and "I've Got You Under My Skin." From *Red, Hot and Blue* came "Down in the Depths" and "It's De-Lovely." From the film *Rosalie* (1937) came "In the Still of the Night."

After 1937, Porter continued to write great songs, but less frequently. His 1938 opus, *You Never Know*, which closed after only 78 performances, produced "At Long Last Love" but nothing else that is still remembered. *Leave It to Me* opened on Broadway the same year and was a success, but it too is memorable for just one song, "My Heart Belongs to Daddy," introduced by the very young Mary Martin (so young, in fact, that she was unaware of the song's sexual implications). Porter's next project was a film, *Broadway Melody of 1940*, also remembered now for only one song, "I Concentrate on You," as was his last Broadway show of the decade, *DuBarry Was a Lady*, which contained "Friendship."

The early 1940s were almost as rough on Porter as they were on the rest of the world. In October of 1940 his show *Panama Hattie* opened on Broadway and, though a success, it produced no outstanding songs. The same can be said of his work for the 1941 film *You'll Never Get Rich*. Consoling himself with travel — a drive across the United States and Canada, a voyage to the South Seas, a trip to Latin America where he baked his legs in the equatorial sun — Porter tried to keep a step ahead of despondency. But the nation was at war and the public had little taste for dry wit and sophisticated love, preferring instead simple and emotionally direct songs, such as Sammy Fain and Irving Kahal's "I'll Be Seeing You" or Berlin's "White Christmas." Though Porter expressed a desire to write "less of the brittle bright poesy with which I've been associated," he was unwilling or unable to align his material with the basic emotions which were then gripping the American public. There was no way that he was going to come up with anything like Berlin's *This Is the Army*, a show which featured soldiers on stage and which went on tour across America and Europe to raise funds for the Allied cause. He did gear two songs for the armed forces, "Glide, Glider, Glide" and "Sailors of the Sky," but neither was effective. Though he praised Berlin's war contributions he himself spent much of his time circumventing rationing and hoarding scarce commodities.

In 1941 there was another Broadway show, *Let's Face It*, which, though moderately successful, produced no hits. Porter was deeply distressed by this. It was obvious by now that the quality of his songs had declined sharply. Moreover, there was much illness to contend with. He had developed a bone growth in his weary left leg and his wife had tuberculosis. He withdrew to his home in Williamstown, Massachusetts, where he read Dick Tracy, listened to *Stella Dallas* on the radio and bought paintings from an elderly neighbor who would later become known as Grandma Moses. His one project in 1942, a film entitled *Something to Shout About*, boasted one good tune, "You'd Be So Nice to Come Home To" but his next play, *Something for the Boys*, was consistently mediocre. That same year Warner Brothers decided not to use any of the numbers he had written for *Mississippi Belle*, abandoning that film project entirely. In 1944 he was back on Broadway with *Mexican Hayride* but it too lacked outstanding songs. Porter's best effort in the score, "I Love You," had been written on a bet. His friend Monty Woolley had wagered $25 that Porter could not make a hit out of such a monumentally trite phrase. Porter got his money when the song topped the hit parade but he knew that it did not measure up to the songs he had been writing in the 1930s. Another break in the clouds came when "Don't Fence Me In" was successfully introduced by Roy Rogers in the film *Hollywood Canteen* (it was sobering, however, to realize that the song had actually been written in 1934). But 1944 ended with what Porter was to call his most miserable experience in the Broadway theater. This was *Seven Lively Arts*, a series of sketches produced by Billy Rose. It and the material he wrote for it failed miserably and, shortly thereafter, Porter was in the hospital for his 31st operation.

He wrote no new songs in 1945, although his screen biography, starring Cary Grant, was completed by Warner Brothers that year. He did come up with a new Broadway score in 1946. This was *Around the World in 80 Days*, based on the Jules Verne novel and directed by Orson Welles (not to be confused with the film made ten years later, music by Victor Young). But it was a bona fide disaster. Beginning with a simple, attractive premise, it, like so many Broadway shows, developed a fatal centrifugal force. Casting changes, script rewrites, producer troubles and show doctors all hacked away at the original idea. It also suffered from one of Porter's poorest scores. At this point the consensus was that he was finished. He was 55 years old, in poor health and spirits, and he seemed to have already had his day in the sun. In 1947, twenty years since his first success and ten since his accident, no new offers of work came his way.

In 1948, however, he was back. The spring saw the release of a Vincente Minnelli picture, *The Pirate*, and for it Porter wrote one of his standards, "Be a Clown." Then, on the penultimate day of that year, *Kiss Me Kate* opened in New York. With the possible exception of *Anything Goes*, it was the best score he ever wrote.

Doing a musical version of Shakespeare's *Taming of the Shrew* had not been Porter's idea. In fact, he had at first refused to join the project, preferring the idea of a soap-opera-ish musical based on the Miss America beauty pageant. Porter had to be talked into his masterpiece, just as Irving Berlin had to be talked into writing *Annie Get Your Gun*. And when he finally did get to work on the project, he was suffering from pain so intense that it sometimes caused him to lose consciousness. Somehow, he was able to write such songs as "Another Op'nin', Another Show" (its main strain is closely related to that of Gershwin's Introduction to *Porgy and Bess* and to Berlin's "There's No Business Like Show Business"), "Wunderbar" (although this consisted of new words only; Porter had written the tune in 1934 for *Anything Goes* and its original title had been "Waltz Me

Down the Aisle"), "So in Love," "We Open in Venice," "Too Darn Hot" and "Where Is the Life That Late I Led."

Kiss Me Kate, which inaugurated the final decade of Porter's creative life, seemed at first to be a stunning rebirth. And it is true that he never again suffered from so dreary a period as that which befell him in the early 1940s. But the pleasure from this success did not last long. In 1949 his weight, normally 150, was down to 131 and he complained of looking like a withered grape. The next year, after the failure of *Out of This World* (its one classic song, "From This Moment On," was dropped from the show before opening night), his weight slipped to 124. He suffered from severe depression, was convinced that his talent was gone, feared that he would receive no new offers of employment. Friends watched him closely in case he attempted suicide. In October he was admitted to Doctors' Hospital in New York for electric shock treatments.

As if all that weren't enough, Porter also had to contend with the death of his mother and the terminal illness of his wife. Nevertheless, he was back on Broadway in 1953 with a successful show, *Can-Can*, whose score was a good one, containing such standards as "C'est Magnifique," "It's All Right with Me" and "I Love Paris." In this work Porter undertook the task of writing songs in the style of the 1890s' French music hall and, to do so, he went back to his old habit of studying up, this time reading and absorbing musical scores printed in that era.

In 1955 he wrote another work for Broadway, *Silk Stockings*. Its score, save for the hit song, "All of You," was not noteworthy. But in 1956 came the very fine film score for *High Society*. It included "High Society Calypso," "I Love You, Samantha," "You're Sensational," "Now You Has Jazz" and "True Love." Of the latter, Max Dreyfus wrote Porter to say "it is truly a simple, beautiful, tasteful composition worthy of a Franz Schubert." It is indeed a lovely song and, as things turned out, it was Porter's last hit. He wrote two more scores, a film, *Les Girls* and a television production, *Aladdin*, but neither contained anything memorable. So it is with *High Society* that his career as an effective writer closed. Thirty years had passed since his first great success, twenty since his riding accident, ten since *Kiss Me Kate*. The years after 1957 were taken up with a prodigious list of health problems, including an ulcer operation in 1957 and the amputation of his right leg in 1958. The amputation may have saved Porter's life but it sent him into a permanent depression. By November of 1960 he was down to 80 pounds. In 1963 he was severely burned while smoking in bed. Shortly thereafter, while listening to a recording of one of his show scores, he was heard to say, "*How* did I ever do it?"

There is no answer to that question. Nor can it be known whether

Porter's catalogue of great songs would have been fattened had Broadway accepted him sooner, or had he refused to mount that nag at the Countess's home in Oyster Bay. But even if his career had not been so truncated, his music would almost certainly have remained earthbound; it would not have taken off as did that of Gershwin and, later, the Beatles. Unlike them, Porter was not fascinated by the possibilities inherent in a musical idea. The idea itself was sufficient for him. He loved the theater well enough but he did not have the kind of mystical attachment to it that helped Rodgers transcend the same kind of limitations. Rodgers was not a greater musician than Porter, but he was able to extend himself through his empathy with exotic characters and situations. Porter, for all his bravery and true grit, did not have that kind of heart. He also had trouble with the other requirement for productive longevity – that is, staying in touch with the source of his original inspiration. The high-spirited, razor-sharp wit of his early songs, both lyrical and musical, became elusive in his later work. It did not disappear entirely: the sexual naughtiness of "But in the Morning, No!" (1939) was matched by "All of You" (1955). Yet Porter's style, which had at one time been the most original and inimitable among the great show writers, became watered down. Ill health was certainly a factor. But his failing to become more than he had been made it inevitable that he would become less.

Harold Arlen: Always the Bridesmaid

Writers and critics are always making apologies when discussing Harold Arlen – not for him but to him: they regret that the public hardly knows his name and they are ashamed that the Broadway theater never took him to its heart, as it did the other five great show composers. Despite the fact that he, more than any of the other five, has been a performer himself, he has somehow always remained in the wings. In 1954, when Truman Capote was asked if he would adapt his short story "House of Flowers" into a Broadway show with music by Arlen, Capote had to ask who Arlen was. A list of the latter's songs was read to him and it was only after hearing such titles as "Over the Rainbow," "I've Got the World on a String," "Paper Moon," "Stormy Weather," "Blues in the Night," and "Old Black Magic," that his interest in the project picked up.

Arlen's career had many other galling moments. There was the time at George Gershwin's house in Beverly Hills when he played a newly written tune for the latter and another guest, the conductor William Daly. The song was "Last Night When We Were Young," one

127

Harold Arlen in the 1960s.

of his best, but his two friends hardly noticed it, so engrossed were they in a conversation about something else. (This song was later plucked from obscurity by Judy Garland who learned of its existence by accident — she had been thumbing through a bin of records and had noticed opera singer Lawrence Tibbett's recording of it.) Gershwin was not always so rude to the younger composer. He promoted Arlen's career on many occasions and it was he who said that Arlen was "the most original of us all" (an opinion seconded by Irving Berlin). Still, Arlen's name never achieved the stature of the others. In a law firm he would have been the associate, they the partners.

The problem was that Arlen never really made it on Broadway, which was where the names of the other five became firmly established in the public's mind. His first successes came not on 42nd Street but uptown, in Harlem's Cotton Club. Established in 1923 and run by gangsters, its entertainers were black — Ethel Waters, Bill "Bojangles" Robinson, Cab Calloway, Duke Ellington — but many of its writers were white and it catered to a strictly white clientele. Arlen and his first lyricist, Ted Koehler, in a series of Cotton Club revues, wrote such songs as "Between the Devil and the Deep Blue Sea," "I Love a Parade" and "Ill Wind" — songs which equaled anything being done on Broadway at the time and which achieved the same kind of general popularity. But the renown and the prestige of Broadway did not come to the Cotton Club songwriters.

By the time the Cotton Club closed (in 1936, a victim of the Depression), Arlen was in Hollywood, where the other great show writers were also at work. But in Hollywood too, though he continued to write classics, fate was against him. He was never awarded that choicest of plums, an Astaire/Rogers film. It is true that he was chosen over Jerome Kern to write the music for *The Wizard of Oz* but that project immediately became associated in the public's memory with its stars and especially with Judy Garland. It was another fifteen years before he worked on a great film again. This was *A Star Is Born*, also starring Garland, and again his songs, particularly "The Man That Got Away," became associated more with her than with him.

It is possible that Arlen was not entirely unhappy with the way things were in Hollywood. He knew that he was writing great songs and he was certainly making a decent living at it. If he did have any regrets, they probably centered on his inability to achieve a definitive success on the Broadway stage. In 1944 he and Harburg wrote a show, *Bloomer Girl*, about Dolly Bloomer, a feminist and underwear innovator of the 19th century. It had a respectable run of 654 performances but it was hardly a classic on par with *Oklahoma!*, *Annie Get Your Gun* or *Kiss Me Kate*. Two years later he and Johnny

Mercer wrote an excellent score for *St. Louis Woman*. But it was an out and out failure, running only 113 performances. Arlen did not return to Broadway for another eight years and when he did, with *House of Flowers*, his and Capote's score faced a similar disappointment. But he kept trying. In 1957 came *Jamaica*, written with his old partner Harburg. This one ran for more than a year, but that was probably due to the magnetism of its star, Lena Horne (who had had one of her first great successes with Arlen's "Stormy Weather") rather than to its songs, which were lacklustre. Then, in 1959, Broadway saw a new Arlen/Mercer show, *Saratoga*, but this one closed after only 80 performances. The same year *St. Louis Woman*, which had achieved a following despite its initial bellyflop, was operatized and renamed *Free and Easy*. But, though a critical success, it could not compete with Rodgers and Hammerstein's *The Sound of Music*, which was produced at the same time.

There is, therefore, no score in the Arlen canon which proclaims and preserves his name. *The Wizard of Oz* almost does this but "Over the Rainbow" has become Judy Garland's song in a deeper sense than "Cheek to Cheek" became Astaire's or "I Got Rhythm" became Merman's. Perhaps that was the price one paid for writing for Garland. When she had a mind to, she could make any song her own. Her hair-raising performance of "Stormy Weather" at the 1961 Carnegie Hall Concert outdid all other versions, even Lena Horne's previously definitive performance in the movie *Stormy Weather*.

In terms of his stage and screen works, therefore, Arlen's career had no momentum. There was no steady progression for him as there had been for Gershwin, who began with revues, progressed to musical comedies, then to Gilbert & Sullivan-style satire and finally to opera. Arlen's sense of his own identity as an artist must have been somewhat humbler than that of his five peers, each of whom, after a string of Broadway hits, got his name indelibly attached to Hollywood assignments (i.e., *Irving Berlin's Holiday Inn*). He was not, like Kern, the inventor of the modern American song or, like Rodgers, the father of the modern American musical; nor was he, like Gershwin, the celebrated colossus of symphonic jazz. Arlen's career had little of the grandeur that theirs had and, thus, less of their momentum. Somewhat like the careers of Berlin and Porter, but without their endless series of hit shows, Arlen's career existed from song to song, rather than from production to production. Nevertheless, he did manage to develop and keep a sense of himself as an author, unlike fellow Hollywood tunesmiths such as Harry Warren or Jimmy Van Heusen. That sense of his own distinctiveness is wrapped up in a proclivity toward what can be called, loosely, the blues. It was in songs like "Blues in the Night" and "One for My Baby" that he built up an identity. He wrote many different kinds of tunes — from ballads to dances to Stephen Foster style Americana — but he defined himself in this bluesy material in much the same way that Porter defined himself with his Hebraic beguines — "From This Moment On," "I Love Paris" — and not with such atypical works as "Don't Fence Me In." Arlen followed no strict blues format — his music was a long way from that of Robert Johnson — but he brought jazz and blues influences to the popular song in much the same way that Gershwin brought them to symphonic music. What the *Rhapsody in Blue* was to a Liszt Hungarian rhapsody, "Blues in the Night" and "Stormy Weather" were to "Whip-poor-Will" or "Night and Day."

Ethel Waters called Arlen "the Negro-est white man," and it is obvious that he identified with black performers and with their kind of show biz blues. He and Koehler wrote some songs specifically for what was then called the "race record market" ("My Military Man," "High Flyin' Man," "Pool Room Poppa," "The Wail of the Reefer Man") and these were recorded by Ethel Waters, Cab Calloway and even by the Empress of the Blues, Bessie Smith herself. Arlen never stopped working with black artists. In addition to the Cotton Club performers, the casts of *Cabin in the Sky, St. Louis Woman, House of Flowers* and *Jamaica* were all black and other Arlen musicals, including *Bloomer Girl* and *Saratoga*, had black principals and themes. In addition, his one large-scale concert work was entitled *Americanegro Suite*. Like Gershwin, he understood and acknowledged his debt to black musicians.

A second facet of Arlen's style, and one which also gave his work continuity and a means of development, was the way he experimented with the length and shape of his songs. He never wrote one so endless as Porter's "Begin the Beguine" (that one weighed in at 108 measures) but he was more consistent in this kind of thing than Porter was, writing songs which were often much longer than the traditional 32 bars. "Blues in the Night" is perhaps the most famous example of this, though, of its 58 measures, most listeners are familiar with only the first four ("My momma done tol' me/When I was in knee pants/My mama done tol' me/Son!"). "The Man That Got Away" (at 57 bars) is another example, as is "I Had Myself a True Love" (64 bars). Arlen referred to these songs as his "tapeworms" — but they are perhaps more accurately (but less graphically) described as short stories. He was intrigued with the shape and structure of his melodies — he liked it when they unfolded slowly, each section a logical outcome of the one that preceded it. This was his game, the way modulation was Kern's. And it is because Arlen did have such a definite style that he could develop despite a moribund career as a theater composer. His art never descended into a lifetime of hunting and pecking for hits. When he sat down to work he had a sense not only of popular music's past, but of his own past and he strived to meet not just his audience's expectations but his own as well.

Arlen's career as a songwriter encompasses forty-seven years — from the publication of "Minor Gaff" in 1926 to music written in 1973 for an unproduced television show entitled "Clippity Clop and Clementine." But his great years were between 1930 and 1954 — that is, between "Get Happy" and "The Man That Got Away." And the era of his prime continues to shrink when one considers that, in the eight years prior to *A Star Is Born* and *House of Flowers*, both from 1954, he had written just one standard, "Hooray for Love." One must really go back to 1946 and *St. Louis Woman* to find Arlen at his peak. It can be said, therefore, that he is remembered for what he wrote in just a decade and a half — from the time he was 25 until he was 40 — a shorter span than Gershwin's prime, though Arlen's lifespan has been more than twice as long.

Part of the post-1954 slackening must be attributed to two factors that were certainly beyond his control. One was his health. In 1954, during the composition of *House of Flowers*, he required three dozen blood transfusions for hepatitis and a bleeding ulcer. His spunk in the face of such distress rivaled that of Cole Porter, for he continued composing from his hospital bed, even when he was reduced to tapping a spoon on a dinner tray. The second circumstance was the death of his wife in 1970 which sent him into almost total retirement.

It is harder to isolate the reason for the inferiority of so much of his work between 1946 and 1954. One can point to the inconsequentiality of his Hollywood assignments but the post-'46 films (*Casbah, My Blue Heaven, The Petty Girl, Mr. Imperium*) were no worse than some of his earlier projects (he and Mercer wrote some very good songs for some very bad films: "Ac-cent-tchu-ate the Positive" for *Here Come the Waves* in 1944, "My Shining Hour" and "One for My Baby" for *The Sky's the Limit* in 1943 and "That Old Black Magic" and "Hit the Road to Dreamland" for *Star Spangled Rhythm* in 1942; in 1939, Arlen even managed to turn out something memorable for a Marx Brothers comedy when he wrote "Lydia the Tatooed Lady" for *At the Circus*). Without ever being able to know just what happens in an artist's head at any given period in his life, one is forced to look at his environment to understand a surge or, as in this case, a decline in his powers. In doing so, it is not too hard to pinpoint a major factor in the mid-1940s which might have contributed to Arlen's slippage. The post-war public's taste for sophisticated pop and theater songs was, after *Oklahoma!*, geared to the new form called the musical play. Richard Rodgers was certainly faring best in this regard. In the latter 1940s he was able to follow *Oklahoma!* with two other financially and artistically successful works, *Carousel* and *South Pacific*. Each of the other living members of The Six saw the writing on the wall and each of them attempted to reconquer Broadway in terms of the new, integrated book musical. Kern died before he was able to give it a try but Porter managed to pull it off with *Kiss Me Kate* as did Berlin with *Annie Get Your Gun*. Only Arlen lived through the decade without finding such a suitable vehicle. He was the youngest of these great writers and yet he had failed to capitalize on and encompass this new trend — a trend which was clearly an artistic step up and one which seemed certain to be the wave of the future. Arlen's lack of a steady, solid partner was perhaps his greatest stumbling block. Rodgers succeeded best, not only because of his long-time desire for and vision of the musical play, but because he had teamed up with Oscar Hammerstein, a man who was not only a capable lyricist but an excellent writer of libretti, as he had shown as early as 1927 with *Show Boat*. Berlin and Porter, who wrote both words and music, had no such partnerships to fall back on. But they did have luck. It was Berlin's good fortune that Dorothy Fields was on hand to write the book for *Annie Get Your Gun* and it was to Porter's great advantage that Sam and Bella Spewack were doing the same for *Kiss Me Kate*. But such happy associations were not permanent ones. Fields and the Spewacks went on to other concerns. Their careers were not fundamentally entwined with Berlin or Porter and both of those men found it increasingly difficult to get the right writers for the right shows. Arlen, for his part, was removed from the running by an extra step. Unlike Berlin and Porter, he needed a lyricist. But his lyricists, able as they were, were not playwrights, as was Hammerstein. Men like Johnny Mercer, Yip Harburg and Leo Robin had little expertise in the construction of book musicals. It is not unreasonable to believe that Arlen, had he gotten to Hammerstein first in the early '40s, might have had something of the second wind that Rodgers received. As it turned out, Arlen tried very hard to make it in the new world of Broadway and he failed, despite such *succès d'estime* as *St. Louis Woman* and *House of Flowers*. His interior momentum was still intact — "The Man That Got Away" and "I Never Has Seen Snow" from 1954 and "Paris Is a Lonely Town" from the 1962 film *Gay Purree* (sung by Judy Garland) continued the bluesy style begun decades before. He was able to continue his development in an idiosyncratic sense. But he was unable to remain abreast of and in command of the times, growing in a way that would excite the public at large — as Rodgers and Hammerstein were doing and as the Beatles would do a few years later.

John Lennon in 1968.

John Lennon: The Great Swan of Liverpool

Lennon's final decade of life — his post-Beatles' career — was spent almost entirely in the United States. In 1970 he and his wife Yoko Ono went to Los Angeles where they both underwent therapy with Dr. Arthur Janov, author of *The Primal Scream*. The Janov book had come to him in the mail and Lennon, unable to resist any new approach to the Infinite, had become enthusiastic about it, as he had in earlier days been enthused about LSD and the Maharishi. It was in the summer of that year, while still under Janov's influence, that he recorded his first solo album of original songs, *John Lennon/Plastic Ono Band*. This work, while it met with critical success, was too morbid to achieve the kind of sales that Lennon had been used to as a Beatle. Fans noticed also that they did not return to this music again and again as they did to their Beatle albums.

John and Yoko spent much of 1971 in Europe trying unsuccessfully to locate Yoko's daughter Kyoko, who was in the custody of her father, Anthony Cox. They returned to the United States on August 13, 1971, and by the end of the year they were in New York City. The Lennons lived in a two-room West Village studio, worked in a So-Ho loft, rode bicycles in the park, took in midnight movies and picked up Sunday papers in Sheridan Square. John was immersing himself in Yoko's territory. She was the daughter of a wealthy Japanese banker who had himself hankered after an artistic career (as a pianist) and she had spent the late 1950s residing in a loft at 112 Chambers Street, gaining recognition as a quirky avant garde artist. Now Lennon was trying to reduce the size of his sphere to that of hers.

Unnerved by *Plastic Ono Band*'s lacklustre sales, he spent July of 1971 recording *Imagine*, a more commercial set of songs. If this seemed to contradict the ethos of the *artiste* so recently adopted by Yoko and himself, well, it was nothing new for Lennon to contradict himself. This time, however, the contradiction was carried into the music itself. He opted for a more saleable sound and, in an attempt to make the songs full-bodied (*Plastic Ono Band* had featured just four instruments: piano, guitar, bass and drums) he hired many musicians; their names would fill a small directory. Though *Imagine* contained some excellent songs (particularly the eponym, as well as "Jealous Guy" and "Give Me Some Truth"), there was none of the stylistic unity of *Plastic Ono Band*. "I Don't Wanna Be a Soldier, Mama" was heavy metal, "Crippled Inside" was in a jug band format and so on. Eclecticism had been a virtue of the *White Album* but

Imagine's potluck selections were not always authoritative. A number of its songs sounded like what they were: filler.

On March 1, 1972, the United States Immigration Service gave Lennon fifteen days to get out of the country. This was ostensibly due to his 1968 drug arrest in England but, as was later revealed, it was actually a project of the Nixon administration, which wanted to get him out of the country before the start of the 1972 presidential campaign. That very week a court in Houston gave Yoko temporary custody of Kyoko and, as this was to be exercised in the United States only, Yoko was put in the position of having to choose between her daughter and her husband. Lennon appealed the Immigration Service's ruling (a chronicle of his litigations in this decade would fill volumes) and in 1975 was finally given status as a permanent resident.

In March of 1972, in the midst of all of these troubles, he recorded his third album of original songs, *Sometime in New York City*. It was his greatest failure, due to its simple-minded polemics, its ephemeral lyrics and to the fact that he shared songwriting chores with his wife, who wrongly believed the god of talent to be, like herself, a strict egalitarian. The album did have its notable moments, particularly the songs "John Sinclair," on which Lennon played even better slide guitar than he had on the Beatles' "For You Blue," and "New York City," a manic song that, had it been by the Rolling Stones, would have entered their permanent repertoire alongside "Jumping Jack Flash" and "Brown Sugar." But sales were relatively poor and Lennon, as he had after *Plastic Ono Band*, turned in a more commercial direction, this time with *Mind Games*. That, as it turned out, was a pallid version of *Imagine*. The cycle was repeating itself and he knew it.

Now came the first of his two retreats, this one to California. Separated from his wife, he went on a year-long bender, accompanied by drinking buddies such as Ringo Starr, Harry Nilsson and Keith Moon. It ended in the summer of 1974 when he returned to New York to record another album, *Walls and Bridges*. Elton John played on one of its songs, "Whatever Gets You Through the Night," and Lennon promised him that, should that record reach number one on the charts, he would join John on stage at the latter's upcoming concert in Madison Square Garden. "Whatever Gets You Through the Night" did reach number one and it was backstage at the ensuing concert that Lennon was reconciled with Yoko.

In October of 1975, with the birth of their son Sean, John and Yoko retired from public life. Lennon had just turned 35 and was consumed with the specter of age. Perhaps he did not know that Irving Berlin had reached that age in 1923, well before he wrote his most memorable songs; or that George Gershwin at that age was just beginning to tackle his life's ambition, an opera; or that Richard Rodgers at that age was still six years away from his partnership with Oscar Hammerstein. In any event, Lennon now became the reclusive elder statesman of rock. Songwriters made a point of calling on him when they were in New York but he would often refuse to let them into his apartment in the Dakota, a Victorian structure with a view of Central Park. (Paul McCartney himself, apparently, was turned away on one occasion.) It was not until the summer of 1980 that he and his wife resumed their careers as artists with the album *Double Fantasy*, which was to be his last.

No one, Lennon least of all, had been prepared for such a disappointing decade. In his final two years as a Beatle, 1968 and 1969, he had been at the very peak of his powers. The songs that he wrote for the *White Album* are among his best: "Julia," "Dear Prudence," "Happiness Is a Warm Gun," "Everybody's Got Something to Hide," "Revolution 1" and "Goodnight." His songs from 1969 are just as good: "Don't Let Me Down," "The Ballad of John and Yoko," "Come Together," "I Want You (She's So Heavy)," "Sun King," and "Because." The decline does not seem to have had any roots in the period which immediately preceded it. This is true of the other Beatles, who were all producing their best work at the very end of their career as a unit. What happened, then? What were the mechanics of this deterioration? In order to reach some conclusions about this, one must leave aside Lennon's biography and the accompanying sociology of the 1970s and take a look at the music itself.

In February of 1968 the Beatles recorded "Across the Universe," a Lennon song, under the direction of George Martin. It appeared on an album entitled *No One's Gonna Change Our World*, a charitable project of the World Wildlife Fund, to which the Bee Gees and other groups also made contributions. Two years later the Beatles, in disarray, gave the recording to Phil Spector to remix, rearrange and otherwise doctor. Although Lennon had little or nothing to do with the revision of "Across the Universe," his first solo albums did use the Spector production style. Spector's version of "Across the Universe" can therefore be seen as a transition between Lennon's Beatle and solo years.

A haunting melody, as if touched by another, better, world, it, like so many Lennon tunes, alternates between verse and refrain like a folk song and its folk roots are also made evident by standard, predictable harmony. Still, the version produced by George Martin is far from simple. It begins with a jest — the sound of ducks as they take flight — which travels from one stereo channel to another, giving the listener the impression that his living room has suddenly turned into a marsh. Then comes a short introduction played by acoustic guitars. It is a distinctive little melody in itself, related to but not

137

congruent with the melody of the verse, into which it evolves. The vocal ideas are especially bountiful on this recording. To Lennon's childlike, faraway voice (the one he reserved for particularly delicate songs like "I'm Only Sleeping" and "Dear Prudence") is added a birdlike, electronically altered voice which, chirping the melody an octave above Lennon, creates a kind of humorous unity with the ducks heard at the beginning. There is also a tricky two-part harmony line, sung as a fill when the main melody comes to a rest. (The Beatles, like Gershwin, were experts at filling in the cracks with good ideas. Rarely did they let an opportunity pass without making good use of it.) Two other instrumental ideas at work in "Across the Universe" are a drone (played on two Hammond organs) which gives musical expression to the mystical lyrics, and a rising phrase in the bass guitar which accompanies the refrain as it fades out at the end. This simple song is thus given a fascinating but unobtrusive complexity that makes one want to hear it again and again.

In Spector's version several of these charming subsidiary ideas have been erased — the ducks, the second voice and the two-part harmonizing after the "nothing's gonna change my world" refrain. In their place Spector added a large mushy choir full of indistinct, ambiguous voices, which effectively destroyed the intimacy of the song. The Beatles' music, because of its care for every line played by every instrument, always had the quality of chamber music — no matter how raucous it became. Spector's reworking of "Across the Universe" is thus a preview of Lennon's later solo efforts in that this gossamer quality was abandoned.

Revealing comparisons can also be made among a trio of Lennon's political songs — "Revolution 1" (1968), "Instant Karma" (1970) and "Power to the People" (1971).

"Revolution 1" appeared on side four of the *White Album*. (Another, less studied version, entitled, simply "Revolution," was released by the Beatles as the B-side of "Hey Jude.") Its melody, which follows a modified blues structure, is simple, yet unpredictable and appealing, full of tied notes and appoggiaturas. Unlike the melodies of many rhythm songs, it does not stay in one place but is a traveller. The harmony is tried and true rock and roll: alternating major and major sixth chords (the Chuck Berry shuffle), in this case C to C6 and F to F6. However, upon the word "destruction" a D-minor chord appears which leads us outside the key of C to A. This makes the return to C via G somewhat jarring and spicy. In other words, the usual ii-V-I progression (in this case D-minor to G to C) has been toyed with, making that first Chuck Berry shuffle, when it returns, more heightened and satisfying. With the studio writers, harmonic novelty was often achieved in this fashion — not with complicated chords (ninth chords are very rare; eleventh chords

138

are almost unheard of) but with chords which were dimly related to the key in question. This is how Lennon attained some of his best harmonic effects in songs like "Strawberry Fields" and "I Am the Walrus."

At first hearing, "Revolution 1" seems to be one of his simpler songs — certainly less complicated than "A Day in the Life" or "Happiness Is a Warm Gun." But looking at its components, one is not so sure. The song begins with an introduction, itself consisting of several subsections: a false start (a Beatles trademark and, by 1968, a consciously applied tool) and a guitar line based on triplets and syncopations. Next is the main twelve-bar melody, altered upon repetition and followed by two releases. The first ("But if you talk about destruction") leads into the second ("Don't you know it's gonna be") which, after a short guitar transition, leads us back to the beginning. These sections melt into each other imperceptibly and with less spectacle than do the segments of "A Day in the Life" but they are there nevertheless. "Revolution 1" is less grandiose than "A Day in the Life" but it is just as full of ideas. And here too, as was usually the case with the Beatles, each instrument is given its own characteristic and notable lines — from the triplets played by the drum, to the bass fill which precedes every repetition of the chorus, to the final electric guitar talk during the fade-out. The instrumentation is primarily guitar, bass and drums, although horns and electric organs tastefully fill out the sound. Also of consequence are the backing voices which sing "shooby-doo-a" to a counter-melody that is later taken up by the instruments during the fade.

The kernel of "Instant Karma" is every bit as good as that of "Revolution 1," but this song was not thought through as completely. Lennon wrote and recorded it in a single day, January 26, 1970, while he was still nominally a Beatle, but apart from the group. Phil Spector produced it and it features Lennon on guitar and electric piano, George Harrison on guitar and piano, Billy Preston on organ, Klaus Voorman on bass and electric piano, Andy White on drums and piano and the hand-clapping of Beatle road-manager Mal Evans. The background chorus featured all of them plus Allen Klein and the patrons of London's Hatchett Club.

The song consists of a verse and a refrain. The verse ("Instant Karma's going to get you"), after some repetitiveness, rises in pitch to create tension which is then released in the refrain ("we all shine on"). This is reminiscent of the Motown approach, where the verse and the refrain usually had the same windup/pitch relationship. "Instant Karma" 's melody is a good one — even if the "we all shine on" section seems to be suspiciously similar to the "love, love, love" verse of "All You Need Is Love" — and the words of this song are among Lennon's strongest and most direct. The sentimental "we all

139

shine on" is not only his best utopian line, it appears to have some scientific basis: the heavy elements that compose our bodies were apparently manufactured in the centers of exploding stars.

But the odd thing about "Instant Karma" is that, although both Lennon and Harrison are playing guitar on this song, no noteworthy guitar lines emerge. In fact, the guitars are pretty much missing from the mix. The piano has taken center stage, but as a rhythm instrument — it only supplies chords. It adds nothing very distinctive of its own. This approach carries over into the chorus. Like "Revolution 1," "Instant Karma" uses background singers. But this time they do not provide the interlocking harmonies and humor of "Revolution 1" 's "Shooby-doo-a." Instead, they have a random quality, like a campfire singalong. It has a certain charm (the Beatles had done the same thing in "All You Need Is Love" and in "Hey Jude" and Lennon had done it on his own in "Give Peace a Chance" with a collection of visitors to his Montreal hotel room) but this kind of impromptu, "oh, what the hell" attitude has its dangers. A laissez-faire approach to music can all too easily become the rule and not the exception.

A year later, in February of 1971, Lennon recorded "Power to the People" (he released it in early March). Production credit goes to himself, Yoko and Phil Spector. The musicians on the record are not identified but the background vocals are credited to "Rosetta Hightower and 44 others."

"Revolution 1" had been deceptively simple but there is no such deception in this song. It is as simple in fact as "Revolution 1" had been at first hearing. Like a much earlier Lennon song, "Nowhere Man," recorded by the Beatles in 1966, it begins with an a capella choral statement of the refrain. But the "Nowhere Man" choir sang three-part harmony. "Power to the People" is sung in unison. The refrain of "Nowhere Man," moreover, was a longer and a more attractive musical phrase than that of "Power to the People;" it led to a release whose minor tonality and unaggressiveness presented a real contrast to the refrain. This does not happen in the later song, whose refrain would have passed muster only as an ancillary motif in Lennon's Beatle days. The entire tune is based on two alternating chords, in this case D and E-minor. Except for a brief cadence involving C, that is all there is. In itself, this extreme harmonic simplicity is no indication of barrenness. Many songs, including great ones by Hank Williams, Buddy Holly, Bob Dylan and Lennon too use no more than three chords. But in those cases the melodies are especially strong. Not here.

Still, the real deterioration represented by this song occurs in its production. The Beatles were always able to work miracles with unpromising ideas, usually by squeezing from them a wealth of attractive subordinate ideas. Those ideas were often in the instrumental and vocal arrangements — arrangements which were so entwined with the construction of a tune that they became an integral part of it. Many later Beatle songs are no more "arranged" than a Mozart string quartet is arranged. They are compositions, not interpretations (which is what the word "arrangement" implies). This was the principal advantage that the best '60s songs had over those of the show composers, just as sophistication in melodic and harmonic writing was the show writers' forte. "Power to the People," however, falls short of this. Its muddy rhythm section consists of drums, bass and handclaps; its large chorus, singing in unison, is exuberant but bland; it brings to the song nothing so charming as the two-part vocal backup on "Across the Universe" or the three-part harmonies of "Nowhere Man." In fact, this chorus sets up an amorphousness which is quickly compounded by a thick mixture of instruments, none of them given distinctive lines. The only player with anything individual to say is the saxophonist but he is merely adding what must have been a very impromptu obligato. One has the impression that Lennon (or Spector) said, simply, "Sax solo here" and when the result proved to be indeed a sax solo, he was satisfied. The saxophone became a curiously ubiquitous instrument in the 1970s. It seemed that no up-tempo song was quite respectable without one; moreover, every sax solo was amazingly like every other one. On "Power to the People," therefore, this "what the hell" attitude had crept not only into the backing voices as on "Instant Karma" but it had also gotten into all of the instruments and the chorus as well. As for the lyrics, it should be noted that in this song Lennon was willing for the first time to adopt the catch-phrases and slogans of others; heretofore he had made up his own.

There were, therefore, two salient factors in John Lennon's decline: his lax attitude toward clarity and his refusal to think out all the ramifications and possibilities inherent in his musical ideas. The ideas themselves were still good. Throughout the 1970s and in his last songs as well, he continued to have a superb melodic gift — "Imagine," "Jealous Guy," "No. 9 Dream," "Watching the Wheels" and "Woman" are as fine melodically and harmonically as his best work in the 1960s. They do suffer, however, if they are compared with Lennon's Beatle tunes as compositions. This was because laziness had crept in. The painstaking energy that was required to wring every possibility out of every idea, to enrich a song without overloading it, slowly dwindled. Lennon was never at any time writing trash. But by allowing himself even once to take the line of least resistance, he had opened up a Pandora's Box. He no longer let the songs stew in the studio over months. For the most part, his musical sins in the 1970s were sins of omission.

141

Another often overlooked factor in Lennon's decline concerns the quantity of his output. After the enormously prolific years of the Beatles' first success, 1964--1966, he began to write less. More and more space on Beatle albums became the province of Paul McCartney's tunes. Of the fourteen titles on the English version of *Revolver*, only five are by Lennon. Only four of the twelve songs on *Sgt. Pepper* are his (and one of those, "A Day in the Life," was a collaboration between him and McCartney). He wrote twelve of the *White Album*'s thirty, four of the eleven songs on *Let It Be*, and two of the six songs on side one of *Abbey Road*. Side two of that album was mostly McCartney territory, with Lennon's four tunes accounting for about seven minutes of the eleven-song, twenty-minute medley. From the August, 1966 release of *Revolver* through the May, 1970 release of *Let It Be*, therefore, he was producing about seven and a half songs a year — songs that were arduously worked over not only by himself but by the other Beatles and George Martin. As a solo performer he averaged one album of new songs a year between 1970 and 1974 and each of those albums contained at least ten tunes. To maintain a level of quality on par with what he had accomplished as a Beatle would have required not only more work but more inspiration — a tall order.

Upon hearing of John Lennon's death many people thought of him in black and white; that is, in terms of early Beatlemania — the television appearances on Ed Sullivan's show, the cover of *Meet the Beatles* and the black-and-white film *A Hard Day's Night*. They are the ones who viewed the murder (even now those words — "the murder" — are so fantastic) with some dispassion. Time had run out on someone from an era long gone. For a second group, Lennon's image was in glaring color, as bright and gaudy as the mismatched hues of a faulty television set. For them his death was something more: an end, once and for all, to the psychedelic extravagances of a tumultuous youth. But there was a third group, one that followed him past the breakup of the Beatles and through the solo years and who felt that they had somehow gotten to know him by snatching up magazines in which he was interviewed. They were disappointed by the unevenness of his new music but heartened by the buoyancy of his talent and by the fact that his mind was as felicitous as ever. For them the end of The Great Swan of Liverpool — as poet Allen Ginsberg called him — was the end of a man who, more than any other member of his generation, was blessed with two human qualities as rare as they were disparate. Songwriting genius was one of them. Moral courage was the other. Lennon was never afraid to speak up for what he believed was just, no matter how much he damaged himself in the process. The fundamental hypocrisy of those who touted violence as a means to just goals — who were violently opposed

142

to violence — was never lost on him. Nor did he fail to note the absurdity of self-proclaimed free-thinkers who were all too ready to prostrate themselves at the feet of heroes — heroes like Lennon himself. Lennon was, in the words of Nicholas Schaffner, "an uncompromisingly honest man who felt uncomfortable with the notion that pop stars should radiate mindless good cheer." He was against mental shackles — whether they were imposed by his elders or his peers, whether they were political, religious or musical. At the same time, he was for the future. He hated the idea that he and the other Beatles were saints and oracles and that the band's reformation was necessary for the moral or even the musical regeneration of the world. At the end of his life Lennon was ready and anxious to participate in a future in which the roles of everyday people would be enhanced, even if his own influence was to be diminished. It was this kind of courage that made people all over the world sense — know — that here was not only a great songwriter but a great man as well. So it is that, for this third group of admirers, his death was a return to black and white, symbolized by that last album cover and by the monochrome that is murder.

Paul McCartney: Keeper of the Flame

It has been said that an autumn leaf, by turning bright colors, is simply giving back in one fell swoop all the sunlight that it has collected through the spring and summer. In the autumn of 1969, as the Beatles were breaking up, they released a burst of light in the form of their beautiful and cumulative last album, *Abbey Road*. Then, suddenly, a second burst came, this time from legions of Beatle admirers who released their collected Beatle memories — only to come up with the macabre and startling theory that Paul McCartney was dead. Intimations of a fatal car crash were found in the lyrics to "Got to Get You into My Life" ("I was alone/I took a ride/ I didn't know what I would find there"), "Strawberry Fields," (where John Lennon seemed to be saying "I buried Paul"), and "Revolution 9" (the spoken words "number nine" were supposed to become "turn me on, dead man" when played in reverse). Then there was the album art work: *Sgt. Pepper*'s cover depicted a grave strewn with yellow flowers in the shape of Paul's bass guitar, a *Magical Mystery Tour* photo had Paul seated behind a sign which read, "I Was," and the *Abbey Road* cover showed a Volkswagen "beetle" whose license plate, 28IF, seemed to suggest McCartney's age had he lived (actually, he was 27 at the time).

Because of these and many other "clues" scattered through the

Paul McCartney in the 1970s.

band's post-1966 work, a lot of Beatle admirers became convinced that McCartney really had died and that the remaining Beatles had somehow found an imposter who not only looked just like him, but who sang, played and wrote like him too. Calmer — if equally suspicious — souls thought the whole thing a hoax engineered either by the Beatles as a group or by John Lennon alone. As for McCartney, he had spent the fall of 1969 in seclusion with his new wife and her family, licking his wounds over continuing disagreements with other members of the group, and it was this absence from the public eye that further inflamed the speculation about his death. Even though he poked fun at the whole thing ("I suppose if I were dead I would be the last to know it"), this strange episode took several months to run its course and by that time he did something which, to fans, seemed even worse than departing this life — he left the Beatles. In the spring of 1970 he released his first solo work, *McCartney* (a true and literal solo work: he played all the instruments), and its unpolished, fluffy spirit, the antithesis of all that the Beatles had stood for, spelled, if not artistic death, then a new and lesser artistic incarnation. To many it suddenly seemed that the rumors of his death had been at least allegorically true.

As it turned out, *McCartney* was the first salvo of the 1970s, a decade when, for some reason, people thought it a virtue to lower their expectations (implying that their expectations had been unvirtuous). But in the spring of 1970 no one knew that pop music was about to undergo a debilitating sea change, and most of McCartney's audience was willing to go along and forgive him for dabbling in minimalism. After all, hadn't Lennon and Harrison done much worse with avant garde and unmusical albums such as *Two Virgins* and *Electronic Sound*? And McCartney's first solo album was at least adhering to 1960s sensibilities in that it expressed a consistent attitute — hominess, modesty and a disinclination to dazzle — which had an important precedent in Dylan's *Nashville Skyline*, released the year before. The consensus was that, like Dylan, McCartney had made this new career move by design.

It was not until the following year, with *Ram* (May 1971), that critics became convinced that he was, in fact, floundering. They zeroed in on McCartney's lyrics. Lines like

> Fly fly in
> Fly fly out
> Most flies they got three legs
> But mine got one

were not only pointless, they were humorless as well. In fact, the whole album was filled with dummy lyrics, which was the last thing people expected of McCartney, for no one had ever thought him lazy. As for the music, it was still obvious that a powerful talent was at work, but this talent was badly in need of an editor. Songs such as "3 Legs" and "Monkberry Moon Delight" should have been rejected. Other songs, while good, needed more work — "Ram On" lacked a release; "Too Many People" had an ineffective instrumental finish; "Long Haired Lady" had several segments, some excellent and some terrible. There were a few songs, such as "Dear Boy" and "Uncle Albert/Admiral Halsey," that were fully realized and brilliant. But the whole of this album was less than the sum of its parts; it, unlike great albums of the 1960s by Dylan, the Stones, the Who, the Beach Boys and the Beatles, had no point of view, no real tone of voice. Its cumulative effect was cuteness and inconsequentiality. Obviously, one more encomium had to be given the Beatles and George Martin of Abbey Road — they were good editors of one another's work. *Ram* made it plain that McCartney needed someone to, in Irving Berlin's words, "splash against."

Further proof that there was no design behind McCartney's post-Beatle career was provided by *Wildlife,* an album released in December of 1971 under the aegis of his new group, Wings. When the minimalist, one-man band approach of *McCartney* had been less than successful, he had swung in the opposite direction, using session players and an orchestra for *Ram.* And when that had not met with much approval, he swung back, this time to an unadorned four-piece combo (including his wife). As a Beatle, critics had always taken their cue from him. Now, he was reacting to them. *Wildlife,* like the previous solo albums, contained some good material — "Tomorrow" being a particular standout — but it was amazing to see how much outright chaff McCartney was willing to publish. Flak from critics was still directed at his weak lyrics — on two of *Wildlife's* songs, "Mumbo" and Bip Bop," he gave up entirely and scatted — and at his imperviousness to the political issues of the day. Reacting to this, McCartney released a topical single, "Give Ireland Back to the Irish," but defenders of the counter-culture found it more significant that he had written the theme song to the Establishment's new James Bond movie, *Live and Let Die.*

In October of 1973 Wings went on the road — literally, in a bus — and Paul McCartney's first post-Beatles concert was given not in any huge arena but at Nottingham University, where the price of admission was a mere 50p. He was trying to get his band and himself in shape by playing to small impromptu audiences, just as his first band had honed its skills in unpretentious surroundings. At the same time, nostalgia for the Beatles was becoming serious. In 1974 the first Beatlefest was held in New York. There, thousands of people who had once been happy to consider themselves very small in comparison to their four heroes, and who were now being robbed of that opportunity as those heroes shrank closer and closer to life size, could again become tiny, this time before tennis shoes imprinted with pictures of the Fab Four. The real Lennon, McCartney, Harrison and Starr, who had seemed superhuman and for good reasons only a few dozen months earlier, were losing their celestial glow.

In the mid-1970s McCartney finally arrived at an acceptable plateau. The album that broke his fall was *Band on the Run*, released in December of 1973. Unlike his previous solo efforts, its songs were consistently good. Critics were also pleased because the title song seemed to suggest an overall theme — was McCartney referring to his efforts to outrun the abnormal expectations of his audience? — and this unity was carried out by the instrumentation, which combined the one-man band concept of *McCartney* (due to sudden personnel changes, Wings was now reduced to two effective members, Paul and sideman Denny Laine) with the brilliant orchestral overdubbing of *Ram*. His next album, *Venus and Mars* (released in May of 1975) was almost as good, though, as if to point out the difficulty of writing an entire album, the songs on the second side are generally inferior to those of side one. But these two works, *Band on the Run* and *Venus and Mars*, set McCartney's new standards. After 1975 he would be measuring up to them and not to his work in the 1960s and that gave him breathing room, as did an unbroken string of gold records. Round two of his career was firmly established; he had no fear of becoming an anachronism.

Since 1975 he has been able to indulge his every musical fantasy and, in so doing, he has become keeper of the Beatle flame — though, at first glance, this would not seem to be so, for the other two songwriting ex-Beatles, Lennon and Harrison, had, more than McCartney, continued to express Beatle-like utopianism and they, just as much as McCartney, indulged in Beatle-ish pranks and whimsy. But McCartney, despite his "death" in 1969 and his disappointing reincarnation in 1970, was truer to the '60s in several very important respects. One was his commitment to the purity of his instrumentation. After *Plastic Ono Band*, Lennon abandoned the unspoken but very real ethos that his songs be written and recorded as chamber music — that each instrument speak authoritatively in its own voice. It was probably to this quality that producer Richard Perry was referring when he said: "The secret of a Beatles record [was that] you felt right next to them." Lennon was lax about that standard, as was Harrison, especially on the latter's *All Things Must Pass*. But McCartney's post-Beatle instrumentation rarely dissolves into an amorphous, soupy sound. In fact, much of the pleasure of his music is in the perfection of his instrumental fills. When he does fall down in this regard it is usually by allowing a less than professional choral backing. For a while he seemed unable to resist adding gratuitous woo-woos to nearly every one of his songs and too often he conceived backup vocal lines in order to give his wife something to do. There was also a puzzling decline in his own bass playing. It was no longer as breathtaking as it had been in such Beatle songs as "Everybody's Got Something to Hide But Me and My Monkey." But these are relatively minor points when measured against McCartney's consistently brilliant post-Beatle orchestration.

There is another manner in which McCartney has remained truer to Beatles' methods than either of his songwriting confreres. This is in his willingness to turn an unpromising idea into a promising one — to milk an idea of its hidden potential. That was a Beatles trademark, for rarely did the group come up with a "natural" or a "discovered" tune à la Irving Berlin. They did not often pull ideas whole and ready out of the heavens. They were more like Gershwin — their fancy was usually caught by an interesting pattern (a chord progression as in "Julia," a circular riff, as in "Day Tripper") which they used as a starting point. The many bootleg recordings of the Beatles' January 1969 rehearsals point this out clearly. Such songs as "Get Back" and "Two of Us" began as rough approximations. But played over and over again, their inherent possibilities became clearer. McCartney continued to operate in this manner. But Lennon and Harrison began to depend on their initial inspirations, packaging them as neatly as possible but not composing from them. Fortunately, their ideas were usually good enough to keep their careers alive, although sometimes just barely so. But McCartney was more willing to let his lesser ideas spawn better ones. In many songs — "Big Barn Bed," "Silly Love Songs," "With a Little Luck," "The Pound Is Sinking" — the initial tune seems disappointingly ordinary. But as the song progresses the first strain gives birth to others while harmony, counterpoint and instrumentation do their part to win the listener over. For this reason, his better songs stand up under the weight of repeated listenings.

Leaving aside what is forgettable in McCartney's music — and if this seems to be a large percentage one must remember that the lion's share of the songs for most musicals by the great show composers was often forgettable — he *has* continued to write masterpieces. These works fall into several categories, some of which are peculiarly his own. In a way, he has been like Cole Porter, who had staked out his own territory with Hebraic beguines ("In the Still of the Night," "Love for Sale," "From This Moment On") and with comic list songs ("Let's Do It," "You're the Top"). One style that McCartney has made his own has been the eccentric ballad. Around 1966, when still a Beatle, his acclaimed series of love ballads ("And I Love Her," "Yesterday," "Michelle") pretty much came to a halt with "Here,

There and Everywhere" (although there have been a couple of notable additions — "Maybe I'm Amazed" and "My Love"). He then began to develop a highly personal form in which his slow melodies expressed not romance but idiosyncratic and sometimes other-worldly subjects. The best of these in his Beatle days were "She's Leaving Home," "The Fool on the Hill," "Mother Nature's Son," "Hey Jude" and "Let It Be." Since 1970 he has continued this tradition with a series of equally good songs, many of them overlooked or too casually dismissed by critics. The first was "Uncle Albert/Admiral Halsey" from *Ram*. For pure British eccentricity this one is hard to beat, though in its nautical references it is similar to "Yellow Submarine" and also to later McCartney songs such as "Morse Moose and the Grey Goose" and "Wanderlust." It has a languid easygoing charm all its own and its harmony (rising chromatic triads on "No one left at home and I believe it's going to rain") and instrumental interludes help give it Beatle-ish complexity. The next McCartney number in this vein was even better, a song called "Little Lamb Dragonfly," from the 1973 album *Red Rose Speedway*. Its lyrics are vague, like those of "Uncle Albert," but the heart-rending quality of the music leads one to believe that, instead of hiding meaninglessness, they are veiling some genuinely felt experience; they add up to a kind of goodbye. The music is in three distinct sections, each in a different key. The first ("I have no answer for you little lamb") is in B-minor, the second (without words, only a la la la vocalise) is in C and the third ("Dragonfly, fly by my window") is in E. A neat and very assured Kern-like modulation is effected between the end of the last section and the repetition of the first, but not before some extraordinary musical thinking has occurred in the instrumentation and in a vocal canon (on "since you've gone I never know/I go on— I miss you so"). It is a very beautiful song.

Band on the Run contained another in this series, the more conventional, folk-like "Mamunia." Its lyric is much more straightforward, admonishing one not to dread but to welcome a rainy day — words which might have been too cloying but for the melody, which is both charming and satisfying (it too changes key, this time from A to C and back). From the 1978 album *London Town* came two other songs in this vein. The first was the title tune, whose vague lyrics, various sections and overriding sadness resemble "Little Lamb Dragonfly." It too is one of McCartney's unique ballad/compositions in which instrumental motifs exist apart from vocal lines and where complicated structure indicates a musical intelligence that is too large to be confined to the traditional limits of pop songwriting. Also on *London Town* is "I'm Carrying," a tune singled out for praise by George Harrison who, up to that point, had been regularly sniping at his former comrade. "I'm Carrying" is, like "Mamunia," less complex

149

in structure than the others and it comes closest of this group to being an old-fashioned love song. Yet, like "Little Lamb Dragonfly," its lyrics are about loss more than love ("Oh, long time no see baby sure has been a while") and the sense of sadness here, underscored by effective use of strings, is just as affecting as it was in the earlier song.

Then, in 1980, came "Summer's Day Song" on *McCartney II*. This is in a world all of its own — one melody of utter simplicity set to a simple lyric about waking up from a bad dream. Most of the song is instrumental, consisting of tender synthesizer music which exactly depicts the promise of the lyric. Though *McCartney II* was released several months before John Lennon's death, and though McCartney's official song in Lennon's memory, "Here Today," appeared in 1982 on the *Tug of War* album, it is hard not to think of "Summer's Day Song" as another, perhaps more profound tribute to his friend. The latter album however, in its title song and in "Here Today," provided additions to this series of very fine slow tunes — not ballads *per se*, and not even songs in the traditional sense, but highly evocative compositions which, if they must be categorized, fall somewhere between songs and tone poems.

A second domain staked out by McCartney has been the parody of what, in his mind, was the essence of the 1920s and 1930s tune, the foursquare, up and down, somewhat silly foxtrot. That this type of song never really existed has not bothered him very much and it ought not bother his audience, because McCartney has really been creating another category of tune, one of which he is not just the master but the lone practitioner. The first one in the series was "When I'm 64," from *Sgt. Pepper* (though McCartney had written that tune several years before). He followed it up with "Your Mother Should Know" from *Magical Mystery Tour*, "Honey Pie," from *The White Album* and "Maxwell's Silver Hammer" from *Abbey Road*. It seemed that none of the later Beatle albums was complete without one of what McCartney called his "Fred Astaire numbers." As an ex-Beatle he waited until 1973 to tackle the form again, in a song from *Red Rose Speedway* called "Only One More Kiss." It is as good as the earlier efforts, with its contrasting major/minor tonalities and its perfect 32-bar form but, instrumentally, it settled for less sophisticated fun. Not so with his two most recent follow-ups. "You Gave Me the Answer," from *Venus and Mars* is probably the jauntiest of McCartney's supperclub series and its artful orchestration is a real cornucopia — from the piano introduction to the strings, muted trumpet, clarinet and trombone — each of which takes a turn in an extended instrumental interlude. There is also the wit of the lyric ("I love you and you — you seem to like me"). Then, for the relatively lackluster album, *Back to the Egg*, released in 1979, McCartney wrote the slower-paced "Baby's Request" which is just as good a tune as its predecessors. Its instrumentation features piano, jazz guitar, horn and trombone solos — all of them right on the mark.

Other standout songs from McCartney's solo career are in various styles. There are excellent examples of old-fashioned rock and roll ("Let Me Roll It," "Name and Address," "I've Had Enough" and "Nobody Knows") and of lightweight skipalong tunes ("Listen to What the Man Said," "With a Little Luck," "Magneto and Titanium Man"). Considering the high quality of much of what he has written since 1970 it seems odd that he has been on the receiving end of so much critical condescension, even contempt. Part of the problem, of course, is that side by side with his best songs are efforts which are not merely inferior, but irritatingly so. Over-cute, under-realized: they seem to be saying, "kick me." Another part of the problem is that McCartney, by sharing his albums of the 1960s with Lennon and, to a lesser extent, with Harrison, got people used to the idea that every track on his every LP ought to be inspired and perfect. Later, as a soloist, not only did he not have Lennon to help him with the middle eight bars of a tricky song — he did not have Lennon's songs to help him fill the gaps between his own ideas.

A third problem has been his lyrics. On some songs it was painfully obvious that he couldn't care less about what words he sang — and that attitude bled over into the music, about which he cared very much. It is significant that on the sleeve of *Tug of War* he is pictured not with a guitar or at a piano but at a table laboring over a lyric. On this album he took more care about his words — the title song, for instance, is an excellent lyric. Also significant about this album is the fact that he shared production chores with George Martin. It was not that Martin's orchestral ideas were so much better than McCartney's had been on earlier albums (though they do show a greater breadth). It was that Martin had the wherewithal to say "no!," declaring, at the album's first session, that only four of the fourteen songs brought to him by his former protégé were good. Thus, the world was spared more songs like "Loop (First Indian on the Moon)" and "Famous Groupies."

McCartney has admitted that he does his best work under pressure. But there has been very little of that commodity since 1970 — everything he records is bought up in the millions all over the world. On the two occasions when the heat was really on him — during the recording of *Band on the Run* under trying circumstances in Lagos in 1973 and during the recording of *Tug of War*, when the world expected something substantial from him in the wake of Lennon's death — he did come through with some of his best work. In the 1960s he had reacted to pressure too. It is said that he dreamed up the idea of *Sgt. Pepper* after hearing the Beach Boys' masterpiece,

Pet Sounds and that he wrote "Helter Skelter" after reading that the Who had just recorded the noisiest song ever. Obviously, competition brings out the best in him. But the 1970s did not produce much stimulation in that respect: though some fine writers were at work in that decade — Elton John, Stevie Wonder, Billy Joel — they were never electrifying, and McCartney seems to need real electric juice to get going. John Lennon did too. But, as Paul has so aptly put it, the creative tension between them in the 1960s turned into an enervating tug of war in the 1970s.

More than most of his contemporaries and certainly more than his Beatle brothers, he has had self-discipline. But it has been incomplete. He can get himself to the studio but once there he is prone to a certain laxness. Take, for example, "Junior's Farm," a rocker released in 1974. In type it is very similar to "Get Back" but it bears no mark of the constant refashioning that gave "Get Back" such jewel-like precision. "Junior's Farm" has good ideas like "Get Back" but it suffers from a case of arrested development. As a solo artist, McCartney has always found it easier to be picky about the production of a song than about the song itself.

On the other hand, even a throwaway like "Junior's Farm" shows the presence not only of McCartney the songwriter but of McCartney the composer, for it ends, like so many of his songs, with a surprise bonus — churchy chords sung in whole notes by a backup chorus. McCartney's continued willingness to experiment has been one of his saving graces and it is a source of much of the anticipation that people still feel about his future work. He has developed an increasingly sophisticated use of medleys, going beyond simple tune-stringing and toward complex, unified compositions by the use of recurrent themes. The second side of *Abbey Road* was his first venture in this regard and, because of contributions by Lennon and Harrison, it remains the richest musically. But some of McCartney's other medleys are structurally at least as ingenious. "Live and Let Die," because of the film for which it was written, was dismissed as reactionary by *Rolling Stone*. But, as music, it was actually more revolutionary than anything that had been done in the pop field in a long time. Other efforts at creating extended compositions have not worked as well — the flimsy "Hold Me Tight/Lazy Dynamite" medley on *Red Rose Speedway*, for instance, or the "Treat Her Gently/Lonely Old People" coupling on *Venus and Mars*. And it is true that he has yet to come up with anything as verbally unified as Rodgers and Hammerstein's "Soliloquy" (from *Carousel*) which depicts the self-contradictory thoughts of a father-to-be. Nevertheless, McCartney may one day produce something very memorable by using his affinity for the medley as a starting point. And he has also continued to grow musically in other ways. He has been one of the few modern pop songwriters to attempt the kind of double song that was Irving Berlin's specialty ("Wanderlust" is the most recent of these efforts) and he has occasionally gone beyond that, with two-, three- and even four-part counterpoint ("Dear Boy," "Silly Love Songs"). Nor should one overlook his mastery of intriguing instrumentation ("Mull of Kintyre") or spoken song dialogue ("Rock Show").

Most important, McCartney has always known instinctively that surprise is an essential element of art. His music has always been full of surprises — some so powerful as the four-minute mantra at the end of "Hey Jude," others so brief and subtle as the false key introduction to "Maybe I'm Amazed." In this century, pop music has had two landmark surprises — Gershwin's *Rhapsody in Blue* and the Beatles' *Sgt. Pepper*. Whether McCartney has it in him to provide another surprise of that magnitude remains to be seen. In the meantime, one must be content with the little surprises which result from his continuing willingness to experiment.

George Harrison: Fall from Grace

George Harrison has written about one hundred and ten songs so far, of which some twenty-four are now or seem destined to become classics:

> If I Needed Someone
> Think for Yourself
> Taxman
> The Inner Light
> It's All Too Much
> Savoy Truffle
> While My Guitar Gently Weeps
> For You Blue
> Something
> Here Comes the Sun
> My Sweet Lord
> Beware of Darkness
> Isn't It a Pity
> All Things Must Pass
> Give Me Love (Give Me Peace on Earth)
> Who Can See It
> It Is He (Jai Sri Krishna)
> Can't Stop Thinking About You
> Beautiful Girl

George Harrison at the "Concert for Bangladesh" in 1971.

Learning How to Love You
Your Love Is Forever
Blow Away
All Those Years Ago
Baby Don't Run Away

This list might seem at first to be too meager to represent the life's work of a major writer. But one ought to remember that of the more than eight hundred songs by the indisputably great Jerome Kern, only some fifty became standards. (In his biography of Kern, David Ewen compiled a list of that composer's great songs and came up with fifty-nine, including "Leave It to Jane," "Nodding Roses," and several others that are hardly ever played today.) It is necessary to point this out because Harrison's stock has never been lower than it is today. He is generally regarded as an anachronism and a dreary one at that. This is in total contrast to how he was perceived in the wake of the Beatles' split when, after a long period as an apprentice songwriter, he suddenly emerged as a tunesmith of the first magnitude. Between 1963 and 1967 the Beatles had recorded just eleven of his songs (if one includes "Flying," an instrumental credited to the whole band) and none of these was outstanding enough to merit release as a single. But in the next two years, 1968 and 1969, they recorded twelve, among them "While My Guitar Gently Weeps" and "Savoy Truffle" (two of the most stunning pieces on the *White Album*), "The Inner Light" (the beautiful if neglected B-side of "Lady Madonna"), "Here Comes the Sun" (the most transcendent song in the entire Beatles catalogue) and the standard ballad "Something" (which was released as the A-side of a single). In 1969 Harrison was in his take-off period as a songwriter. It was a time in his life analogous to Cole Porter's glory years of the mid-1930s. Somehow, everything had fallen into place for him — he had finally equaled Lennon and McCartney as a composer.

After the breakup in 1970 he did not falter as they did but instead emerged with a new and fully developed style. His work — lyrics, melodies, singing and guitar playing — had been revamped in an effort to express his devotion to Eastern religion and mysticism. The anomaly here was that, while his post-Beatle music did not sound like what he had written in the 1960s, he was nevertheless the one commanding figure from the 1960s who seemed to have retained the spirit of that decade. He was the only ex-Beatle with a consistent and positive sense of himself. He had what McCartney in particular (soon to be followed by Lennon and Dylan) lacked — an attitude.

All of this — the new musical style and the philosophic certainty — was expressed in *All Things Must Pass*, a triple album released in the fall of 1970. Writers for *Time* magazine, inspired by the sheer size of the work, dubbed it "Wagnerian." They and other observers were beginning to look on Harrison as the Beatles' last, greatest surprise. *He* would carry the grandeur of the group into the future — a prospect that became more certain a year later when, in an act of Olympian generosity and clout, he assembled an extraordinary lineup of musicians (including the reclusive Bob Dylan) to play in the Concert for Bangladesh, an event which exceeded all musical (if not financial) expectations. Lennon and McCartney were both tottering but Harrison was on top.

But it was not until mid-1973 that Harrison was heard from again. In June of that year, a full two and a half years after *All Things Must Pass*, he released his next batch of new songs, an album entitled *Living in the Material World*. This was an unusually long and daring stretch for a pop songwriter to be without a product but in Harrison's case the public, instead of forgetting him, was filled with great expectations — so much anticipation that the new work could hardly be anything but a disappointment. It was not that it was a step down from the previous album. It was that, in the euphoric desire for a Beatles' succession, the real nature of *All Things Must Pass* had been overlooked. Its sheer bulk and its grandiose themes had fooled the public into believing that Harrison was something other than what he really was, a painstaking, unprolific writer, one who was not given to bold conceptions and who was not at home with the eclectic, smorgasbord approach to pop that had been characteristic of Lennon and McCartney. *All Things Must Pass* had fooled them because it had given the impression of expansiveness while it had really been a retrenchment. On closer inspection, it was not all that Wagnerian. Its size was relatively conventional. One of its three records consisted of some 28 minutes of uninspired between-take jamming by Harrison and his studio musicians, while the other two contained just about half as many original tunes as had the Beatles' *White Album*, itself a two-record set. *All Things Must Pass* did have sixteen new originals (including "I'd Have You Anytime," for which he provided music to a Dylan lyric), but this was really only two songs more than the English editions of such single Beatle albums as *Rubber Soul* and *Revolver*.

Nor was this work as infallible as a genuine Beatle album. The "Wagner" behind it all was producer Phil Spector, who had recently worked on the Beatles' final issue, *Let It Be*, and on Lennon's first solo efforts. In many of the album's cuts Spector's production sounds as if the recording had been made in a well. Favoring opaque backings, he took pleasure in distorting and even concealing the nature and identity of various instruments. There were some brilliant uses of this technique — the effective background chorus on "My Sweet Lord," for instance, was no chorus at all but a layering

156

upon layering of George Harrison's voice. Yet, on the whole, Spector's production did a real disservice to Harrison, who was in the middle of his great years as a songwriter and who was creating masterpieces with impressive regularity. "Wagnerian" size and sound notwithstanding, *All Things Must Pass* was a stylistic contraction for Harrison. He was no longer trying his hand at such various pop forms as the blues ("For You Blue") or folk ("Here Comes the Sun") or straight rock ("Savoy Truffle") or psychedelia ("It's All Too Much"). He had chosen a very narrow musical scope for his themes and those themes were themselves a very specific and circumscribed set of concerns. Beginning with *All Things Must Pass*, nearly all of his lyrics would express his religious beliefs and, like most prayers, they tended toward repetitiveness. As for his music, he did what the Beatles had never been willing to do: he cut the tether between himself and the pulse of rock and roll. Starting with *All Things Must Pass* and continuing with *Living in the Material World*, his up-tempo music would sometimes have the kind of liveliness that can be found in folk music, but never again would it have a rock beat. On most tracks it would be his strummed acoustic guitar that would establish the rhythm; he would play electric guitar sparingly and then only as a color instrument, like a horn or a cello, and not as the central rhythmic impetus. So it was that his first solo works gave the overall impression of slowness, an impression compounded by Harrison's voice which intoned his serious and often melancholy lyrics in a dreary, lugubrious manner. The cumulative effect was unappealing. Just as McCartney's *Ram* had left one with the taste of cotton candy, Harrison's first albums, despite their many fine musical moments, left one with the feeling of plodding mournfulness — a most un-Beatle-ish quality.

From here on, this would be the public's sense of him: slow, preachy, willing to have some occasional fun but only on his own self-indulgent, obscure and not very amusing terms (in such songs as "His Name Is Legs" and "Save the World"). This was an image that was solidified by the many references in his lyrics to weeping. It seemed more than a little odd that a man who was so rich, famous and spiritually content should spend so much of his time in tears.

To many critics and fans he had fallen out of his eyrie. But what they failed to perceive was that, in spite of this self-limiting retrenchment, he was still producing great songs and doing so at a pace that was not unlike the one he had maintained in the 1960s. *All Things Must Pass* had contained a half dozen memorable tunes. The reputation of one, "My Sweet Lord," has become tarnished since a court ruled that Harrison had unconsciously plagiarized it from "He's So Fine," an early 1960s hit by the Chiffons (it is true that there are overwhelming similarities between the two songs, though the middle of "My Sweet Lord," which amounts to a short development section, is superior musically) but there were two other masterpieces ready to rush in and take the place of their fallen comrade. One, "Beware of Darkness," was a brooding quasi-aria written while Harrison was still with the Beatles. It is intriguing to imagine how they might have played it, for its eerie and despairing aura would have profited from the kind of precise and haunting production given "Come Together." The other was the title tune, "All Things Must Pass," which was also written when Harrison was still a Beatle (there is even a bootleg recording of the Beatles rehearsing it). Because of its simplicity, Spector's arrangement probably does not differ all that much from what the group would have done with it.

Another fine song, "Isn't It a Pity," is pivotal in Harrison's development because it both displays and overcomes two tendencies which marred his later work. First, it was obviously written not as a melody but as a set of chord changes and though the tune rides these changes gracefully and even soars off on its own, later Harrison melodies would not be so lucky. Second, "Isn't It a Pity" was the first of Harrison's songs to show an infatuation with and a dependence on diminished chords. The diminished seventh, once such a rarity in rock, is used effectively here (it first appears on the last word in the phrase "forgetting to give back") but by the late 1970s, Harrison would be using it to bail himself out whenever he was faced with writer's block.

Other good songs in *All Things Must Pass* include "Apple Scruffs," Harrison's tribute to Dylan (in 1970 the two of them were spending time and writing together) which, with its tuneful verse and refrain and its simple guitar/harmonica instrumentation (a backup chorus is used sparingly), bears a resemblance not only to Dylan's early style but to his return to that style in the mid-1970s, especially on songs such as "You're Gonna Make Me Lonesome When You Go." "Apple Scruffs" is also a tribute to all of the faithful Beatlemaniacs who waited on the steps of Apple Corps day and night with the hope of seeing one of the four. "The Ballad of Sir Frankie Crisp (Let It Roll)," named after the first owner of Harrison's palatial home, is another fine melody, although it suffers more than some others from the production style of the album.

Living in the Material World, half the size of *All Things Must Pass*, contained half as many exceptional pieces. One was "Give Me Love (Give Me Peace on Earth)," a companion piece to and every bit as good as "My Sweet Lord." A second, "Who Can See It," is that very rare commodity in pop music — a melody that manages to achieve grandeur without displaying any bombast. The third, "Don't Let Me Wait Too Long," is an enjoyable piece of up-tempo folk, similar to "Apple Scruffs." Other songs on this album, while not masterpieces, are nevertheless interesting and entertaining. One is "Living in the Material World" which, by contrasting Western music in its refrain with Eastern music in its remarkable release, encapsulates the theme of the entire project (materialism and spirituality — life's ironic duality). Another is an ambitious waltz, an epic of sorts, entitled "Try Some, Buy Some." This song was originally written for Phil Spector's wife Ronnie and it was produced by Spector in an attempt to outdo his great opus of the '60s, "River Deep, Mountain High." Spector almost succeeded, though Harrison has some difficulty hitting all the notes, as the backing had been recorded in Mrs. Spector's key.

Late in 1973, for Ringo Starr's successful *Ringo* album, Harrison wrote the music to an excellent pop song, "Photograph" (Ringo wrote the words), which became a huge hit. And in 1974 the much scorned album *Dark Horse* contained another trio of superior songs: the title tune — with its abrupt and surprising key change at the refrain, "Far East Man" — a lovely, if not fully realized melody, and "It Is He (Jai Sri Krishna)" — whose natural jauntiness equals that of Dylan's great "You Ain't Goin' Nowhere." On 1975's *Extra Texture* there was a solitary masterpiece, "Can't Stop Thinking About You," whose sincere and heartfelt lyrics (secular this time) were more than matched by a touching melody. *Thirty-Three and a Third* appeared at the end of 1976 and it had three more great songs: "Beautiful Girl" is of a kind and just as good as "Can't Stop Thinking About You;" "Learning How to Love You" is one of Harrison's loveliest and most characteristic melodies (it is a haunting tune, slow to unfold, and he gave it the best guitar solo of his post-Beatle years), and the catchy hit "Crackerbox Palace." Three years passed before the 1979 release of *George Harrison*, but this one was probably his best solo work. Not the least of its assets was its modest and tasteful approach to studio production. It did not quite have the chamber music clarity of a Beatles LP but Harrison had molted out of the Spector studio style in favor of a functional simplicity. By the mid-'70s his instrumental lineup almost always consisted of acoustic guitar, electric slide guitar, a rhythm section and electric keyboards (with the addition here and there of unexpected but apropos instruments — a marimba, a string harp, a glockenspiel). Because this sound became more predictable with every new album, casual listeners were easily fooled into thinking that the songs themselves were predictable — even interchangeable. But that was not the case. Harrison at his best is able to acheive considerable variety within this restrained and unambitious orchestration. On *George Harrison* there were some very fine songs, including "Dark Sweet Lady," "Here Comes the Moon," "Blow Away," "Soft Touch" and two indisputable masterpieces: "If You Believe" (a joyous and infectious call to positive thinking) and "Your Love Is Forever" (another one of his earnest and gorgeous melodies — this one, like "Learning How to Love You," with an unforgettable guitar solo).

Harrison's melodic gift is as strong as that of any songwriter of his generation and it must be galling to him when his best songs receive so little acclaim or attention. Perhaps the poor impression left by such washouts as "Save the World," which appeared on the 1981 album *Somewhere in England*, absorbs the luster of the best of their companions. That album, one of Harrison's least distinguished efforts, nevertheless contained a couple of excellent numbers: his Lennon tribute, "All Those Years Ago," in which he, for the one and only time since the demise of the Beatles, played rock guitar (if only for a few seconds) and "Life Itself," an effective and affecting melody, something like "Far East Man." *Gone Troppo*, released at the end of 1982, was a return to the self-assured and graceful style of *George Harrison*. It is chock-full of good, singable songs: "That's the Way It Goes," "Gone Troppo" (literally, "gone nuts"), "Mystical One," "Unknown Delight," "Dream Away" (the theme of the Harrison-produced film *Time Bandits* and a relative of his 1976 hit "Crackerbox Palace") and one more masterpiece, "Baby Don't Run Away."

Critics with unjaundiced ears might do well to listen again to some of the above-mentioned songs. It is time for Harrison, now safely off his pedestal, to undergo a re-evaluation. This is not to say that he has no real faults. His lyrics can be preachy or whiny or both and often they are poorly wrought (he has been especially careless about rhyming — "Bangla Desh" was paired with "looks like a mess" — and, at other times he has shown all the awkwardness of a high school poet: "While waiting on the Light/How patience learned to grow/Endeavor could relieve me/Left alone with my heart/I know that I can love you"). His singing has rarely been more than adequate and whole albums of his voice are hard to take. (As a Beatle, following the examples of Lennon and McCartney, he changed his vocal attack to suit the needs of each particular tune. His singing style on "Roll Over Beethoven" was quite different from the voice he used on "Blue Jay Way," for instance. But on his solo albums he has been content to use one vocal style, just as, excluding a few rare if brilliant acoustic solos, he has abandoned every style of lead guitar playing except for an increasingly vestigial brand of slide guitar.) Unpolished lyrics and monotonous tendencies as a singer and guitarist have thus detracted from his real abilities as a songwriter.

In short, Harrison has given up on eclecticism and much of the element of surprise that goes with it. But in return he has gotten stylistic unity and, with that, he has been able to achieve the kind of home base, the kind of attitude or point of view that eluded Dylan,

Lennon and McCartney in the 1970s. It has been a trade-off. The advantage of stylistic unity is the same as the advantage of religious belief: one is sure of one's place in the universe, only this time it is the musical universe. But there is a common disadvantage too. Adventurousness and the desire to break through barriers is apt to dwindle. Harrison could have found a way around that impasse — after all, many composers from the highbrow side of the fence and a few from the pop fold have been able to explore new territory while retaining their own identifiable styles — but he chose not to follow through on the paths that beckoned to him. Kern's point of departure was his interest in unusual and witty modulation. Rodgers' was in expressing the predicaments of fictional characters. McCartney's has been in joining unrelated tunes to make extended songs and medleys. Harrison might have followed up on his interest in Indian music. He had shown distinct if fitful progress in this respect when he went from the all-Eastern sounds of "Within You Without You" and "The Inner Light" to the East/West mixture of "Living in the Material World" and "It Is He (Jai Sri Krishna)." But he has been reluctant to follow through. His inclination toward retrenchment has always gotten the better of him. He has, therefore, not only failed to touch base with his roots in rock and roll, he has also failed to keep in touch with the experimental mood of the late 1960s. He is now a complacent, steady-state composer.

Nevertheless, as was the case with Lennon and as is still the case with McCartney, Harrison's talent is intact. He has not lost the ability to write good and sometimes great music — something that happened to so many of his fellow travellers of the 1960s. It is a peculiar thing but fate has never seemed to want to pick its favorite among the three songwriting ex-Beatles. McCartney may have been more prolific and more commercially successful but, at their best, all three were always at just about the same level. "At their best" was how one would describe them when they were a unit, each an editor and a presence in the other's work. Now the great songs of McCartney and Harrison are scattered — not only across separate albums, but across the detritus of their own individual failures. Still, they are there.

Mick Jagger and Keith Richards.

Mick Jagger and Keith Richards: Poseurs

A thumb and four fingers — that is how Conrad Silvert described the relationship between Mick Jagger and the other Rolling Stones. Jagger dominates the group. It is his face that appears most prominently on the album covers, in photo magazines and in the more serious journals too. His past, his present, his morals and his art are ritualistically pondered every time the Stones issue a new record and every time they embark on a tour. For the casual fan, it might seem that Jagger *is* the Rolling Stones; that he has the kind of relationship with his band that Buddy Holly had with the Crickets, who were really just hired hands. These days the other Rolling Stones do seem like Mick Jagger's hired hands. But it was not always so.

In the beginning there was a rough equality within the group, on the model of the Beatles, though, like the Beatles, some members were always more equal than others. Drummer Charlie Watts and bass player Bill Wyman remained in the background. Singer Jagger and guitarists Keith Richards and Brian Jones were prominent. Jones, the founder and titular head of the Stones, was the best musician of the lot, able to play almost any instrument after a couple of hours' practice. But he did not write songs. That task was left up to just two members, Jagger and Richards (again following the Beatles' pattern), leaving Jones at a disadvantage. In a decade which made heroes out of songwriters, he could not compete with Jagger as a celebrity (Richards, though a pivotal figure in the band, was content to stay out of the limelight); nor could he compete with Jagger as a partner to Richards. Over the years his input into the group declined steadily and he finally quit the band in the spring of 1969. A few days later he died, drugs having replaced music in his life.

It was in 1969, therefore, that Jagger became the leader of the band and, with that settled, the Rolling Stones were able to avoid the rivalries that afflicted the Beatles. The Jagger/Richards songwriting partnership has survived every other great songwriting team in rock: Lennon and McCartney, King and Goffin, and Holland-Dozier-Holland to name the most prominent. They have been together twenty years now, longer than Rodgers was with Hammerstein and, though they may not realize it, they are going for the all-time record for exclusivity held by Rodgers and Hart, who were with one another for twenty-five years. In fact, the Jagger/Richards relationship is more reminiscent of the show writers' generation than it is of their own: it is like the long-running teams of Rodgers and Hammerstein, Kern and Hammerstein and the Gershwin brothers —

163

which leads one to conclude that they have even more in common with the earlier writers than mere mutual tolerance. For one thing, there is the personality mix. The show writing teams often had a Mutt and Jeff quality: if one of them was outgoing and dynamic (George Gershwin), the other was slow and phlegmatic (Ira Gershwin). If one was straight and upright (Richard Rodgers), the other was dissolute and erratic (Lorenz Hart). If one was serious and high-minded (Oscar Hammerstein), the other was full of the devil (Jerome Kern), and so on. The exuberant Jagger and the shadowy Richards have followed this pattern. But they also echo the older teams in another and more fundamental way: they are the mating of a word-smith (Jagger) to a tunesmith (Richards). Of course, this line of de-marcation has been much more elastic with them than it was with Kern and Hammerstein. Jagger does have input into the music, es-pecially when a tune results from improvisation by the band as a whole. In some sessions, as he has described them, the melody has begun with a guitar riff played by Richards in conjunction with rhythmic groundwork provided by Watts and Wyman, while Jagger improvised words and a tune on top of that. It is possible that Jagger has even written whole songs on his own, both words and music. But he has never been the complete songwriter. He has never been con-fident of his ability to do the whole job himself. Nor has Richards. Their need for one another is much more obvious than was Len-non's need for McCartney or vice versa. That is why the Stones have stayed together so long. It has been an ideal combination of elements in terms of both personality and talent.

But this confluence of factors, though it has enabled the group to survive, has also put its limitations on the development of their music. With Richards in the background and with Brian Jones gone, the music's personality, its attitude, has become Mick Jagger's per-sonality and attitude. And Jagger, for all his brilliance as a writer of lyrics, has always been a musical poseur: growling like a black rhythm and blues man or twanging like a country singer, he must al-ways be somebody else — someone from another country or another race. This becomes all the more obvious when one compares his onstage with his offstage personality. Away from an audience Jag-ger is the model of cool rationality, while onstage he is a master of histrionics — and it is the histrionics that have won out in the Stones' music.

Not that acting is a new or even an unwelcome element in the art of songwriting. After all, the creation of a song is itself always a performance of one sort or another, whether that performance is at a guitar or a piano or in the solitude of one's thoughts. But it was only after World War II, with the rise of country and western music and then of rock and roll, that performance became central to the art of songwriting. It was when writers became performers that their personalities entered into and became the basis of their songs. An analogous situation had arisen in film when the great screen stars began playing themselves as opposed to characters thought up by scriptwriters. Gary Cooper playing Gary Cooper and Cary Grant playing Cary Grant were not so very different from Hank Williams singing Hank Williams or Little Richard singing Little Richard; certainly, Williams and Little Richard expressed their own personalities in a more elemental way than did Rodgers, Kern or Arlen. But the Rolling Stones, dominated by the personality of Mick Jagger, went farther. Jagger was never himself. He was always trying to be someone else: a black man, a hillbilly. Of course, he was not alone in this. The same thing was true of every British group at the time — the Beatles, the Who, the Kinks and the Animals all began by aping the sounds of popular music in the United States. The Beatles could successfully imitate any number of different musical styles because they had what in baseball would be called a good bench. Lennon and McCartney could, between them, sing convincingly in almost any imaginable style from Carl Perkins to Trini Lopez. Moreover, they and George Harrison were all gifted songwriters, multifaceted instrumentalists and instinctive record producers. The Stones' bench was not so deep but, as musicians with a broad knowledge of various pop styles, they were able to give the Beatles a good run for their money in the mid to late '60s.

In those days the fact that they were imitators was a positive thing for, by absorbing many influences, they were testing and stretching themselves. By 1965 their work showed competence in a wide range of styles. "As Tears Go By," which appeared in November of that year on the *December's Children* album, was their answer to the Beatles' "Yesterday" in that it was another ballad that employed the effective and unexpected use of strings. "Yesterday" recalled the kind of well-crafted songs that had appeared in the 1920s and the 1930s (even the title reminded many of Kern and Harbach's "Yesterdays"), while "As Tears Go By" had an even older, almost Elizabethan flavor. On *Aftermath,* which was released in June of 1966, Jagger and Richards continued to delve into a stylistic grabbag with another Elizabethan entry, "Lady Jane," an extended, bluesy song called "Going Home" and rock classics such as "Paint It Black" and "Under My Thumb." Their richest album appeared six months later, in January of 1967: this was *Between the Buttons*, which showed the team's ability to write excellent ballads ("Ruby Tuesday"), up-tempo numbers ("Let's Spend the Night Together") and even vaudeville tunes ("Something Happened to Me Yesterday"). It is interesting to note that Mick Jagger did some of his most unaffected singing on the records of these middle years — that is, singing straight in his own natural voice without any pretended accents or inflections and with less of the trumped-up malice that would later become the norm with him.

After *Between the Buttons* came *Their Satanic Majesties Request* in November of 1967. That year had been a troubled one for the Stones. Jagger, Richards and Jones were all arrested on drug charges and this album probably suffered from the upheaval. Despite some good music it was not a success. The public and critics saw it as an imitation of *Sgt. Pepper* — its songs and their production seemed to be an attempt to out-psychedelize the Beatles' opus, as did the album cover — and it was at this point that it became clear to the Stones and to everyone else that they could not effectively compete with the Beatles as masters of pop music's wide spectrum. Not only had "As Tears Go By" been reminiscent of "Yesterday" — "We Love You," a single, had followed "All You Need Is Love" by just a few weeks. It was time for the group to consider its own pride and rethink its image. And this is what they did with their next album, *Beggars Banquet*, released in November of 1968. By this time Jones was a vestigial member of the band. Jagger had taken over completely. It is very possible that he, an intelligent and deliberate man, carefully thought through the new direction, though it is just as likely that he and the others had been heading that way willy nilly all along. In any case, they chose to become the underside of the Beatles. Where the Liverpudlians sang about love, preached nonviolence and seemed (sometimes despite themselves) to radiate good will, the Stones began to toy with allusions to evil, destruction and the Devil himself. The first song on the new album, "Sympathy for the Devil," was their credo in this regard, though it was hardly their first brush with Lucifer. A negative, bad-boy image had surrounded them from the very beginning. Early photos of them had often been determinedly anti-social. One publicity still even showed them tipping over a baby carriage. There was also Brian Jones' fascination with Nazi paraphernalia — an interest which was apparently shared by the group as a whole when, in 1966, they considered doing a film based on Dave Wallis' book *Only Lovers Left Alive*, about a fascist Britain ruled by teenagers. Then came the allusions to black magic and voo-doo. On the cover of *Between the Buttons* the image of a black cat can be discerned around the two buttons at the base of Charlie Watts' coat, and *Their Satanic Majesties Request* was a title that left no doubt as to how Jagger and the rest were beginning to bill themselves. But this image really gathered momentum with the composition of "Sympathy for the Devil." At the end of the 1969 U.S. tour when the Stones gave a free concert at the Altamont Speedway near San Francisco, it was to this tune that the Hell's Angels (whom they had hired as ushers) murdered a young man just a few feet from the stage. Shortly before that tour, Jagger and Richards had gone to Brazil where they had, according to Richards, met and studied with a magician who practiced "both white and black magic," and references to the forces of darkness now began to appear regularly in their work: "The Midnight Rambler," from the 1969 album *Let It Bleed*, "Sway" from *Sticky Fingers*, released in 1971 ("It's just that demon life has got me in its sway") and "Dancing with Mr. D" in 1973 from *Goat's Head Soup*. This fascination with devilry continues to this day: the inner sleeve of the 1982 album *Tattoo You* features a goat's foot in a high-heeled shoe. Then, of course, there is the image of the two principal Rolling Stones. Jagger, even without his image of carefully manicured decadence and by his name alone, which sounds like a combination of dagger and jagged, would give one pause. Richards, with drugged and glowering eyes, has the heavy brow of a hunter-gatherer. They have certainly achieved their goal — they can no longer be confused with the lovable Beatles. Actually, it was only briefly that the Stones aspired to the aura of humanity which came so effortlessly to the Beatles, for that was not easy to achieve. Paul Simon was perhaps the most intentionally "humane" writer of the 1960s and he did not become the kind of human touchstone that the Beatles became. The Stones, going in the opposite direction, developed a riveting and viable image. But if it helped them to survive in the ephemeral world of pop music, it also eventually thwarted them as songwriters. As the pose was perfected, it solidified. As Jagger became locked into this posture the songs he wrote with Richards followed suit. What they gained in unity they lost in variety. That, in turn, led to the downfall of melody.

To younger Stones' fans, it must come as a surprise that the band was once so versatile. Not only were mid-'60s Stones songs different one from another, there was much richness and surprise within the songs themselves. Unusual instruments were often expertly added to the Stones' basic lineup. On *Between the Buttons* Brian Jones played dulcimer on "Lady Jane," flute on "Ruby Tuesday," and marimbas on "Yesterday's Papers." The organ on "She Smiled Sweetly" is a perfect touch, as is the bawdy piano on "Cool, Calm and Collected." There was also consistent use of a backup chorus on this album (though the Stones sang in unison, not in harmony, and roughly at that). In addition, the Stones used to enjoy changing tempos within a song: the frenetic chorus of "Let's Spend the Night Together" alternated with the sudden hush of its release. On "Ruby Tuesday" a slow and dreamy verse was separated from a more insistent and emphatic chorus by a bar of staccato drumming. And there was the comic speed-up at the end of "Cool, Calm and Collected." Harmonically too, this album was a high point for Jagger and Richards. To be sure, the harmony is rudimentary by the standards of the theater writers. But it is certainly beyond the three-chord harmony of blues and country songs and beyond that of the songs the Stones would write in the 1970s. "Yesterday's Papers" displays a consciousness of songwriting tradition by switching to a minor mode for its release. In "Connection" the listener is led to expect a release in the home key of D but is instead given a surprise, for the release begins outside the key of the song, in F-sharp (though it quickly makes its way back home). "She Smiled Sweetly" contains no such surprises, but its harmony, based on six chords, is well-rounded and the song is notable for its shapely and pleasing melody. That Jagger and Richards were able to write a good tune – the first and most essential requirement of a songwriter – is shown again and again on this album. As a melodic line, "Ruby Tuesday" can certainly hold its own with the best of any generation. The same can be said for "Something Happened to Me Yesterday," whose playful melody has an affinity with Berlin's "Let's Have Another Cup of Coffee."

But in the years that followed *Between the Buttons*, as the band's image became fixed and one-dimensional, their songs gradually lost range and variety. *Beggars Banquet* was a fine album (it contained two of the most powerful rockers ever recorded, "Sympathy for the Devil" and "Street Fighting Man," songs which did what great music has always done – they successfully captured, bottled and preserved human energy); yet, this album held the seed of a future wrong turn. In it there was little love for the playfulness and inventiveness that lies at the heart of all viable music. Jagger and Richards were choosing an attitude – brawny, pitiless rock and roll aligned with up-to-date politics – over musical fun and exploration. Melody, harmony, instrumentation were still more than adequate (in fact, they seemed at this point to have benefitted from the band's new tightness and focus) but the sameness behind each of these songs presaged a decline. In a way, *Beggars Banquet* was to the Stones what *Nashville Skyline* was to Dylan: a masterpiece of concentration and unity which had the unfortunate effect of setting up the only paradigm to which the composer would turn when writing new, ever more pallid works.

In 1969 came *Let It Bleed* which, with "Gimme Shelter," "Midnight Rambler" and the inevitable big finale, "You Can't Always Get What You Want," showed that Jagger and Richards were still willing and able to write good tunes. Yet, there was even less variety here than there had been on *Beggars Banquet*. The songs were all cut from the same bolt of cloth – cut brilliantly, to be sure, but that would not always be the case. *Sticky Fingers*, released in 1971, was the first Stones album to suffer seriously from an absence of good melody. Not that there were no great moments. "Brown Sugar" is another one of the Stones' untouchables, in the same class as "Street Fighting Man" and "Jumping Jack Flash" (the latter, released in May of 1968, is, arguably, the finest piece of rock and roll ever recorded). Similarly, "Wild Horses" is another of the Stones' rare great slow numbers (they have since equaled it only once, with "Angie," from *Goat's Head Soup*). But by 1971 their musical canvas had shrunk, as had their emotional range. Sex (usually allied with cruelty), drugs and death were the incessant subjects. Truly good musical ideas became harder to find. Though it was still inconceivable that a Stones album would be without its good and sometimes great moments (on 1972's *Exile on Main Street* there were "Tumbling Dice" and "Happy") the same thing was happening to the Stones as was happening to the solo Beatles. Most of their new numbers were filler.

If the Stones felt that they had to radically streamline the melodic and the harmonic content of their music in order to get to the meat of rock and roll, they were wrong. The truth is that powerhouse rock has always depended on melody. Any number of examples, from "Peggy Sue" to "Johnny B. Goode" to "Ticket to Ride" (the latter, slowed down, could easily make it as a ballad) to "Jumping Jack Flash" might be offered as proof of this. No amount of posturing or acting can replace this essential ingredient. Volume and frenzy are useless in themselves.

But by the end of the 1970s it had become plain that Jagger's persona, based on overweening hipness and sexual chauvinism, was now at the core of the Stones' musical decline. And the more unyielding his posture became, the more the melodic content of the Stones' music was sapped. (One ought to place some of the blame on Richards, since he was the main composer. Moreover, his physical debilitation due to a serious drug problem could not have helped matters. In a sense, Jagger is being used here as a lightning rod for criticism which ought to devolve on them both, for it is the confusion of musicianship with role-playing that is being faulted, and both were guilty of that.) One now had to pick through the songs carefully in order to come up with a decent musical tidbit — the "ha ha ha" chorus on "Miss You," for instance, on which the last "ha" makes a neat, swift change from D-minor to D-major (although this song sounds a lot like an earlier, better Stones tune, "Mother's Little Helper") — but to enjoy these songs, one had to give them the benefit of the doubt and that was something that had not been necessary in the Stones' salad days. Melodically, they were uninspired. Harmonically, the songs were so rudimentary as to seem musically cynical. There were no interesting changes, as there had been in "Ruby Tuesday," whose tonality alternated between a B-minor verse and a D-major chorus, or "Sing This Song All Together,"

169

Bob Dylan in 1978.

whose chorus in D alternated with a release in B-flat, or "Street Fighting Man," whose great moment (at "but what can a poor boy do") is the result of a sudden change from the key of F to the key of G. The Stones were losing consciousness as songwriters. They were not thinking anymore.

This is the fate of all spent songwriters: their music falters because of a dearth of melodic and harmonic inspiration and they, lacking the ability or the desire to think about melody, harmony, rhythm and instrumentation, unable to see that conscious manipulation is a possibility, allow themselves to write watered-down versions of their old successes. For aging athletes, the legs are the first thing to go. For songwriters, it is melody. When that happens there is nothing left to do but rekindle one's imagination. It is not an easy thing to do. Songwriters, more than other creative artists, are used to bolts from the blue. But if the bolts stop coming to you you must go to them. In other words, the lowbrow must, however reluctantly, become highbrow.

Bob Dylan: Tunesmith

The word "poet" is tied to Bob Dylan much more frequently than the word "composer" but that does not alter the fact that every great moment of his career has been a musical one. It was his singing that attracted the attention and the respect of Woody Guthrie and John Hammond. It was the melody of "Blowin' in the Wind" that lifted him head and shoulders above other folksinger/songwriters — a melody that was recognized instantly as a classic and one which was effective in any setting, whether it was performed a capella by street demonstrators or without words by the Boston Pops. Certainly the lyrics to "Blowin' in the Wind" were excellent and important but it was the tune that did for Dylan what the melody of "Alexander's Ragtime Band" had done for Berlin and what first great catchy tunes always do for songwriters: it gave him his stripes.

After "Blowin' in the Wind" it was the composition of a second great tune, "Mr. Tambourine Man," which gave Dylan his next big boost. "Mr. Tambourine Man" 's free-association lyrics, though not unimportant, were hardly as intelligible as the words to "Blowin' in the Wind" — they lay like an intriguing patina on top of the tune, piquing the curiosity of Dylan's listeners and thereby increasing the lifespan of the song — but it was the warmth of the music that stuck in the mind. A lush arrangement by the Byrds in 1965 helped usher in the era of amplified folk music called folk-rock. Inspired by them

171

and by other groups, Dylan decided to turn to folk-rock himself and his new sound — one of the rawest and, at the same time, most melodic in pop — enabled him to again take the kind of jump with which his career was now becoming identified. For the next two years he wrote in a bluesy rock and roll manner that, for sheer energy, matched any music that had ever come out of America.

The next milestone in Dylan's career came late in the psyche- delic year of 1967. He had not been heard from in some time and there was great curiosity and anticipation over what was next on his agenda. Ostensibly, he was recuperating from a motorcycle accident (Dylan fell off his Triumph 500 a little less than thirty years after Cole Porter fell off his horse), but it is more likely that he was sit- ting out the year, puzzled by the rapid changes that were taking place in the music business. He had been in the vanguard of the pop innovators in 1965 and 1966 but the Beatles and others were now conducting even stranger musical experiments; for them, the use of electric guitars was old hat. Their music had entered the age of multi- track recordings and this was a slow, painstaking process, one that Dylan did not like; nor did he like *Sgt. Pepper*, which had taken nearly half a year to record. It was important to him that music be immediate and that the performer be tangible. He did not like elaborate orchestration and he could not understand why one would want to put so many tricks between the breath of the singer and the ears of the listener. Finally, in October of 1967, he went to Nashville to record his next album, *John Wesley Harding*. Backed by just three other musicians, Dylan finished it in a few days and, upon its re- lease in January of 1968, the quiet restraint of its music single-han- dedly ended the psychedelic era. Once again a major moment in his career was a musical one.

In the years between 1961 and 1968 he had placed his unique mark on four distinct musical styles: folk, rock, blues and country — and he had done so without in any way diminishing them. He had so strong a personality that every time he turned to a new musical format he enhanced it. In this respect he was the American counter- part of the Beatles. But Dylan's music in each of these styles was al- ways primal. All of the musical elements in his work — melody, harmony, rhythm, structure and instrumentation — were all always utterly simple, no matter what his brand of pop was at any given time. Sometimes it seemed as if he were heading into new musical terrain — the extended length of "Sad-Eyed Lady of the Lowlands," for instance — but he never really was. That song was actually only a brief, if lovely melody, made long by many repetitions. When Dylan seemed to be pushing back musical frontiers he was actually doing so in terms of style and fashion: he introduced folk lyrics to rock and roll and vice versa; he made loud music fashionable among

172

folkies and then he made quiet music fashionable among rockers. He was certainly a more sophisticated writer than Guthrie or Carl Perkins or Chuck Berry, but this was because he entered his prime in more sophisticated times. Contemporary writers such as the Beatles and Paul Simon were far ahead of Dylan in their harmonies and in their instrumental thinking. Actually, Dylan preferred not to *do* any real musical thinking. His idea of orchestration, for instance, was to let his backup band play what they liked. As long as the sound they made was more or less what he had in mind he was happy. The arrangements for *Nashville Skyline, Planet Waves* and *Blood on the Tracks* were typical in that they were quickly improvised in the studio. The violin continuo on *Desire* was the result of a chance encounter between Dylan and a young woman, Scarlet Rivera, who had been walking to her violin lesson when Dylan spotted her on the street. His music, therefore, was all instinct and, luckily for him, his instinct was usually right on the mark. He was especially fortunate in that melody, the one musical element which must by its very nature be instinctive, was his greatest gift.

But Dylan-watchers have always spent most of their time picking over his words. Never before had anyone attempted to apply the fiery visionary style of Blake and Ginsberg to popular song. Still, no one would have given this a second thought had it not been for the music. Professional critics knew — or ought to have known — that it is not all that difficult to write apocalyptic poetry and that such material, like late night auto accidents, is one of the hazards of adolescence. Not that Dylan did not have a special flair for it ("Subterranean Homesick Blues," for instance, was a masterpiece of extraordinary, if disconnected imagery). But if he had written no music — if he had only written poetry — he might at best have won a niche in the popular culture next to Lawrence Ferlinghetti. He would never have become a dominant figure.

It is not clear whether Dylan himself ever realized that this was so — that the rungs of his career were all musical ones. Certainly in the early days he considered words more important than music. "If you take away whatever there is to sing — the beat, the melody — I could still recite it," he told a friend. And he was, like Guthrie, not above copping a good tune from another source if it suited his ends. "Don't Think Twice," a song from 1963, is based on a folk tune discovered by Dylan's friend Paul Clayton in Appalachia — a fact that was eventually acknowledged by Dylan's publisher when Clayton was paid royalties.

Sometimes, he would write a powerful and coherent lyric such as "Maggie's Farm." And there were times too when his wordsmithing was undeniably tender, as in "Just Like a Woman." He could also catch rhythms of speech that were quintessentially American, as in

"It Takes a Lot to Laugh, It Takes a Train to Cry." But much more frequently he was turning out random and delirious images. These were often evocative enough to inspire daydreams and even a nightmare or two. But as one became used to the novelty of this kind of thing the effect began to wear off.

Dylan's real contribution as a lyricist in the mid-'60s was actually his unself-conscious mastery of colloquial speech. And in this respect he was not all that different from traditional pop lyricists such as Johnny Mercer and Frank Loesser. He had a great knack for making additions to the national supply of buzzwords and catch-phrases. Just as "Life is just a bowl of cherries," "Brother, can you spare a dime" and "Praise the Lord and pass the ammunition" were phrases from songs which, while in vogue, possessed overtones which spoke to genuine and generally felt national moods, so did Dylan's catch-phrases. His ability to come up with them was probably greater than anyone else's — and doing so became his trademark: "I'm a long time a-comin'/I'll be a long time gone," "The times they are a-changin'," "I was so much older then, I'm younger than that now," "Love is just a four-letter word," "Don't follow leaders — watch your parking meters," and on and on. Many of his surreal, apocalyptic songs are really just collections of random images placed around a brilliant catch-phrase, which is often the only real idea.

Certainly Dylan did have great talent as a lyricist — that was no illusion. Apart from his knack as a phrasemaker, he had always shown the ability to write words with simplicity and warmth. "Blowin' in the Wind" had had those qualities, as had other, less famous songs such as "Tomorrow Is a Long Time," "Girl from the North Country," and "Walls of Red Wing." But in the early days, he lost more battles with control than he won. Perhaps it was his eagerness to avoid what he considered the slickness of the professional that made him use a line like "And they threw him in the waters to cease his screaming pain" in "The Death of Emmett Till." But it is more likely that he was just too sloppy to root out errors of syntax and grammar. The lack of editing is evident in much of the early work: "A finger fired the trigger to his name" from "Only a Pawn in Their Game" and "As her thoughts pounded hard/Like the pierce of an arrow" from "Eternal Circle" (a song Dylan never recorded) are just a couple of examples. Urgency won out over fastidiousness again and again: "Come gather 'round people wherever you roam," from "The Times They Are A-Changin'," is, when thought about, a logistical impossibility. "But you who philosophize disgrace and criticize all fears" from "The Lonesome Death of Hattie Carroll" is the kind of pretentious mumbo jumbo that is all too easily seen through. Maybe Dylan turned to wild personal imagery in the mid-'60s to get beyond the need for self-editing and, at the same time, beyond the reach of

Bob Dylan and Joan Baez in 1963.

grammarians. But by *John Wesley Harding* he was becoming uncomfortable with verbal excess. He still felt as if he ought to play the bard and most of the songs on that album certainly tried very hard to appear imponderable, yet all that striving melted away in the last two cuts. In "Down Along the Cove" and on "I'll Be Your Baby Tonight," Dylan relaxed and allowed himself some simple, comprehensible and moving lyrics. And it was at this point that his words caught up with his music — they became equally effortless and equally eloquent. With these two songs and then with the songs from *Nashville Skyline*, which appeared in 1969, he picked up the thread in his work that lay with "Girl from the North Country" and "Walls of Red Wing."

Toward the end of the 1960s the lyrics of the major songwriters — Dylan, the Beatles, the Stones and Paul Simon — sought to break away from the tradition of the simple love song. In the eyes of these writers that form was a trap that had locked popular song in a vice-like grip for generations. To break free Paul McCartney wrote about an aging spinster in "Eleanor Rigby," John Lennon tackled his childhood in "In My Life," Mick Jagger worked up a short history of evil in "Sympathy for the Devil," and Paul Simon wrote about suicide in "Richard Cory." They were all following Dylan's lead, in a way, for he had touched on all those subjects in his startling songs of the 1960s. But with *Nashville Skyline* he, of all people, went back to the love song. At the time, many saw this as a terrible atavism, as an indication of fatigue and mindlessness. But *Nashville Skyline* was really Dylan's first attempt to keep his lyrics on a short leash. That kind of control had always been evident in his music but the music had been so quick and effortless that controlling it was instinctive, a reflex. It was understandable, therefore, that, as Dylan saw it, consciousness was not to be wasted on the music, for that was a snap. If consciousness were to be applied, then it should be applied to the words. And the lyrics of *Nashville Skyline are* the work of a craftsman.

> Once I had mountains in the palm of my hand
> And rivers that ran through ev'ry day.
> I must have been mad.
> I never knew what I had.
> Until I threw it all away.

These lines from "I Threw It All Away" show the unmistakable touch of a man with genuine poetry in his soul. And from this point on, every one of his songs would have an understandable point to make and nearly all of them would do so with economy, deftness and class.

But while the lyrics were catching up, what was happening to the music? Up to and including *Nashville Skyline* Dylan's talent as a melodist had been robust. But then came that fateful year of 1970 — as tragic a time for the studio writers as 1937 had been for the theater writers. The Beatles broke up, Janis Joplin and Jimi Hendrix died, and Bob Dylan issued his first stunning disappointment, a double album called *Self Portrait*, which contained only a smattering of new material, most of it second drawer. *New Morning*, following *Self Portrait* by just four months, was Dylan's attempt to regroup and it did show an improvement in his tunesmithing ("If Not for You" was just as good as the best of *Nashville Skyline* and "Winterlude" was a happy skater's waltz). But other tracks on the album were more memorable for their lyrics. (The new maturity of Dylan's lyric writing was most obvious in "Day of the Locusts," a song in which he marshalled his old apocalyptic artillery behind the description of a single specific scene — the day he received an honorary degree from Princeton University — and it is a convincing depiction of the kind of suffocating claustrophobia that can arise at an official ceremony.)

Still, however much one wanted to see in *New Morning* a suite of songs equaling Dylan at his best, the truth was that these songs were a musical cut below his work in the 1960s. The new decade, which was to have a debilitating effect on nearly every one of the great young songwriters of the '60s, had already gotten its mitts on Dylan. After *New Morning* he actually came down with a four-year case of writer's block — something that must have come as quite a jolt to a man who had once been seen writing four songs at once, flipping the pages of a steno pad back and forth. He did compose three good songs during this period — "Watching the River Flow," "When I Paint My Masterpiece" and "Knockin' on Heaven's Door" — but he mainly confined himself to redoing some of his old numbers (excellent versions of "I Shall Be Released," "You Ain't Goin' Nowhere," and "Down in the Flood," recorded by Dylan and guitarist Happy Traum in 1971, appeared on the *Greatest Hits, Volume II* album) and to playing on the records of Doug Sahm and others. This hiatus lasted until 1974 when he returned to the spotlight with a national tour and a new album, *Planet Waves*. As if there had been no interruption, that album continued where *New Morning* left off. All of the lyrics were polished and several of them, with recurring images of frozen lakes and cold winter nights, were beautiful. Musically, there were great moments too. "On a Night Like This" was a wonderful opener, made all the more winning by Garth Hudson's playful accordion. "Never Say Goodbye" and "Something There Is About You" are two of Dylan's finest inspirations, each an ideal matching of words and music. But other songs did not come off so well. "Hazel" is uncomfortably similar to that old standard,

"Abilene," and other numbers, particularly "Dirge" and "Going Going Gone" are uninspired. They gave the album an overall impression of unevenness, which was unsettling when one considered that these songs had to account for nearly half a decade of Dylan's artistic life.

The next year, however, Dylan's musical decline was suddenly reversed. For *Blood on the Tracks* his melodies were consistently marvelous. How so much originality and emotion could be packed into such utter simplicity is beyond analysis. It will be recalled that Gershwin, in such pop songs as "They Can't Take That Away from Me" and "A Foggy Day," achieved surreptitious emotional effects through the use of such subtle harmonic maneuvers as pedal points and altered chords. Only in *Porgy and Bess* did he wear his heart on his sleeve, that being an operatic tradition. Now, forty years later, Dylan was doing the same thing, but with the barest kind of harmony and without any of the grand gestures of a highbrow. Not that the work is devoid of subtle music. In "You're a Big Girl Now" the melody achieves its most poignant moment in the last beat of the fifth bar where Dylan's voice rises up a major seventh, landing on F-sharp, to create a dissonance against the supporting chord of G. Dylan then holds the note across the bar line while the harmony changes to C, so that for the first beat of the new bar he is singing a second, more disturbing dissonance. It will be remembered that something very similar happened during the release of Gershwin's "I Can't Be Bothered Now." But Gershwin's double dissonance (on the same two chords) relied on an F-natural, which expressed a lilting gaiety. Dylan used an F-sharp, which resulted in a memorable piece of pathos. Still, most of the songs on *Blood on the Tracks* make do without unusual harmony or structural idiosyncrasies — unless utter simplicity is unusual and idiosyncratic. Eight of the album's ten songs are without releases. That is, their form is not the traditional AABA or even ABA but, simply enough, A. That Dylan's melodies here were good enough to entertain with a minimum number of surprises, with little help from supporting harmony, with few if any attention-getting turns and without being offset by subsidiary sections, is an indication of how great they were.

But after *Blood on the Tracks* the ominous turn that had been foreshadowed by *New Morning* and *Planet Waves* came to pass, and with a vengeance. On the 1976 album *Desire* parts of "Oh, Sister" sounded suspiciously like "Girl from the North Country." "Romance in Durango" was a derivative and predictable piece of ersatz Mexicana. "Black Diamond Bay" and "Sara" were equally hapless. Though he continued for a while to display his mastery of the tightly executed song lyric, Dylan's musical muse was gone. *Street Legal*, which appeared in 1978, did have one strong number, "Baby

Stop Crying," but otherwise it was the slimmest of musical pickings. And, without good music, the lyrics, while still many cuts above those of other pop writers, were left high and dry. Inevitably, they withered too. Dylan's conversion to Christianity was a potentially interesting subject but, unfortunately, it led him to write lyrics which were as vapid as his new music.

Faced with writer's block in 1971--1974, Dylan had chosen not to record any albums at all. Now, faced with the same problem, he seemed to be trying to write his way out of the impasse. Following *Street Legal* were *Slow Train Coming* (1979), *Saved* (1980) and *Shot of Love* (1981). All were to no avail. Dylan was in a difficult situation. He had always taken melodies as they came. Often they were good but, good or bad, he did not like to think about them. As a musical mind, he was the opposite of Gershwin, Kern, Simon and McCartney. He was unwilling to try to make more out of less, to see what extraordinary possibilities lay in an ordinary idea. None of music's elements excited him as a field for exploration — not harmony, melody, form, meter or instrumentation. He was that rarity: a highly intelligent man who relies almost entirely upon instinct. Until 1975 he was wise to do so for his muse was generous. Now, however, when it is not, he can do little but follow it into a kind of musical lockjaw. It may well be time for Dylan to start thinking about the unthinkable — about harmony and counterpoint. Otherwise he will have to wait for the good tunes to return and, as is evident from the the fate of the Rolling Stones, that wait can be a long one.

Carole King: The Perils of Philosophy

If catchy tunes are ever successfully subjected to mathematical analysis it will be a sad surprise — for melody, like the universe, would lose something if its secret were to become known. Still, it is possible to identify factors that effective tunes have in common. And, by doing so, one can begin to understand what makes them tick.

First and last, a good melody must create anticipation: it must make the listener want to know what will come next and then it must make him want to hear it all again. Usually, this is done in one of the following two ways:

Motif development. In "The Way You Look Tonight," Kern takes a phrase consisting of four quarter notes and keeps moving it higher and higher, punctuating it each time with a whole note pause. The first pause is on F, the second is on G and the final one comes on E-flat, the root, providing a resolution. In the meantime, the listener has been kept in a state of pleasant expectation.

The same sort of thing happens in Rodgers and Hart's "Bewitched," where a simple phrase is manipulated so that on each repetition it comes to rest on a high note. In this case, however, the high note remains the same while the lower note — the first of two stepping stones — is always a half tone higher. But the effect of upward movement and of rising tension is the same. Motif development is a technique that is particularly effective in ballads, and any number of other examples can be cited, including "Embraceable You," "Long Ago and Far Away," "I'll Be Seeing You" and, more recently, "You Light Up My Life" (the Debbie Boone hit by Joe Brooks; a song of the same title by Carole King does not qualify in this regard).

The hook. Melodic hooks can come in any number of guises. They can be rhythmic and syncopated, as in "Mountain Greenery" and "Puttin' on the Ritz" and they can be based on intervalic leaps, as in the first two notes of "Over the Rainbow" or the last two notes in the title phrase of "I Want to Hold Your Hand." They can also be based on child-speech: the way children emphasize certain syllables, almost to the point of singing them. Such baby-talk hooks have been a chief ingredient in the success of many songs, including "The 59th Street Bridge Song (Feelin' Groovy)," "Baby Love" and "Staying Alive."

What distinguishes hooks from motif development is that they do not have to be closely related to the song as a whole. The closest that a hook comes to that kind of unity is when it is part of a call and response pattern, as in that eminently catchy tune, "On the Atchison, Topeka and the Santa Fe," where an initial melodic phrase ("Do you hear that whistle down the line") is answered by the hook ("I figure that it's engine number forty-nine"). Other hooks consist of departures from, rather than extensions of, what has gone on before. In "Stormy Weather," for example, the first surprise occurs on the opening note which, being an A-sharp, is outside the key of the song, that being G. This A-sharp is only a leading tone and it is immediately followed by a B-natural, which *is* part of the key — but this chromatic moment has piqued the interest of the listener. A little later there is an unexpected, unrelated octave leap (on "weather") which is yet another melodic surprise. "Stormy Weather" and songs of its ilk do not achieve their effectiveness by pushing a single motif toward a climax. Instead, they take the listener on a journey whose scenery has one or more unique points of interest. One of the best of the latter-day practitioners of this type of song is Paul McCartney. In "The Fool on the Hill," for example, the melody makes its way pleasantly through fourteen bars in the key of C until

Carole King publicity photo from the early **1960s**.

it suddenly (on "but the fool on the hill") takes on a darker hue, backed by a C-minor chord. McCartney's longer compositions, such as "London Town" and "Tug of War," are extended journeys of this kind.

The show writers were adept at both kinds of writing, though development was more characteristic of Broadway songs, while hooks were more typical of tunes written for Hollywood. One of the best of the Hollywood hook-writers was Harry Warren, whose "Atchison, Topeka and the Santa Fe," has been cited above and whose other works include "Jeepers Creepers," "That's Amore," "About a Quarter to Nine," "Lullabye of Broadway," "You Must Have Been a Beautiful Baby," "I've Got a Gal in Kalamazoo," "Chattanooga Choo Choo," and "You'll Never Know." Warren's songs do not express a persona, a style of musical thinking, in the same way as do those of The Six. He never developed into an author. Yet, his tunes have retained their appeal. Those that he wrote in 1933 for the Busby Berkeley film *42nd Street* have recently been used in a successful Broadway production of that name; and it was not too long ago that Art Garfunkel had a hit with a version of the Warren/Dubin song, "I Only Have Eyes for You."

Composers like Warren were the prototypes for the Brill Building writers of the early '60s. Neil Sedaka, Jeff Barry and Carole King wrote not as authors but as musical short-order cooks. In King's case, the songs that she wrote with her lyricist/husband, Gerry Goffin, were peddled to performers with very diverse styles. They wrote hits for Steve Lawrence ("Go Away Little Girl"), Tony Orlando ("Halfway to Paradise"), The Monkees ("Pleasant Valley Sunday") and Aretha Franklin ("Natural Woman"). Unlike Dylan, the Stones, the Beatles and Paul Simon, King's melodies were not based in folk music. They were rooted instead in Harry Warren's kind of writing and in Tin Pan Alley — which, by mid-century, had become a generic term for all well-crafted songs that did not aim quite so high as the Broadway theater song. At its worst, Tin Pan Alley was a home for the musical hack. But at its best, it produced songwriters whose works were, like all great tunes, miraculous.

From 1960 to 1970 King and Goffin had seventy songs on the charts — an astonishing achievement that ought to have made them famous. Not so. In those years Carole King was well known in the music industry and to a few aficionados, but not to the public at large. (Many years later, the musicians in a Colorado-based band called Navarro, with whom she was recording, were astonished to learn that she was the one who had written "The Locomotion," sung by Little Eva back in 1962.) But in this way too she was following in the footsteps of Warren who, despite an impressive catalogue, achieved little public recognition. Perhaps that is why King became restless in the mid-'60s. The age of the songwriter as author had arrived and those tunesmiths who did not measure up were being left behind. Measuring up meant that you *had* to sing your own songs. Otherwise, your work was left to the mercy of a performer. It is not hard to imagine the frustration of trying to develop a body of work when the only way that it could see the light of day was through a Tom Jones or an Engelbert Humperdink. And it is easy to imagine why, given those circumstances, a songwriter might want to establish the kind of control over his output that had traditionally resided with the highbrows, for the composer of a symphony can rest assured that any competent orchestra will give it an accurate, if not necessarily an inspired, reading. But with pop songwriters, there is much less control. It is always possible that a song will die a-borning due to a self-indulgent interpretation. And even if a song does succeed, it is next to impossible to get the public to take note of one's particular songwriting style and the progress of one's musical thinking if its follow-up is sung by a different vocalist or group. Who would notice the continuum of one's harmonic or rhythmic discoveries if one song, done by the Drifters, was followed by another, sung by the Everly Brothers? As authors, songwriters are at an enormous disadvantage. Unlike their highbrow cousins, they cannot even take refuge in the printed version of their work — sheet music — since pop music publishers have never been anxious about accuracy or thoroughness. It is now nearly a half century after Gershwin's death and there has as yet been no complete edition of his songs; nor is one being contemplated.

Therefore, Carole King faced a tricky situation in the mid-'60s. Songwriters had at last come into their own as authors — but this was because they were successfully performing and arranging their own works. What's more, it was becoming apparent that great music in the rock idiom could best be written from inside the nucleus of a band. The Beatles, fathers of art-rock, had in each other an experimental orchestra, just as Joseph Haydn, father of the symphony, had the orchestra of Prince Esterházy at his disposal. In the mid-'60s King became aware of this new state of affairs and she wanted to participate in it, but it took her some time to decide what to do. She made her first move along the road to authorhood by trying to establish her identity apart from Don Kirshner's publishing company, Aldon Music. She and Goffin established their own record company, called Tomorrow. It was not a success but its formation was the first in a series of events which eventually led to her emergence in the early 1970s as one of the greatest of all the performer/songwriters. Tomorrow Records had signed a group called The Myddle Class and King broke up with Goffin to marry their bass player, Charles Larkey. In 1968 she joined Larkey in a new group

183

Carole King in the early 1970s.

called The City and they released one album, *Now That Everything's Been Said*. It was not commercially successful but it did contain three fine songs: "Hi-De-Ho" (later a hit for Blood, Sweat and Tears), "Wasn't Born to Follow" (written earlier for the Byrds) and "You've Got a Friend" (which later appeared on her *Tapestry* album and which also became a huge hit for James Taylor).

This work with The City was an intermediate step, for King's success was still primarily as a writer, not as a singer. Nevertheless, she was admirably equipped to take advantage of the new circumstances in which songwriters were finding themselves. She did not have a professional singing voice — but neither did Dylan, the Beatles, Mick Jagger or Paul Simon. Trained voices were, if anything, a drawback. What was required and what King had in abundance was the ability to sing honestly and communicate feeling. Her talent in this regard had been known for years within the music industry. The demonstration tapes by which she presented her songs to vocalists and singing groups were renowned. Many who heard them thought that her performances were better than the ones which eventually made the songs famous. In addition, she had all of the other trappings that went with writer/performer stardom. A pianist since the age of four, she was able to accompany herself in public and on recordings. As her own lyricist, she could write words that were to the point and eloquent. Topping it off, she was physically attractive in the unglamorous, earthy '60s manner.

At the end of the decade she moved from New York to Los Angeles and there she consolidated her new role as a performer by playing on albums by James Taylor and John Stewart. By 1970 she was ready to record her first solo album. Somewhat apologetically, she called it *Writer*, as if to warn her audience that she was new to the performing game. Though it did not sell well, it was a *succès d'estime* and she was encouraged by her mentor, Lou Adler (who produced the album and who owned the label, Ode, on which it was released) to continue.

It was at this time that the age of the *solo* singer/songwriter was dawning. The Beatles had broken up, each to follow that road, and so had Simon and Garfunkel, and Crosby, Stills, Nash and Young. New writers, who were taking control over all aspects of their work, from the music to the lyrics to the performance and the arrangement, included Joni Mitchell, Randy Newman, Van Morrison and Don McLean. But it was Carole King who struck the first gusher. In 1971 she released *Tapestry* and it quickly became the best selling LP in history (by 1978 it had sold more than 14 million copies, though it eventually lost the number one spot to the Bee Gees' soundtrack for *Saturday Night Fever*). *Tapestry* was appealing because it combined the solid and dependable professionalism of a long-time veteran (her first success, "Will You Love Me Tomorrow," was in 1960, two years before Dylan came to prominence with "Blowin' in the Wind" and four years before the Beatles conquered America with "I Want to Hold Your Hand") with the excitement that always attends a new writer who is finding a voice. When, later in the same year, she released a third solo album, *Music* — one that was every bit as good as *Tapestry* — she reached the pinnacle of her profession.

But then, in 1972, with her next opus, *Rhymes and Reasons*, a slow descent began, one that has continued to this day. As it turned out, King was not immune to the decade's dispiriting gravitational pull. There was the occasional good song — "Jazzman," from the 1974 album *Wrap Around Joy* and "I'd Like to Know You Better," from *Thoroughbred* in 1975. But her period of invincibility had really lasted only a very short while, just about a year.

Of all the disappointing tumbles taken by songwriters in the 1970s, hers was the most puzzling. It seems as if she ought to have been immune to the decline and fall syndrome, for she had been writing good songs before any of the other writers had come along and she was just reaching her prime after many of them had peaked.

To understand what happened, one must go back to that fateful decision, taken in the mid-'60s, to come out of the shadows and become not just a songwriter/songplugger, but a voice and author. Up to that point, King's songs had always been models of structural conciseness, making their point (which was inevitably a quick, melodic hook) with graceful economy in the face of the straitjacket limitations of the A.M. radio marketplace. In nearly every one of her hits the hook could be found in the title phrase and it was inevitably a self-contained snippet that, once finished, left no loose ends. Rarely did she engage in any slow, steady motif building as Kern was so wont to do. In the creation of her hooks, King occasionally came up with an intriguing baby-talk phrase ("Something tells me I'm into something good" is one) but her real distinction was the development of a style of hook that depended on the contrast between major and minor modes. In the phrase "One fine day, you're gonna want me for your girl," for instance, the first two words are supported by a bar of F-major and then on "day" there is a sudden shift to the relative minor, D-minor. This shift creates a sense of expectation that is immediately satisfied by an F-major cadence. In its entirety, the hook has lasted just five bars. But it is the essence of the song. This sort of contrast is behind the charm of many of King's early numbers, including "The Locomotion," a call and response song in which the call ("Everybody's doin' a brand new dance now") is a syncopated motif riding the chord of E-flat, while the response ("C'mon, baby, do the Locomotion") does the same over

C-minor (again, the relative minor). And the same kind of harmony is at work in "Go Away Little Girl," where the refrain is in G and the release is in E-minor (also the relative minor).

Because King was not yet writing to express her own personal point of view and because she was not yet writing her own lyrics she could spend all of her time fashioning these hooks in the succinct manner that had always been called for in pop music. She continued to do the same thing in her first solo albums and with great success. In *Tapestry*, there were "I Feel the Earth Move," "Beautiful," "It's Too Late," "Way Over Yonder," and "You've Got a Friend," which all had hooks that landed on the title phrase and that made good use of the major-minor contrast. On *Music* the same process was at work in "Growing Away from Me," "It's Going to Take Some Time," "Some Kind of Wonderful," and "Song of Long Ago." Other numbers, such as "Carry Your Load" and "Sweet Seasons," based their hooks on major tonalities but led up to them with alternating major and minor chords. In "Surely," a very beautiful song, the unusual key of D-sharp minor predominates until the end, when its relative major, F-sharp, comes to the fore. "Music," the album's eponym, also has its major-minor contrasts but it is essentially a brief, inspired up-tempo waltz in a style that is reminiscent of Richard Rodgers at his best. In other words, King, though she had opted for prominence as a composer/lyricist/singer/philosopher, had not yet abandoned any of the tricks of the trade that had accounted for her success when she was anonymous. Though the new songs were often more complex than the old ones they always did what they were meant to do — they each created an instant or two of melodic magic.

In artistic growth, as in biological evolution, the core of the old is retained but something new and quite unexpected is always being added. In this way, *Tapestry* and *Music* had evoked the canyons of Malibu with music that kept its Manhattan muscletone. In succeeding albums, however, King let her tunesmithing atrophy while she placed emphasis on her newly won position as a songwriter with "something to say." She lost touch with the kind of songwriting that had brought her success in the first place. Her musical hooks became ill-defined, uninsistent. Instead of taut little five-bar dynamos they became weak engines that could not prevent the rest of the tune from rambling. In many of her later works the melodies tipped their hands — they were like badly written mystery stories. Or they simply bided their time between chord changes — changes that were almost always predictable. And, even when these changes were unusual, they were less than exciting, since it is commonplace for a composer who is at a loss to simply jump out of one key and into another without any real plan in mind. In "You Go Your Way, I'll Go Mine" (from *Wrap Around Joy*), King took a turn around the cycle of fifths from

187

E (on "you've cut the binding ties") and then from E-flat (on "making love seems so unkind") without producing any of the dizzy fun of a Kern modulation. Throwing in a "wrong" chord every now and then became her new mannerism. But chords, like notes, are only exciting in relation to one another — in patterns, such as Gershwin's string of augmented chords in "Who Cares" and Hugh Martin's series of suspended dominant ninth chords in "The Boy Next Door."

Productive longevity requires that one keep in touch with the source of one's early inspiration. But, by the late 1970s, King's songs were no longer built around brief, memorable hooks. Nor was she successfully following the second injunction of productive longevity — experimentation. She was in a real predicament. It was next to impossible for her to consciously develop her strong point, since that strong point was the five-bar stinger, the hook, which, by its very nature resists development. Unlike Gershwin, who had always experimented with subtle harmonizations, and unlike the Beatles, whose experiments had from the beginning concerned orchestration, King's music did not have any obvious point of departure, any path that was crying to be explored. Exotic harmony was not her forte: she could come up with nothing better than an unexpected chord or two. Neither was modulation. At the 17th bar of the song "Time Alone" (from *Simple Things*), there is a sudden change from A to G (since it comes on the phrase "no sign of the changes we have come through," it might be a musical pun of sorts) that packs no punch at all. A few bars later the song moves for no apparent reason into the key of B, where it stays, the original key of A having been forgotten. On *Welcome Home*, released a year later in 1978, there are equally gratuitous modulations in several songs, including "Changes" (another in-joke, perhaps), "Morning Sun," and "Wings of Love."

King's other experiments usually involved song structure: adding second releases, extending refrains, inserting instrumental introductions and breaks. Unfortunately, these worked against her because they tended to destroy the tight and seamless construction that had been the hallmark of her earlier work. Because she was now writing to express herself, she no longer had to meet the specifications dictated by pop groups who wanted only to get A.M. radio airplay. Her move from New York to Los Angeles (and then from Los Angeles to Idaho) was, literally and metaphorically, a move from A.M. to F.M. radio. She had a larger canvas now but her gift had always been for that musical miniature, the hook.

The lyrics to her new songs, whether they were by herself, by David Palmer or by her third husband, Rick Evers, were full of good intentions and utopian ideals. But they were usually vague and amorphous. They often lacked a focal point, unlike the lines written in the 1960s by Gerry Goffin or those written in the early 1970s by

King herself. Lyrics like the following, from "One" (on *Simple Things*) certainly took their toll on King's music:

> He is one
> She is one
> A tree is one
> The earth is one
> The universe is one
> I am one
> We are one
> It just amazes me that I can be part of the
> Energy it takes to serve each other.

True to her decision in the mid-'60s, she did become an author with a recognizable style and point of view. In the process, however, she seemed to forget what medium she was working in. She had forgotten that her odyssey as an author was supposed to have been a musical one. Philosophy was all very well, but it was not her profession.

Holland-Dozier-Holland: The Thousand Days

While it is hard to understand how Carole King could have failed in the 1970s, it is not hard to see what brought Holland-Dozier-Holland down. More than King — more than any of the other great songwriters of the '60s — they were tied to a specific time and place. Their great days, from 1963 to 1967, coincided with the golden age of the Motown family, which had been assembled by Berry Gordy, Jr., in much the same way that Jack Warner assembled his family in Burbank in the 1920s and '30s. HDH were contract players (one of their first assignments was to help a Detroit disc jockey move into his new house) who worked with other players such as Smokey Robinson, Marvin Gaye, the Four Tops, and the Supremes. All of these singers had their own styles but each of those styles was really a sub-species of the overall Motown sound. It was a synthesis of sophisticated pop songwriting and thumping gospel, written and produced for the monaural, tinny tone of automobile radios. Until the 1970s, when Motown singers such as Stevie Wonder, Marvin Gaye and Michael Jackson began to evolve along their own distinct paths, these were qualities that all Motown products had in common — again, it was not unlike the Warner Brothers' imprint on early talking motion pictures.

Holland-Dozier-Holland shortly after they left Motown. Lamont Dozier is on the left, Eddie Holland in the center, and Brian Holland on the right.

The greatness of HDH was inextricably linked with those times. In fact, their great period might well be called The Thousand Days, since the solid core of their successful output was written in 1964, 1965 and 1966 — years which produced a body of work that is one of the great achievements in the history of popular music. Here is a partial list:

(Love Is Like a) Heat Wave	1963
Mickey's Monkey	1963
How Sweet It Is (To Be Loved By You)	1964
Baby I Need Your Loving	1964
Where Did Our Love Go?	1964
Baby Love	1964
Come See About Me	1964
Stop! In the Name of Love	1965
I Can't Help Myself	1965
It's the Same Old Song	1965
Back in My Arms Again	1965
I Hear a Symphony	1965
My World's Empty Without You	1965
You Keep Me Hanging On	1966
Reach Out, I'll Be There	1966
Standing in the Shadows of Love	1966
Reflections	1967

These and other HDH songs written in those years can stand beside the Beatles' output for the same period. That Lamont Dozier, Eddie Holland and Brian Holland are not as well know as the Beatles — that they are, in fact, nearly anonymous — is an unjust situation and one which ought to be corrected. The fault probably lies in the 1960s' overwhelming fascination with the performer/songwriter. Of the three, Dozier was the only one to follow that route with any perseverance. But by the time he did so, in the 1970s, his creative powers had waned considerably.

In 1967, due to a dispute over money, they left Motown — only to find themselves out in the cold. Denied the hothouse atmosphere of Gordy's young corporation and without the great singing groups for whom they had cranked out classic after classic, they were lost. What was worse, lawsuits and countersuits between them and Motown put them out of action as a songwriting team. They were literally enjoined from writing songs together between May 1969 and early 1972, when a settlement was finally reached (eventually, they began selling songs to Motown on a free-lance basis).

Though litigation is common in the music trade, and though many composers of stature have become entangled in civil actions,

191

no lawsuit had ever before become a significant stumbling block in the career of a major songwriter. George Harrison had to pay a half million dollar settlement for "unconsciously plagiarizing" the tune to "He's So Fine" in his composition "My Sweet Lord." But that ruling was no great hardship on him, either artistically or financially. John Lennon, accused by Chuck Berry's publishers of using a Berry line in "Come Together" ("Here comes old flat top, he come groovin' up slowly"), was forced to record other songs from that publisher's catalogue to avoid being taken to court. But, to him, this was no more than a minor irritant. Irving Berlin, as has been seen, was brought to court in the mid-1950s by a writer named Joseph Smith, who claimed that Berlin had used his, Smith's, melody in "You're Just in Love." And Berlin, who won that case, was not above initiating his own suits when he felt that his work had been tampered with. In what is perhaps the most famous instance of his litigious spirit, he sued *Mad Magazine* (unsuccessfully) in the 1960s over their parody of "A Pretty Girl Is Like a Melody," called "Louella Schwartz Describes Her Malady." Jerome Kern was brought to court by a composer named Fred Fisher, who claimed that Kern's song "Ka-lu-a," had used the bass line to "Dardinella," a song that Fisher owned (but had not written). During the colorful trial, an eight-piece band played those two songs as well as musically related selections from the highbrow repertoire, and the principal witness for Kern was Victor Herbert, who demonstrated several of his points at the cello. The final decision in this case was made by Judge Learned Hand who ruled that Kern had unconsciously plagiarized the bass line. But it was a Pyrrhic victory for Fisher, who was awarded only $250 in damages, and Kern's career was unaffected.

The case of Motown v. Holland-Dozier-Holland was entirely different. This team of enormously successful songwriters was told that they could not write music together. And for the next three years, they were unable to function as anything but producers and arrangers. Yet their work for Motown had always been a combination of writing and producing and it was next to impossible for them to be successful at one without, at the same time, practicing the other. As songwriters/producers they had become involved in an experimental try-anything atmosphere that was similar to that of the Beatles' recording sessions (to get the thundering Motown beat, Dozier would strike the underside of a piano keyboard with a hammer every time a chord was pounded out from above). The HDH songs for Motown were, like the Beatles' efforts, not just songs but compositions, tied intimately to instrumental riffs and sounds.

And, as if all of these problems were not enough, the team members began fighting amongst themselves. In the threesome there had always been an inherent imbalance. Dozier was the chief composer and

Eddie Holland was the main lyricist, but Brian Holland's function was never all that clear. He might well have become the odd man out but for the fact that he was Eddie Holland's brother. So it was that when squabbling developed it was Dozier who left the team. This was in 1973, shortly after the suit with Motown was settled, and the three men did not regroup until 1979 when they wrote some new songs and re-recorded some of their old ones for a Motown compilation called *Yesterday, Today and Forever*. When that project failed to catch fire with the public, Dozier again split from the brothers to pursue his own course.

Without Motown and then without each other, Dozier and the Hollands found themselves adrift. Unlike Carole King, who had taken a logical step in moving away from Aldon Music, HDH had no clear idea where they were going when they left Motown in 1967. They were not used to free-lancing, nor had they groomed a new singing group to take the place of the Four Tops and the Supremes. They started their own record company, Invictus, but it was really just a subsidiary of Capitol Records and, in any case, they had none of Gordy's organizational talent. They had left Motown without any plan, without thinking things through.

For all of the above-mentioned reasons, therefore, it is tempting to say that HDH's time in the sun was an unavoidably brief one and that, because their music was so bound up in a specific era, there was never any real chance that they, as artists, would outlive it. Yet, to believe that, one would have to ignore the fact that the songs that they wrote for the Motown singers were and are good enough to live on, apart from those first recordings and apart from the Motown imprimatur. "(Love Is Like a) Heat Wave," recorded by Martha and the Vandellas in 1963, was in the Top 10 twelve years later in a version by Linda Ronstadt. "How Sweet It Is (to be Loved by You)," recorded by Marvin Gaye in 1964, was successfully revived by James Taylor in 1975. "Standing in the Shadows of Love," done initially by the Four Tops in 1966, was covered by Barbra Streisand a decade later.

It must be remembered as well that the HDH songs were not, as some critics have said, a formula product. That word, "formula," implies that they were a fad, like cha-cha music. If that had been so, then HDH's work certainly would have been ephemeral. But it was not. Over those thousand-plus days their style was constantly evolving — was, in fact, following those two prerequisites for productive longevity. They became more and more sophisticated while remaining true to their pop and gospel roots.

A case in point is "How Sweet It Is," written in 1964. Harmonically, this is as simple as a nursery rhyme, using the elementary chords so dear to amateur pianists who like to pound out "Heart and Soul." The only musical element here that is at all complex is the syncopated melody, which is particularly effective in the pause between "I wanna stop" and "and thank you baby." The same thing can be said of other HDH songs of that year. "Baby I Need Your Loving" also depends on melodic syncopation and bone-simple harmonies – in this case, they are churchy chords such as E-flat, A-flat and C-minor which give the tune real grandeur. "Come See About Me" is another simple song from 1964 though, by some standards, its harmony is relatively sophisticated – certainly more erudite than most Dylan tunes or any latter-day Stones song. From the beginning, Dozier was a knowledgeable composer, a deft and intelligent craftsman who, like Carole King and her Brill Building companions, knew his trade. King made much use of the contrast between major and minor modes in constructing her hooks. Dozier often went a step further by using this contrast to heighten a song's emotional moments. In "Come See About Me," he underlines the phrase "crying baby for you," with E-minor and F-sharp-minor chords, so that the word "crying" has real feeling in it. Still, "Come See About Me" is uncomplicated and relatively tension-free when compared to the songs that HDH were writing in 1966, two years later.

"You Keep Me Hanging On" and "Reach Out, I'll Be There," both from that year, are darker and more urgent. They have an anxious, jumpy quality that is the product of brilliant, meticulous production and tense, unusual harmony. "Reach Out" is the greatest example of HDH's mastery of the verse/refrain format, which has already been likened in this book to a windup and a pitch. The windup is a long series of alternating A-minor and D-major chords. The pitch begins on the words "reach out" when a G-major chord suddenly takes the floor and then, out of nowhere, a B-major chord appears. It is as if the harmony too is reaching out. That B-major sound is a good example of the perfect use and execution of an unexpected chord. Hitting the listener with a jolt, it makes for a thrilling moment – something that fails to happen in so many of Carole King's songs of the late 1970s, where sudden, improbable chords land in the middle of a song with a disappointing thud.

That HDH continued to refine and expand their musical range throughout their Motown days is shown in one of the last songs that they wrote under contract, "Reflections." It possesses the same sense of urgency and the same musical sophistication as "Reach Out," and HDH's mastery of electronic sound in its production equals what the Beatles and the Beach Boys were doing at the same time.

But after 1967 came all of the unhappy vicissitudes that made for a swift decline. Not that this decline did not bottom out. Though the Holland brothers spent most of the 1970s in inactivity, Dozier embarked on a reasonably successful career as a vocalist, recording his own songs as well as songs written by others. He was a true child of the times in this regard for, like King, the Beatles, Dylan and so many other artists who were primarily songwriters, it turned out that he too was a first-rate singer (in 1974 Billboard Magazine voted him pop vocalist of the year). His solo voice was not much suited to the kind of material that HDH had written for vocal groups, so there was a fissure between his 1967 style of composition and the style displayed in his albums of the early 1970s, such as *Out Here On My Own* and *Black Bach*. Nevertheless, these albums display solid evidence of his talent. On *Black Bach* (undue modesty, apparently, was not one of his problems) there are a number of excellent songs, such as "Shine," "Put Out My Fire" and "I'm All Cried Out" (in which he again demonstrates his ability to musically underscore the emotional content of a lyric). This album also has a neat, brief instrumental interlude called "Intermission" (orchestrated by McKinley Jackson) which has a Gershwinesque charm.

Dozier's talents were certainly no mirage. But he has been unable to pick a direction and stick to it. Sometimes he tries to jump on an existing bandwagon (there was a disco album in 1976 called *Bitter Sweet*) and on other occasions he tries to start one of his own (in 1980 he was enthusiastic about Gypsy music). His rudderlessness is probably due in large part to the fact that he will not forsake the need to be a hitmaker long enough to develop a sense of himself as an author. Solid success, therefore, continues to elude him. Certainly, he and the Hollands will never get back together and write for the Supremes. But these talented men should not be forgotten — or counted out.

Paul Simon: Contemporary Lieder

As with Mick Jagger and Keith Richards, the creative partnership between Paul Simon and Art Garfunkel was an ill-defined, mysterious one. Simon's role was clear but it was hard to know the nature of Garfunkel's contribution. While his fine tenor voice, when coupled with Simon's, gave the pair a depth that Simon's somewhat thin voice did not have, it was Simon who was credited as both the composer and lyricist. Sometimes it was said that Garfunkel helped out with the arrangements, particulary with the vocal harmonies which, on such numbers as "Scarborough Fair/Canticle," were relatively tricky. But as the instrumentation of Simon and Garfunkel records became more intricate — and it did with them as it did with nearly

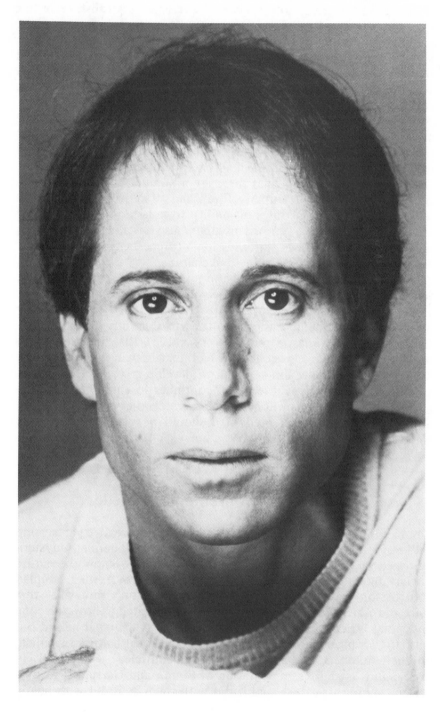

Paul Simon in 1982.

everyone in the 1960s — Simon began to indicate that the main responsibility for the arrangements lay with him. So it was that in the late 1960s, when just about every top writer but Dylan was in some way psychologically dependent on an intense and ill-defined partnership, Simon had the best of both worlds. He had his partner but, as a songwriter, he had his solo career too. When he and Garfunkel split in 1970 he was well-prepared to go it alone.

Simon also had other things going for him as the '70s came along. For one thing, his final album with Garfunkel, *Bridge Over Troubled Water*, had been a huge success, selling over eight million copies, and the public was more than ready to listen to anything new that he might produce. For another, his highest ambitions were as yet unfulfilled. Despite his success in the late 1960s, he had never been considered the equal of the Beatles, Dylan or the Stones. In part, this was because he was not as prolific as they were. Where Dylan's three great rock albums had come out in the space of fourteen months, Simon was apt to wait a year and sometimes two between albums. He was also denied parity with the Big Three because he was not a rock and roller. He could write a good rouser — as "Mrs. Robinson" and "Baby Driver" showed — but he did not have the earthiness that his generation required of its idols. From Bogart and James Dean in films and then from the Kennedys in politics this prerequisite had been transferred to pop music and those coming of age in the 1960s demanded that their heroes show strength *before* they showed heart. With Simon it was always the other way around. Yet he was never in the other camp either — the one dominated by descendants of the show tune writers, such as Bacharach and Sedaka. His instincts and his sympathies were always with the counter-culture writers. Like them, he saw the LP as a new art form. Like them too, he performed his own material. And his songs were timely, like theirs — they were barometers for national and world issues and events. He was also in the counter-culture fold as a lyricist, for he wrote the words to his songs with all the self-importance of a poet.

By 1970 the brunt of his professional jealousy (or chagrin) was directed at Dylan. They had always had the most in common. Both were singer/guitarists, both were composer/lyricists and both were Jewish/Americans. Simon certainly had good reason to compare himself to Dylan and to wonder whether the latter's preeminence had more to do with intangible factors such as charisma than with solid talent. Point for point, he could vie with the legendary troubadour. As a singer his voice, if less commanding, was purer. He was by far the better guitar player. His music was much more complex while, at the same time, his melodies were at least as hummable. Lyrics were said to be Dylan's forte but they were Simon's specialty too and the latter was more willing to sit down and attempt thematic unity and syntactical precision. Dylan's words sometimes had the randomness of buckshot. Moreover, Dylan, by 1970, was showing signs of fallibility. *Nashville Skyline*, released in 1969, had been seen (albeit wrongly) as his first flirtation with triviality and then, in June of 1970, he had issued a surprisingly undistinguished double album called *Self Portrait*, which was a hodgepodge of second-rate original songs and impromptu, ill-conceived covers of the songs of other writers, including Rodgers and Hart's "Blue Moon" and Paul Simon's own "The Boxer." It must have pleased Simon that Dylan was turning for the first time in seven years to non-original material and that one of the chosen tunes was a Paul Simon composition at that. He may have surmised that the tide was turning in his favor.

By 1972, when he was ready to release his first solo album, Simon must have sensed that popular music had undergone a significant transition. Though he had been part of the '60s sensibility, he had nevertheless remained separate from its core (one could not, for instance, imagine him playing at Woodstock) and only as the "counter-culture" blended into the "establishment" did he have the chance to be judged on his pure talent.

The new decade was made for him. Once-impenetrable boundaries were melting away. Rock and roll had come to Broadway in such productions as *Hair* and *Jesus Christ Superstar*. Broadway had come to rock and roll via Bacharach's songs for Dionne Warwicke. It was therefore with little or no risk of critical calumny that Simon began to explore his roots not just down to the folk-rock of Dylan and the Byrds or to the rock and roll of Chuck Berry and the Everly Brothers, but farther back to the works of the great theater writers. "When I listen to Dylan," he told *Newsweek*,

> I think "Oh, no, not the same 3- or 4-chord melody again . . . The staple of American popular music is all 3- or 4-chord country- or rock-oriented now. There's nothing that goes back to the richest, most original form of American popular music — Broadway and Tin Pan Alley — in which sophisticated lyrics are matched by sophisticated melodies . . . . When I started writing I didn't think there was any space for me between Dylan and the Beatles — they had it covered . . . . Now I'm trying to get closer to Broadway and Tin Pan Alley.

It was in this consciousness — even self-consciousness — that Simon differed from Dylan, the ex-Beatles and the Rolling Stones in the 1970s. He was less willing to rely on instinct. He was not afraid to look at himself and his work in perspective — to see what was good about it and what had always been good about it and to see too what areas there were for improvement. "Your ears don't suffer if you know more," he told *Rolling Stone* in 1970. He had been discussing his intention to learn the art of orchestration ("it's just frustrating to me that if I want to write a horn part I have to call in a guy and sing a horn part to him") and, in this way too, he was like the theater writers, who were continually thinking up reasons to learn or to avoid learning about instrumental writing. Simon also echoed them by frequently expressing his desire to write for the stage. He never got very far in this regard (the studio writers were often tempted by Broadway but for some reason they always held back) and it was not until 1980 that, in writing the songs for the film *One Trick Pony*, he attempted to set any narrative to music. Still, because of his self-consciousness and because of his knowledge of what has gone on in the popular music of this century, Simon has given his work a depth and a breadth matched in recent years only by Paul McCartney (who seems to have absorbed various musical styles by osmosis, rather than by contemplation).

These were the pluses with which Simon entered the 1970s: his experience as a solo writer, his unfulfilled ambitions, the relaxation of musical categories, and his willingness to learn. But there were minuses too. For one thing, he was a slow worker. Three years passed between the final Simon and Garfunkel album, *Bridge Over Troubled Water*, and the first solo album, *Paul Simon*, released in 1972. He was apt to labor over a single song for three months or more. This went against pop music tradition, where the usual sign of intense creativity has been quickness — from Richard Rodgers' seven-day miracle, *Oklahoma!*, to Irving Berlin's four-song weekend during the writing of *Annie Get Your Gun*, to the Beatles who, in the early days, could knock off enough songs for an album in a week (John Lennon continued to work this way — both *Walls and Bridges* and *Double Fantasy* were written in a few days), to Holland-Dozier-Holland's amazing string of fine songs in the mid-'60s. Simon has never been like that and, with his deliberate and painstaking approach to songwriting, he has had to buck tradition and work against the odds — he has had to make himself the exception to the rule.

A greater drawback was his tendency to play up his own personal angst. In this regard he was like Lennon and Dylan. But they could turn depression into electrifying rock and roll (Lennon on "I'm So Tired," Dylan on "Memphis Blues Again") while Simon's self-pity often had an enervating effect on his music. As subject matter, it was also self-limiting. There are only so many ways that a writer can express his world-weariness without seriously sapping the strength of his audience. One might argue that the theater writers were even more self-limiting in their endless reworking of the falling in love

Simon and Garfunkel in the late 1960s.

theme. But those lyrics could be witty or sad, clever or basic and, more important, their authors never pretended to be deep or meaningful. Ira Gershwin, for instance, claimed he had written only one line in his life that could be remotely mistaken for poetry (this was "Birds in the trees sing their dayfull of song" from "I Got Rhythm"). But Simon did take pride in the poetic value of his lines. In the early days his models were not Larry Hart, Johnny Mercer or even Chuck Berry. They were those poets long favored by American college freshmen: Amy Lowell, Edward Arlington Robinson and Edgar Lee Masters. Simon himself had taken a B.A. in English literature from Queens College and this shows in such songs as "Richard Cory" (from Robinson) and "Patterns" (from Amy Lowell). His early attempts at "poetic" lyric writing were extremely awkward. Confessions such as "Kathy's Song" and "The Dangling Conversation" (a title inspired by Saul Bellow's novel, *Dangling Man*) made Simon and Garfunkel the white hopes of English teachers everywhere. But they were not nearly as original as Berry's "School Days" or Gene Vincent's "Be-Bop-a-Lula." There were, to be sure, occasional brilliant lines and catch-phrases but, on the whole, Simon's lyrics of the 1960s were overrated. Real poetry eluded him, and his prosody could not help but suffer when compared to Dylan's best work. None of Simon's love songs had the power of "Just Like a Woman." None of his Americana rang as true as "It Takes a Lot to Laugh, It Takes a Train to Cry." Simon's attempts at sarcastic comedy in songs like "A Simple Desultory Philippic" could not compete with the Dylan of "Rainy Day Women" and his dabblings in the surreal, such as "Punky's Dilemma," were no match for any of a number of songs by Dylan or Lennon.

But Simon had one quality that the others lacked. He was able to come to his own rescue. By 1969 he had just about rooted out every trace of pretention in his lyrics. On *Bridge Over Troubled Water* there are occasional moments of bad poetry ("New York City winters bleeding me" from "The Boxer," for instance) but most of the songs have a simple point to make and they make these points well. Humorous songs such as "Why Don't You Write Me?" hit their marks squarely; even the surreal numbers ("So Long Frank Lloyd Wright" and "Baby Driver") are straightforward — that is, they are not trying too hard. With "Bridge Over Troubled Water" Simon wrote one of the truly great pop songs. Had he come up with it a year or two earlier he might have been unable to avoid bombast but now he just skirted it. He was still being self-consciously sensitive (the same theme was treated much more colloquially and with equally good results by Holland-Dozier-Holland in "Reach Out" and by Carole King in "You've Got a Friend") but these lines work well in their gospel setting. As the 1970s came along and as the great writers of the '60s, living the insulated lives of royalty, found that they had less and less to write about, Simon was just getting a handle on his abilities as a lyricist and he was bringing his talent under control.

The stage was set for him to become one of the finest lyric writers of the 1970s — and this was what he did, beginning with the first song on his first album of the decade, "Mother and Child Reunion." Here, in the oblique but unmistakable references to death and in the haunting title phrase (said to have been discovered by Simon in a fortune cookie), is real poetry. If Simon could still be faulted for his lyrics it would no longer be for their self-conscious sensitivity. It would be for his occasional use of incomprehensible dummy lyrics such as "Everything Put Together Falls Apart" and "Armistice Day." For it is a good bet that the words in both of those songs are the first that popped into his head.

But such moments were becoming rare. Though the lyrics on *There Goes Rhymin' Simon*, an album from 1973, were again a product of his weltschmerz, they were generally as excellent as they were straightforward; their meanings were clear and well-stated. "Tenderness" is a return to one of Simon's earliest subjects — honesty between lovers — but with more perception and less of the artiness of earlier days. "One Man's Ceiling Is Another Man's Floor" is proof that Simon, like Larry Hart and Cole Porter, could take a funny premise (expressed in the title, as they liked to do) and build an entire song around it. Being a product of the '70s and not the '30s, Simon's humor is more mordant and violent than what Porter or Hart would have produced, had they taken up the theme. But the technical prowess is much the same.

Simon's musical progress was even greater than his progress in lyric-writing. Over the course of the decade he turned out just three albums. But this trio constituted one of the great achievements in popular music. "Contemporary lieder," *The New Yorker* called his songs, for every one of them now displayed Simon's adherence to the two virtues essential for productive longevity: the care and maintenance of one's roots and the willingness to let one's imagination have its way. That these two ingredients are not mutually exclusive has been shown by great creative artists throughout the ages and, in the 1970s, Paul Simon joined their ranks. As experimental as the songs on *Paul Simon* (1972), *There Goes Rhymin' Simon* (1973) and *Still Crazy After All These Years* (1975) could and did become, they never stopped being viable and accessible as pop songs. The public assimilated them very quickly — as it had assimilated the best and trickiest of Kern's last songs. This is because Simon's songs were always either melodically or rhythmically catchy. While most of the great '60s writers were having trouble maintaining rhythmic vitality in the new decade, Simon gave himself a shot in the arm by turning to Latin and South American music. He had already made a tentative move in that direction in 1969 with "El Condor Pasa," a folk tune to which he set English lyrics, and now he broadened his palette with songs like "Mother and Child Reunion," "Duncan," "Me and Julio Down by the Schoolyard," "Take Me to the Mardi Gras," and "Was a Sunny Day" — tunes whose rhythmic underpinnings were derived from a variety of Latin sources, including Jamaican reggae and Columbian folk music. In this respect he was part of a tradition among American composers. In the 1930s any number of concert works had been inspired by Latin music — the most famous were probably Copland's *El Salon Mexico* and Gershwin's *Cuban Overture* — and Gershwin, toward the end of his life, had gone to Mexico to see if he might derive some inspiration from the folk sounds of that country. But it was Simon who best assimilated these south-of-the-border influences without diluting or parodying them.

He also maintained the pulse of his music by turning in the direction of gospel. Where "Bridge Over Troubled Water" had been slow and hymn-like, "Loves Me Like a Rock" and "Gone at Last" were up-tempo and full of good-time momentum. Rare now was his use of rock and roll rhythm. He had never been particularly comfortable with it and now, as it became less a sign of one's social and political purity, he just about abandoned it altogether. "Kodachrome" was the major exception and parts of "My Little Town," "Fifty Ways to Leave Your Lover" and "Paranoia Blues" used rock rhythms too. But they did so sparingly, taking an almost pristine, musicological approach. Yet, he was able to avoid the kind of slowdown that affected so many others, especially George Harrison, by conscious use of the rhythms of other types of popular music.

In his ballads Simon came up with his best and his most unusual creations — or concoctions, for in them one can note many diverse influences: Broadway, jazz, folk, rock, even atonal music. Yet he never forgot the need or lost the ability to create memorable melody, and this was what saved him from going off the deep end. In "Papa Hobo," for instance, he daringly puts off the first hook of the song (it comes on "sweep up") until an extended verse and then an instrumental solo have come and gone, and even then the main hook ("Detroit, Detroit") is still some fifteen bars away. The song is successful because the music during that long wait is good enough to hold the listener's attention. A ballad with an even more unusual structure is "My Little Town." This song is composed of four separate melodic sections plus one orchestral interlude. The unusual layout begins with an unaggressive 16-bar melody ("In my little town") — itself already a departure from standard 8-bar openings. Then comes a more hard-nosed second

203

section ("coming home after school") which lasts 14 bars. It contains the first of the song's real hooks — one that is to be found not in the melody itself but during a two-bar rest, an interim in which the piano makes an abrupt modulation from the key of G to that of B-flat. The third section ("and after it rains") is also 14-bars long and it is a temporary return to tranquility. It is followed by another melodic idea, this time a melancholy phrase played by a horn, which in turn is followed by the real chorus of the song, a violent outburst ("nothing but the dead and the dying back in my little town"), which is at last followed by the long-awaited repetition of the opening. But here too Simon pulls off a surprise. That first section does get repeated but the repetition is in a new key, A-major, which is a fourth above the key of its initial statement in E-major. This allows for a smooth transition into the "nothing but the dead" section (it is in D-major), bypassing everything in between. The craft in "My Little Town" is nothing short of spectacular. Kern and Gershwin would have been amazed by it. Its structural, harmonic and rhythmic ingenuity (there are frequent metric changes) would have made them consider it an "art" song — the province of concert hall recitals. Yet, when released as a single, it became a hit on A.M. radio.

Simon is a master of modulation but he also knows of other ways to achieve harmonic variety. In this respect he has been a light year ahead of other 1960s alumni (with the possible exception of Joni Mitchell — although her harmonic experiments have been in a jazz more than a pop context). "Everything Put Together Falls Apart" refuses to alight on any particular key. At first it seems to be heading for a cadence in B-flat but suddenly the tonality of E-major dominates and then, just as quickly, we are in the vicinity of C-major (on "Uh huh, I ain't blind, no"). At the end, the key of E wins out, for it gets an emphatic cadence. But the interesting thing about the song is that one is hardly aware that the laws of harmonic gravitation have been tampered with or suspended. On later albums, Simon would again fool around with key centers — on "Silent Eyes" and "Night Game" from the *Still Crazy* album, for instance. He also kept his partiality to spectacular modulations, as in the leap from an A-major chorus to a D-flat release in "I Do It for Your Love" (the songs goes on to end in G-major). But he has mostly kept his harmonic thinking within the boundaries of a single key. There are the strange and disquieting chords at the beginning of "Fifty Ways to Leave Your Lover" (harmony which did not prevent the song from doing well on the radio) and the complicated chordal patterns in "Tenderness," "American Tune," and others.

In these albums Simon also broke just as much ground with his rhythmic experimentation. Even though some of his songs are straightforward examples of certain types of beats, such as reggae and gospel, many others show a rhythmic ambiguity that matches his multi-tonal tendencies. "Something So Right," for instance, changes meter every two or three bars — usually from common to three-quarter time. "Have a Good Time" and "Night Game" alternate between common and waltz time so regularly that they might actually be thought of as two very rare pop examples of 7/4. The same kind of thing happens to a lesser extent in other songs, including "Everything Put Together Falls Apart," "Armistice Day," "Tenderness," "American Tune," "Silent Eyes," and "My Little Town."

Melodically, there are moments in each of these three albums that place Simon in the same league as Kern and Rodgers. "Run That Body Down" is bouncy, singable and memorable. "St. Judy's Comet" is an exceptionally beautiful lullabye (and an unusual one in that, though played softly, it is up-tempo). "Still Crazy After All These Years" is a marvelous slow waltz with a particularly fine release ("Four in the morning") and "I Do It for Your Love," with an equally touching release ("Found a ring in an old junk shop") is another melodic gem.

Instrumentally too, these albums reveal the highest kind of musical intelligence. Simon is less partial to instrumental motifs than is the McCartney of "Summer's Day Song"; his songs are less apt to become extended compositions. But the instrumental solos are often so tastefully and so meticulously crafted that they become separate and distinct sections of a song (as in "My Little Town"). Simon's albums also have a quiet clarity. More than anyone but the Beatles he respects and understands various instruments and their combinations. When a solo appears on a Simon record, one can be sure it will be worthy of the instrument and that the musician will be preeminent in his field. "Night Game" features Toots Thielmans on harmonica. On "Hobo's Blues" there is Stephane Grappelli on violin (he is also co-composer). "Loves Me Like a Rock" has the Dixie Hummingbirds as a backup chorus. On "Gone at Last" there are Richard Tee on piano, the Jesse Dixon Singers as the gospel backup, and Phoebe Snow, who sings a chorus.

Simon's achievement has thus been due not just to talent but to his willingness to think his songs through, to profit by his own mistakes and those of others. He is the most self-conscious of the studio writers and in this way he has more in common with Gershwin and Kern than he has with Berlin and Rodgers. Yet he is more closely related to Berlin and Rodgers than he is to Dylan, who has relied almost entirely on instinct. Only very rarely does Simon write a snappy straightforward 32-bar chorus. Yet he has not fallen into the trap of complexity for its own sake — certain quicksand for any pop songwriter. Even his most complicated songs are sprinkled with enough instantly likeable bits of melody, rhythm, harmony and instrumentation to carry his audience willingly into more esoteric territory. There is only one tendency that seems to hold him back. This is his continuing preoccupation with the kind of angst that, in comedy, has become the domain and perhaps the downfall of his New York neighbor, Woody Allen. Rarely does Simon ever write an out-and-out positive song. Most of his love songs — "Tenderness" is an example of this — are negative statements, complaints. Simon may see them as his answer to the traditional and banal "Hey, I'm in love!" category of lyric. But sighing songs about depressing relationships are, by now, just as ubiquitous and predictable. Even in a cheerful ditty like "Take Me to the Mardi Gras" he slips in a reference to his "burden" and laying it down. As with Harrison, who is always referring to the tears that he has cried, one is apt to wonder if Simon doth protest too much. Does he want his audience to believe that he is unhappy so that they will not envy him his obvious good fortune? A way out of this impasse might well be for him to turn to the writing of musical comedy or musical drama. He certainly has the technical equipment to enter the domain once dominated by Gershwin and Kern. As has been noted, he has already made one tentative move in that direction with *One Trick Pony*, a film produced in 1980. For that, he wrote the script and the songs and he starred in it too. Unfortunately, the story was so downbeat that, rather than serving as a pick-me-up and a new point of departure, it made his songs even more depressing. If he is going to write music for shows or films, he might do better by setting someone else's storyline to music.

AFTERWORD

In the 1920s there was a lot of talk about Third Stream music, a confluence of highbrow and jazz. Gershwin's concert works were thought to be part of this movement, as were certain self-conscious and less than characteristic pieces by such composers as Ravel, Stravinsky, Milhaud and Copland. But the Third Stream never really got off the ground, despite the fact that subsequent composers, including Leonard Bernstein, Gunther Schuller and Duke Ellington, gave it a good college try. It seemed as if the fundamental concerns of the two domains were not easily reconciled. Highbrow composers have always been most interested in the manipulation and transmogrification of ideas — they are paper and pencil men; jazz composers are more interested in improvisation — they are stream of consciousness thinkers. As time went on it became apparent that no amount of consciousness or self-consciousness on the part of either camp was going to successfully bridge the gap.

But the time may have come to revive the concept of the Third Stream — only this time the confluence ought to be of the theater and the studio writers. After all, pop songwriters in every generation approach music with a similar outlook and disposition. They are never very interested in the logical development of musical ideas or in stream of consciousness improvisation. They are interested in the lone, isolated musical idea: a quantum of melody or harmony or rhythm or instrumentation. The theater writers, with more theoretical training and with melodic and harmonic lifelines to the highbrows, were more self-conscious. The studio writers, with a lesser sense of musical history and theory and with greater reliance on their own performing capabilities, wrote on a more instinctive level. But both groups trafficked in the same kinds of musical ideas.

Third Stream pop songwriting, based on an awareness of what has been best and most useful about the methods of both the theater and the studio writers, might be a way out of pop songwriting's current impasse. It might be a way of braking the slide from music to showmanship. The theater writers were always wise or lucky enough to remain behind the scenes. They did not have to worry about keeping their "acts" up to date. Vaudeville came and went, Broadway and movie musical styles changed regularly and radically, but because these writers were dealing with musical quanta — ideas that were governed by more fixed, even eternal laws — they were able to continue working successfully, despite changing fashions in entertainment. That was their lesson to future generations of songwriters — a lesson that, unfortunately, was not always learned or heeded. The studio writers, for their part, discovered that a songwriter could not only become an author, but could admit to being one — could grow in his art by assuming control over the orchestration and the presentation of his work. But without the influence of the first stream, without the theater writers' musical erudition, orchestration all too easily becomes a hollow shell.

The concept of the pop songwriter as an author has been a presence throughout this book, though usually an implicit one. Now it is time to meet it head on. Just how necessary is it that pop songwriters be authors? After all, every year brings its crop of good songs, even when the composers of those songs are one-hit writers who never will be heard from again. Worthy tunes come and go these days in the Top 40 just as they came and went in the Hit Parades of past decades. And, for those listeners who are interested only in the songs themselves, these are not such bad times. They are people who might rightly point to a kind of hypocrisy in all of this talk about musical decline. Good individual songs are still out there. So what if no two are by the same writer? Why not take the songs as they come and stop worrying about who wrote them and whether or not the writer had "progressed"?

That line of thought can be carried even farther. Isn't there an extra-musical factor in all of this talk about authorship? Isn't the cult of the author just an excuse for the existence of high class groupies? Fans of Dylan in the 1960s were often pleasantly surprised to learn that a hit by the Byrds or the Band had actually been penned by their hero. Armed with this new information, they immediately liked the song all the more. Conversely, one can easily imagine the wrath of Mozart lovers should it be discovered that it was Haydn who had really written the *Jupiter Symphony*. In this sense the concept of authorship is wrapped up in loyalty and gratitude. It is a non-musical reason for loving music and one can rightly conclude that there is something fatuous about it.

On the other hand, no one can deny that authorship is a source of genuine pleasure and that it accounts for a lot of the euphoria that music audiences feel, no matter what their musical orientation. It certainly accounts for much of the headiness that young people in the 1960s felt about their generation of songwriters.

There is also this to consider: If, through his work, you get to know the personality of an author, with all of his quirks and with all of his hopes and intentions, then you are going to be better able to understand what he has achieved. And, once you get a sense of his achievement, a sense that comes with a knowledge of how his works exist in the continuum of his life and his career, then you can arrive at the core of the matter: you can begin to measure and appreciate the composer's heart. A lot of popular music is cold these days. But that does not mean that we have progressed beyond our own humanity. To hear a Kern ballad now, nearly forty years after that composer's death, is to be handed an eternal shot of brandy against the endless night. The same can be said of the great works of the other theater composers and of the best work of the studio writers. When they were at their best — when each was expressing his individual genius — they all had that ideal combination of heart and intelligence, of soul and point of view, that is, in the last analysis, the definition of authorship.

INDEX

Abbey Road, 48, 152
"Across the Universe," 137-138
Adler, Lou, 185
Aldon Music, 13, 14, 183
Aftermath, 165
Alexander II, 1-3
Alexander III, 2
Alexander, Jack, 2
"Alexander's Ragtime Band,"
  2, 3, 119, 122, 171
Ali, Muhammed, 33
"All I've Got to Do," 71
"All the Things You Are,"
  105-107
All Things Must Pass, 32, 158
"All Things Must Pass," 158
"All Those Years Ago," 160
"All Together Now," 87
"All You Need Is Love," 81
Allegro, 42, 111
Allen, Woody, 206
American Popular Song, 85
Anderson, Eric, 12
"Angie," 169
Animals, The, 25
Annie Get Your Gun, 77, 107,
  117, 125, 133, 199
"Another Op'nin', Another
  Show," 125
Ansky, S.A., 4
Anything Goes, 76
"Apple Scruffs," 158
Arlen, Harold, 4-5, 17-18, 34,
  46, 52-53, 67, 72, 93, 97,
  127-133
Around the World in 80 Days,
  125
"As Tears Go By," 165
Askey, Arthur, 23

Astaire, Fred, 16, 17, 21, 74-76,
  77, 78, 105, 119, 129, 130,
  150
Astor, Mrs. Vincent, 76
Avalon, Frankie, 68

"Baby I Need Your Loving,"
  194
"Baby's Request," 151
Bacharach, Burt, 197, 198
Baez, Joan, 72
Balin, Marty, 28
"Ballad of Sir Frankie Crisp,
  The," 158
Ballet Russe de Monte Carlo,
  53
Band on the Run, 147
Barrie, Elaine, 18
Barry, Jeff, 182
Barrymore, John, 18
Bart, Lionel, 25
"Because," 98
Beach Boys, The, 146, 151, 194
Beatles, The, 22-25, 31-37, 48-
  49, 61-64, 69-70, 73, 87, 89
"Beautiful Girl," 159
Bee Gees, The, 137, 185
Beethoven, Ludwig Van, 51, 54,
  91-93, 98
Beggars Banquet, 166, 168
"Begin the Beguine," 131
Belafonte, Harry, 63
Bellow, Saul, 201
Bennett, Robert Russell, 53, 56,
  64
Bennett, Tony, 60
Benny, Jack, 114
Berkeley, Busby, 182
Berlin, Irving, 2-4, 16-17, 51-52,

72, 75, 77, 93, 113-121
Bernstein, Leonard, 60, 94, 207
Berry, Chuck, 25, 60, 64, 68, 71, 138, 173, 192, 198, 201
"Bess You Is My Woman," 77, 97
Between the Buttons, 165, 166, 167-168
"Beware of Darkness," 158
"Bewitched," 109, 180
Black Bach, 195
Blake, William, 63, 84, 173
Blitzstein, Marc, 86
Blood on the Tracks, 178
Blood, Sweat and Tears, 185
Bloomfield, Michael, 63
"Blow, Gabriel, Blow," 76
"Blowin' in the Wind," 171
"Blue, Blue, Blue," 104
"Blues in the Night," 131
Bogart, Humphrey, 197
Bolero, 104
Bolger, Ray, 5
Bolton, Guy, 34, 102
Boone, Debbie, 180
Boone, Pat, 68
"Boxer, The," 201
"Boy Next Door, The," 188
Brahms, Johannes, 1, 91
Bridge Over Troubled Water, 201
"Bridge Over Troubled Water," 89, 201
Bringing It All Back Home, 84
Brooks, Joe, 180
Broonzy, Big Bill, 26
"Buckets of Rain," 89
"By Strauss," 97-98
Byrds, The, 171, 185, 198

Calloway, Cab, 129, 131
Can Can, 76, 126
"Can't Stop Thinking About You," 159
Capote, Truman, 46, 127, 130
Carmichael, Hoagy, 16, 29

Carousel, 41, 109, 110
Casady, Jack, 28
Charnin, Martin, 46
Chekhov, Anton, 1
Chess Records, 25, 27
Chevalier, Maurice, 44, 73, 74, 77, 116
Chiffons, The, 157
Chopin, Frédéric, 91
City, The, 185
Clayton, Paul, 10, 173
Cohan, George M., 73
"Come Together," 158, 192
"Come See About Me," 194
"Connection," 168
Cookies, The, 13
"Cool, Calm and Collected," 167
Cooper, Gary, 165
Copland, Aaron, 52, 53, 203, 207
Cotton Club, 5, 129
Coward, Noel, 6, 122
Cox, Anthony, 135
"Crackerbox Palace," 159
Crawdaddy, 84
Creedance Clearwater Revival, 28
Creem, 84
Crickets, The, 163
Crosby, Bing, 18, 119
Crosby, Stills, Nash and Young, 35, 185
Cummings, Jack, 18
Cybriwsky, Oresta, 97

Daly, William, 127
"Dardinella," 192
Dark Horse, 159
"Dark Horse," 159
David, Hal, 14
Davis, Miles, 68
"Day of the Locusts," 177
"Day Tripper," 148, 169
Dean, James, 10, 71, 197
"Dearly Beloved," 107
"De-Lovely," 76

212

De Mille, Agnes, 42
De Sylva, Buddy, 16
Debussy, Claude, 67
Del Ruth, Roy, 18
Desire, 173, 178
Diddley, Bo, 25
Dietz, Howard, 16
DiMaggio, Joe, 83
d'Indy, Vincent, 52
Dixie Hummingbirds, The, 205
Do I Hear a Waltz?, 113
Domino, Fats, 25
Donaldson, Walter, 34
Donnegan, Lonnie, 22-23
"Don't Let Me Wait Too Long," 158
"Don't Think Twice," 173
Double Fantasy, 137, 199
"Down Along the Cove," 106
"Down in the Depths," 76
Dozier, Lamont, 27-28, 72, 73, 189-195
Dreyfus, Max, 102, 104
Drifters, The, 13, 14, 183
Drifting Cowboys, 60
Dryden, Spencer, 28
Dubin, Al, 182
Duke, Vernon, 34, 101
Durante, Jimmy, 19
Dybbuk, The, 4
Dylan, Bob, 9-13, 63-64, 70-73, 77, 79, 80, 83-85, 88, 89, 170-179, 197-198, 201

Eastman, Lee, 37
Eisenhower, Dwight D., 114
"Eleanor Rigby," 61, 69
Ellington, Duke, 129, 207
Elliott, Ramblin' Jack, 8, 10, 11
"Embraceable You," 96
Epstein, Brian, 37, 44, 45
Evans, Mal, 139
Everly Brothers, 183, 198
Evers, Rick, 188
"Everybody's Got Something to
Hide," 148
"Everything Put Together Falls Apart," 204
Ewald, William, 117
Ewen, David, 155
Exile on Main Street, 169
Extra Texture, 159

Fabian, 14, 68
Fain, Sammy, 124
Falstaff, 93, 117
"Far East Man," 159
"Fascinating Rhythm," 54, 104, 119
Felix, Seymour, 18
Ferber, Edna, 103
Ferlinghetti, Lawrence, 173
Fields, Dorothy, 16, 34, 105, 107, 133
Fields, Herbert, 108
Fields, Lew, 107
"Fifty Ways to Leave Your Lover," 204
"Fine Romance, A," 105
Fisher, Fred, 192
Fogerty, John, 28
"Foggy Day, A," 59, 99, 101, 109, 178
"Fool on the Hill, The," 180-181
Foster, Stephen, 91, 107, 131
Four Tops, The 28, 189, 193
Francis, Connie, 13
Franklin, Aretha, 182
Friml, Rudolf, 108
Frost, Robert, 81
"Funny Face," 4

Gable, Clark, 18, 51
Garbo, Greta, 51
Garcia, Jerry, 28
Garfunkel, Art, 14, 35, 182, 185, 195, 197, 199, 201
Garland, Judy, 17, 129, 130, 133

Gaye, Marvin, 26, 189, 193
George Harrison, 159-160
Gerry and the Pacemakers, 23
Gershwin, George, 3-4, 5, 12,
    19-22, 23, 34, 53-60, 61, 62,
    67, 72, 75, 76, 85, 91-101,
    102, 104, 127-129
Gershwin, Ira, 3, 16, 17-18, 19-
    22, 34, 39, 63, 80-81, 86-87,
    89, 94, 96, 97, 99, 101, 122,
    201
"Get Back," 152
"Get Happy," 5
"Get Off My Cloud," 82
Gilbert and Sullivan, 25
Ginsberg, Allen, 143, 173
"Girl," 82
Girl Crazy, 76
"Give Me Love," 158
"Give Peace a Chance," 88
"Go Away Little Girl," 187
Goddard, Paulette, 21
Goetz, Dorothy, 2
Goffin, Gerry, 13, 182, 183,
    188
Goldfadden, Abraham, 4
Goldmark, Rubin, 53
Gone Troppo, 160
Gordy, Berry, 26-27, 189, 191,
    193
Gorme, Edie, 13
Graduate, The, 83
Grant, Cary, 125, 165
Granz, Norman, 76
Grappelli, Stephane, 205
Grateful Dead, 28, 29
Greenfield, Howie, 13
Greenwich, Ellie, 14
Gregg Smith Singers, 97
Grofé, Ferde, 55, 64
Grossman, Albert, 11
Guthrie, Woody, 8, 9, 10, 11,
    63, 171, 173

Hambitzer, Charles, 53

Hammerstein, Oscar II, 5, 6, 16,
    34, 39-44, 45, 48, 79, 103,
    104, 105, 107, 108, 110, 133,
    137, 163
Hammerstein, William, 39
Hammond, John, 11, 171
Hand, Learned, 192
Handley, Tommy, 23
Harbach, Otto, 17
Harburg, Y.A., 16, 17-18, 34,
    86, 129, 130, 133
"Hard Rain's A-Gonna Fall," 83
Harlow, Jean, 18
Harms Music House, 102
Harnick, Sheldon, 46
Harrison, George, 29, 71, 85,
    153-161
Hart, Larry, 6, 7, 19, 34, 37-39,
    44-45, 53, 63, 73, 74, 79, 81,
    88, 89, 107-108, 113, 122,
    163, 198, 201, 202
"Have a Good Time," 205
Haydn, Joseph, 91, 183, 208
"Heart and Soul," 193-194
Heine, Heinrich, 37
"He's So Fine," 157-158, 192
"Hello, Young Lovers," 79
"Help!", 69
Hendrix, Jimi, 177
Henie, Sonja, 16
Herbert, Victor, 5, 67, 103, 192
"Here Today," 150
"Hey Jude," 153
Heyward, Dorothy, 94
Heyward, DuBose, 21, 94
"Hi-Ho," 97
Hill, Billy, 9
Hollies, The, 25
Holly, Buddy, 45, 60, 64, 68,
    69, 140, 163
Hope, Bob, 76
Hopkin, Mary, 72
Holland, Brian, 27-28, 189-195
Holland, Eddie, 27-28, 189-195
Horne, Lena, 130

Houdini, Harry, 111
"How Sweet It Is," 193-194
"How'd You Like to Spoon
    With Me?" 102
Hudson, Garth, 177
Humperdink, Engelbert, 183

"I Am the Walrus," 73
"I Can't Be Bothered Now,"
    98, 178
"I Do It for Your Love," 204,
    205
"I Dream Too Much," 105
"I Get a Kick Out of You," 88
"I Got Rhythm," 201
"I Had Myself a True Love," 131
"I Love Paris," 7
"I Love You," 124-125
"I Threw It All Away," 176
"I Won't Dance," 105
"I'd Have You Anytime," 156
"If You Believe," 159-160
"I'll Be Your Baby Tonight,"
    176
"I'll Build a Stairway to Para-
    dise," 96
"I'm All Cried Out," 195
"I'm Carrying," 149-150
Imagine, 135-136
"In the Still of the Night," 7,
    98
"Instant Karma," 139-140
Institute of Musical Art (see
    Juilliard School of Music)
"Intermission," 195
"Isn't It a Pity," 158
"Isn't This a Lovely Day," 119
"It Is He," 159
"It's a Lovely Day Today,"
    116, 119
It's Only Rock 'n Roll, 70
"I've Got Beginner's Luck," 80
"I've Got the Sun in the Morn-
    ing," 119
Ives, Burl, 8

Ives, Charles, 67

J & M Studios, 25, 27
Jackson, McKinley, 195
Jackson, Michael, 189
Jagger, Mick, 24, 47, 71, 72, 87,
    162-171
Janov, Arthur, 135
"Jealous Guy," 89
Jefferson Airplane, 28, 29
Jesse Dixon Singers, 205
Jessell, George, 24
Joel, Billy, 152
John, Elton, 64, 136, 152
John Lennon/Plastic Ono Band,
    32, 115, 135
"John Sinclair," 136
John Wesley Harding, 64, 172,
    176
"Johnny One Note," 79
Johnson, Robert, 131
"Jolly Tar and the Milk Maid,
    The," 98
Jolson, Al, 16
Jones, Brian, 24, 47, 163, 164,
    166, 167
Jones, Spike, 62
Jones, Tom, 183
Joplin, Janis, 28, 177
Joy of Music, The, 94
Juilliard School of Music, 53
"Julia," 69, 148
"Jumping Jack Flash," 169
"Junior's Farm," 152
"Just Another Rhumba," 97

Kahal, Irving, 124
Kahn, Otto, 56
"Ka-Lu-A," 192
Katz, Sam, 18
Kaukonen, Jorma, 28
Kay, Hershey, 64
Kennedy Family, 31, 33, 197
Kennedy, John F., 31, 187
Kern, Jerome, 5-6, 17, 34, 52, 57,

67, 91, 101-107, 179-180, 209
Kilenyi, Edward, 53
King, Carole, 13, 14, 72, 73, 89, 179-189
"King of Swing," 96, 97
Kinks, The, 24, 25
Kirshner, Don, 13, 183
Kiss Me Kate, 125-126
Klein, Allen, 37, 139
Koechlin, Charles, 52
Koehler, Ted, 4, 34, 53, 129, 131
Kooper, Al, 63
Kostelonetz, Andre, 52
Kreidel, John, 84

Lady Patachou, 116
Laine, Denny, 147
Landau, Jon, 27, 60, 84
Larkey, Charles, 183
"Last Night When We Were Young," 127-129
"Last Time I Saw Paris, The," 107
Lawrence, Gertrude, 16, 49
Lawrence, Steve, 13, 182
"Learning How to Love You," 159
Lee, C.Y., 42
Lehár, Franz, 67, 110
Leiber, Jerry, 14
Lennon, John, 23, 24, 46-47, 61, 71, 72, 81, 85, 87-88, 89, 98, 135-143, 147, 164
Lerner, Alan Jay, 45
Let It Bleed, 168
"Let's Do It," 7
"Let's Have Another Cup of Coffee," 168
"Let's Spend the Night To-gether," 167
Levant, Oscar, 101
Lewis, Jerry Lee, 14, 25, 68
"Life Itself," 160

Liszt, Franz, 131
Little Eva, 182
"Little Lamb Dragonfly," 149
Little Richard, 9, 25, 68, 165
"Live and Let Die," 152
Living in the Material World, 156-159
"Living in the Material World," 159
"Locomotion, The," 182, 186-187
Loesser, Frank, 174
Loewe, Frederick, 46
Logan, Joshua, 42, 116
"London Town," 149
"Long Ago and Far Away," 101
"Look for the Silver Lining," 57
Lopez, Trini, 165
"Love Is Here to Stay," 59, 99-101
"Love for Sale," 7
"Love Walked In," 99-101
Lowell, Amy, 201

McCarten, John, 117
McCartney, 32, 145
McCartney II, 150
McCartney, Paul, 24, 44-48, 61, 71, 82, 85, 143-153, 164, 180-181
McLean, Don, 185
MacDonald, Jeanette, 17
McDonald, Country Joe, 28
McGowan, Jack, 18
McHugh, Jimmy, 105
Mackey, Clarence, 2-3
Mackey, Ellin, 2-3, 51, 115
"Maggie's Farm," 87
"Magic Melody," 104
Mahler, Gustav, 1, 67, 68
"Mamunia," 149
"Man I Love, The," 54, 56, 96
"Man That Got Away, The," 131
Mancini, Henry, 34

"Mandy," 119
"Manhattan," 108
Mann, Barry, 13
Mardin, Arif, 64
Martha and the Vandellas, 27, 193
Martin, George, 61, 63, 64, 137, 142, 146, 151
Martin, Hugh, 188
Martin, Mary, 48, 124
Marx Brothers, The, 24, 132
Masters, Edgar Lee, 201
Matassa, Cosimo, 25-26
Matlowsky, Samuel, 53
Maxwell, Elsa, 123
Mayer, Louis B., 16, 18, 19
"Maybe I'm Amazed," 153
Mendelssohn, Felix, 1
Mercer, Johnny, 34, 107, 129-130, 132, 133, 174, 201
Merman, Ethel, 16, 74, 76-77, 78, 116, 117, 130
"Michelle," 61
Michener, James, 116
Milhaud, Darius, 7, 207
Miller, Charles, 52
Miller, Steve, 28
Mind Games, 136
Minnelli, Vincente, 97, 125
"Mimi," 77
Miracles, The, 27
"Miss You," 169
"Mr. Monotony," 77
Mr. President, 117
"Mr. Tambourine Man," 171
"Mrs. Robinson," 83
Mitchell, Joni, 15, 64, 185, 204
Molnar, Ferenc, 41
Monk, Thelonius, 68
Monkees, The, 182
Moon, Keith, 136
Morrison, Van, 185
Moses, Grandma, 124
"Mother and Child Reunion," 202

"Mother's Little Helper," 169
Motown, 14, 26-27, 139, 189, 191, 192, 193
Mozart, Wolfgang Amadeus, 54, 59, 91, 141, 208
Music, 186, 187
"Music," 187
"My Funny Valentine," 89
"My Heart Belongs to Daddy," 4
"My Little Town," 203-204, 205
"My One and Only," 4
"My Sweet Lord," 157-158, 192

Nash, Graham, 15
Nashville Skyline, 64, 168, 176, 177
Navarro, 182
Nevins, Al, 13
New Morning, 177
"New York City," 136
New York College of Music, 102
Newman, Randy, 64, 123, 185
Nicholson, Nick, 1
"Night and Day," 75
"Night Game," 204, 205
Nilsson, Harry, 136
Nixon, Richard, 136
"No Other Love," 111
"Nobody Else But Me," 104
Now That Everything's Been Said, 185
"Now You Has Jazz," 76
"Nowhere Man," 140

Ochs, Phil, 8, 10, 11, 86
Offenbach, Jacques, 1, 67
"Oh, What a Beautiful Morning," 109
Oklahoma!, 41, 199
"Old Fashioned Wedding, An," 117
"Old Man River," 98, 103
"On a Night Like This," 177
"On the Atchison, Topeka and

the Santa Fe," 180, 182
"One," 189
"One Fine Day," 186
"One Man's Ceiling Is Another
   Man's Floor," 202
One Trick Pony, 199, 206
"Only One More Kiss," 150
Ono, Yoko, 35, 135-136, 140
Orlando, Tony, 182
Otello, 93
"Over the Rainbow," 17-18

Palmer, David, 188
"Papa Hobo," 203
Paramount Pictures, 74
Parker, Junior, 26
Parsifal, 93
Paul Simon, 199-202
Paxton, Tom, 10, 11
Penniman, Richard (see Little
   Richard)
"Penny Lane," 89
Perkins, Carl, 25, 68, 165, 173
Perry, Richard, 64, 147
Peter, Paul and Mary, 11
Phillips, Sam, 25, 68   ·
"Photograph," 159
"Pick Yourself Up," 105
Pinza, Ezio, 48
Planet Waves, 177-178
"Play a Simple Melody," 77,
   116, 117
Pomus, Doc, 14
Porgy and Bess, 4, 56-59, 62,
   94-95, 109, 115, 178
Porter, Cole, 6-8, 18, 52, 67,
   75-76, 88-89, 93, 121-127
Porter, Mrs. Cole (Linda Lee
   Thomas), 123
Powell, Eddie, 18
Powell, Eleanor, 18
Power, Tyrone, 16
"Power to the People," 140-141
Presley, Elvis, 14, 23, 26, 44,
   48, 58, 69

Preston, Billy, 139
Price, Charlie, 25
Prince Esterházy, 183
"Promenade," 59, 96
Rachmaninoff, Sergei, 104
Ram, 145-146
Ravel, Maurice, 67, 68, 96, 104,
   207
Ray, Ted, 23
"Reach Out, I'll Be There," 194
Red, Hot & Blue, 76
Reed, Jimmy, 9
"Reflections," 194
"Revolution," 87, 138-139
Revolver, 61
Rhapsody in Blue, 23, 153
Richard, Cliff, 25
Richards, Keith, 24, 47, 85, 163-
   171
Rivera, Scarlet, 173
RKO, 21, 94
Robin, Leo, 133
Robinson, Bill "Bojangles," 129
Robinson, Edward Arlington,
   201
Robinson, Smokey, 26, 27, 189
Rodgers, Jimmie, 60
Rodgers, Richard, 6-7, 19, 34,
   37-46, 48, 53, 55-56, 73-74,
   77, 93, 107-113, 127, 180
Rogers, Ginger, 16, 17, 21, 129
Rogers, Roy, 125
Rolling Stone, 84, 152, 199
Rolling Stones, The, 24-25, 47,
   69-70, 73, 87, 163-171
Romberg, Sigmund, 16, 122
Ronstadt, Linda, 193
Rory Storm and the Hurricanes,
   23
Rose, Billy, 125
Rubber Soul, 48, 61
Rubenstein, Anton, 23
Ruby, Harry, 12, 16
"Ruby Tuesday," 167, 168, 169
Rumshinsky, Joseph, 4

218

"Run That Body Down," 205

"Sad-Eyed Lady of the Low-
    lands," 172
Sahm, Doug, 28, 177
"St. Judy's Comet," 205
St. Louis Woman, 67
Sainte-Marie, Buffy, 8
Sally, 103
Sargent, Winthrop, 43, 110
Say It with Music, 117
Schaffner, Nicholas, 143
Schillinger, Joseph, 53
Schoenberg, Arnold, 1, 60, 67,
    91
Schubert, Franz, 1, 54, 126
Schuller, Gunther, 207
Schwartz, Arthur, 16, 34
Schwartz, Charles, 4
Scriabin, Alexander, 67
Secunda, Sholom, 4
Sedaka, Neil, 13, 14, 182, 197
Seeger, Pete, 11
Self Portrait, 177
Selznick, David O., 17
Sgt. Pepper, 23, 48, 153, 166,
    172
Shakespeare, William, 1, 48,
    125
Shapiro-Remick Company, 102
"She Came in Through the
    Bathroom Window," 82
"She Said, She Said," 61
"She Smiled Sweetly," 168
Shelton, Robert, 11
Shirelles, The, 13
Show Boat, 103
Shuman, Mort, 14
"Silent Eyes," 204
Silvers, Sidney, 18
Silvert, Conrad, 163
Simon, Paul, 14, 15, 64, 72, 73,
    82-83, 87, 89, 195-206
Simon, Simone, 21
"Sing of Spring," 97, 98

"Sing This Song All Together,"
    169-170
Sirmay, Albert, 122
"Slap That Bass," 86-87, 98
Slick, Grace, 28
Smith, Al, 114
Smith, Bessie, 131
Smith, Joseph, 116, 192
"Smoke Gets in Your Eyes,"
    104
Snow, Hank, 60
Snow, Phoebe, 205
"So in Love," 7
"Soliloquy," 152
"Someone to Watch Over Me,"
    54, 96
"Something Happened to Me
    Yesterday," 168
"Something So Right," 205
Sometime in New York City,
    136
Somewhere in England, 160
Sondheim, Stephen, 43, 46
"Song Is You, The," 104
"Sound of Silence, The," 14
Souza, John Phillip, 44
Spector, Phil, 14, 60, 137-138,
    139, 140, 141, 156, 158, 159
Spector, Ronnie, 159
Spewack, Bella, 133
Spewack, Sam, 133
Springsteen, Bruce, 64
Stafford, Jo, 60
Starr, Ringo, 32, 35, 37, 39, 47,
    49, 85, 136, 147, 159
Steele, Tommy, 25
Stein, Gertrude, 65
Steinbeck, John, 42, 111
Stewart, Jimmy, 18
Stewart, John, 185
Sticky Fingers, 168-169
Still Crazy After All These Years,
    202, 204
"Still Crazy After All These
    Years," 205

Stillman, Albert, 96
Stockhausen, Karlheinz, 61
Stoller, Mike, 14
Stooges, The Three, 19
"Stormy Weather," 180
Strauss Family, 1
Stravinsky, Igor, 109, 207
"Street Fighting Man," 168, 169, 171
Street Legal, 178-179
Streisand, Barbra, 193
"Subterranean Homesick Blues," 173
Sullivan, Arthur, 67, 130
Sullivan, Ed, 142
"Summer's Day Song," 150, 205
"Summertime," 56, 57
Sun Records, 25-26, 27, 68
Sunny, 103
Supremes, The, 28, 189, 193, 195
"Surely," 187
Sutcliffe, Stu, 24
"Swanee," 96, 97
"Sweet and Low Down," 54
"Sweetest Sounds, The," 113
Swingtime, 105
" 'S Wonderful," 4
"Sympathy for the Devil," 84, 166-167, 168, 176

"Take Me to the Mardi Gras," 206
Tapestry, 185-186
Taylor, James, 185, 193
Taylor, Samuel, 111
Tchaikovsky, Peter Ilych, 110
Tee, Richard, 205
Temptations, The, 27
"Tenderness," 202, 206
Thalberg, Irving, 16, 19
"They Can't Take That Away from Me," 59, 98-99, 101, 178

"They Didn't Believe Me," 102, 104
Thielmans, Toots, 205
Their Satanic Majesties Request, 166
There Goes Rhymin' Simon, 202
Thirty-Three and a Third, 259
Thomas, Ned, 123
Thomashevsky, Boris, 4
"Three Legs," 145
Tibbett, Lawrence, 129
"Time Alone," 188
Tolstoy, Leo, 1
"Top Hat, White Tie and Tails," 119
"Touch of Your Hand, The," 104
Traum, Happy, 177
"True Love," 121, 126
"Try Some, Buy Some," 159
Tug of War, 150, 151
"Tug of War," 150, 151

"Uncle Albert/Admiral Halsey," 149

Van Heusen, Jimmy, 130
Van Ronk, Dave, 10, 12
Varèse, Edgar, 61, 62
Vee, Bobby, 10, 13
Venus and Mars, 147
Verdi, Giuseppe, 52, 93, 117
Verne, Jules, 125
Vincent, Gene, 201
Voorman, Klaus, 139

Wagner, Richard, 67, 93, 156
"Walking the Dog" (see "Promenade")
Wallis, Dave, 166
Walls and Bridges, 136, 199
"Waltz in Swingtime, The," 105
Warner Brothers, 124, 125, 189
Warner, Jack L., 16, 189

Warren, Harry, 16, 34, 130, 182
Warwick, Dionne, 14, 198
Waters, Ethel, 129, 131
Waters, Muddy, 9, 25
Watts, Charlie, 24, 163, 164, 166
"Way You Look Tonight, The," 105, 179-180
Webb, Jimmy, 26
Weill, Cynthia, 13
Welcome Home, 188
Welles, Orson, 125
Wells, Mary, 27
Wexler, Jerry, 64
"Whatever Gets You Through the Night," 136
"When I Lost You," 115
"Where or When," 110
White, Andy, 139
White, Josh, 8
Whiteman, Paul, 52, 53, 55
Whitfield, Norman, 27
Whiting, Richard, 34
Who, The, 24, 25, 146, 152
"Who Can See It," 158
"Who Cares," 188
"Wild Horses," 89, 169
Wilder, Alec, 85, 99
Wildlife, 146
Willemetz, Albert, 116
Williams, Hank, 9, 60, 62, 63, 64, 140, 165
Williams, Joe, 10
Wilson, Brian, 60

Wilson, Meredith, 53
Wilson, Tom, 14
Wings, 146, 147
Wizard of Oz, The, 5, 129, 130
Wodehouse, P.G., 34, 103
Wonder, Stevie, 27, 64, 152, 189
"Wonderful Guy, A," 109, 110
Woodin, William Hartman, 34
Writer, 185
"Wunderbar," 125
Wyman, Bill, 24, 163, 164

"Yellow Submarine," 61
"Yesterday," 82, 165
"Yesterday's Papers," 168
"You Gave Me the Answer," 150
"You Go Your Way, I'll Go Mine," 187-188
"You Keep Me Hanging On," 194
"You Never Know," 121
"You'll Never Walk Alone," 110
Youmans, Vincent, 5, 16
Young, Victor, 125
"Your Love Is Forever," 160
"You're a Big Girl Now," 88, 178
"You're Just in Love," 77, 116, 117, 192
"You've Got a Friend," 89

Zoppola, Countess di, 121, 127